Wayward Women

Sex, Friendship and the Midlife Reset

RHONDA CARRIER
AND TRACEY DAVIES

Wayward Women

Sex, Friendship and the Midlife Reset

First published in the UK in 2026 by Bedford Square Publishers Ltd,
London, UK

bedfordsquarepublishers.co.uk
@bedfordsq.publishers

© Rhonda Carrier and Tracey Davies, 2026

A Maxim Jakubowski book

The right of Rhonda Carrier and Tracey Davies to be identified as the authors of this work has been asserted in accordance with the Copyright, Designs and Patents Act 1988. All rights reserved. No part of this book may be reproduced, stored in or introduced into a retrieval system, or transmitted, in any form or by any means (electronic, mechanical, photocopying, recording or otherwise) without the written permission of the publishers.

Any person who does any unauthorised act in relation to this publication may be liable to criminal prosecution and civil claims for damages.
A CIP catalogue record for this book is available from the British Library.

ISBN
978-1-83501-359-5 (Trade Paperback)
978-1-83501-360-1 (eBook)

2 4 6 8 10 9 7 5 3 1

Typeset in 12.75 on 15.7pt Bembo Std
by Avocet Typeset, Bideford, Devon, EX39 2BP
Printed and bound in Great Britain by
CPI Group (UK) Ltd, Croydon CR0 4YY

The manufacturer's authorised representative in the EU for product safety is Easy Access System Europe, Mustamäe tee 50, 10621 Tallinn, Estonia
gpsr.requests@easproject.com

AUTHORS' NOTE

Thanks to those who appear in this book. We changed names/initials and/or identifying information when appropriate or desired. Events are as we remember them but we recognise and respect that everyone has their own take; that this is our version of our story/ies.

To all the wayward women, especially those who left us too early but who walk, swim and dance beside us, always.

PART I
ADRIFT

CHAPTER 1

MERMAIDS

Tracey

*'I have heard the mermaids singing, each to each.
I do not think that they will sing to me.'*
– T.S. Eliot, The Love Song of J. Alfred Prufrock

A child of the *Splash!* era, I longed to be Daryl Hannah: half-hottie, half-mackerel – and boning Tom Hanks. Mermaids are often depicted in film and literature as sexy sirens or bloodthirsty nymphs, voluptuous sea creatures with perky tits and pretty, scaly tails surfacing from the sea to manipulate men and help them shuffle off their mortal coil. And as someone going through an acrimonious divorce and often feeling like I'm treading water or sinking in mud, I feel the mermaids are doing God's work.

But mermaids also represent the ultimate in sisterhood: femininity, rebellion and transformation. It's these aspects of the mermaid lifestyle that I'm most drawn to, especially as I reach midlife. So when my friend Rhonda and I get the opportunity to train with the real mermaids of Florida, we totally flip out.

Apart from the tan, the two best things about being travel writers are the adventures we have and the people we meet. At Tampa International Airport, Rhonda fires up Bumble within minutes of landing to see if she has a message from Daniel, a man from a nearby town called Holiday, a name he described to her as 'wildly inappropriate for the presence of the humans who reside within'. So far, so Florida.

I'm contractually obligated to state that Rhonda Carrier is *not* an international cougar and does *not* fuck her way around the world. Although a self-confessed horn dog, she uses Bumble's travel mode to chat with and sometimes meet interesting people around the world. And that's how she found Young Daniel.

I say young, but there have been younger. That's another story, though. Young Daniel is thirty-nine, Rhonda is fifty-four. I know she really wants to meet him but I'm not sure how she's going to swing it given our packed schedule.

Driving along the highway in our rented Ford Mustang – roof down and filthy ear-blistering German techno on the stereo – I glance over at her, the warm Floridian wind whipping her hair vertical, and I feel my heavy heart lighten.

Okay, indulge me a little. I've had a rough ride these past few years. A delicious life cocktail of marital woe, surprise debt, grief and perimenopause, all shaken up with the unrelenting pressure and responsibility that comes with being a parent. It's no wonder depression has been as regular a visitor as a randy milkman. And each time it's made me feel like I've fallen down a well. This trip has very much come at the right time. There's only so much heavy lifting my dear Prozac can do.

After more than two decades of marriage and parenthood, and now going through a divorce, I crave the freedom of travel more than I crave two Greggs sausage rolls and a Diet Coke after a heavy night. I crave it more than love, I crave it more than sex. I crave freedom even more than acceptance. And now, as I speed towards the wet wilds of Florida sat next to Rhonda in my favourite car, freedom – albeit just for a week – finally feels within reach.

The first stop on our Floridian adventure is Crystal River, famous for its manatees and its mermaids. And I'm obsessed with both. Did you know that manatees actually perpetuated the myth of mermaids? They were often mistaken for the sirens of the sea (well, that's what the near-sighted, amorous sailors said...).

The Italian explorer Christopher Columbus wrote that he'd spotted three 'mermaids' floating in the water near the Dominican Republic. In his log, he said, 'Yesterday, when I was going to Rio del Oro, I saw three sirens that came up very high out of the sea. They were not as beautiful as they are painted, since in some ways they have a face like a man.'

Rude.

We skid the Mustang to a halt outside the Crystal Blue Lagoon, a marvellously kitsch B&B on King Spring, with cheery nautical decor and mermaid and manatee regalia – everything I'd hoped for on our mermaid adventure. We dump our bags and head straight to the Seafood Seller, a brightly lit local joint for 'gator mac and cheese and blackened shrimp po'boys – and numerous margaritas. As a baptism into the Crystal River community, the jolly manager introduces us to his best friend Darryl, a live crayfish (yes, you heard right). For we mermaids, it's love at first sight.

I wake up the next morning to a dolphin splashing noisily outside my bedroom window, and the feeling that I'm in a Disney film continues.

'Not now, Flipper,' I say, shaking a cream cheese and grape jelly bagel at him. 'I'm carb-loading for mermaid school.'

Coming in at number 1,847 of weird things I thought I'd never say or do, attending mermaid school in a tiny watery enclave of west Florida is right up there. I've done some strange things in my career as a travel writer. I trained as a spy in Finland, a safari guide in Kenya and a sommelier in, er, Guildford, and I even went to zombie school in London. And now, I'm learning to be a mermaid. Of course.

Since turning fifty, I have developed the confidence of an unattractive trust fund baby. I think I can do anything. After decades of worrying about what everyone thought of me, now I don't care a jot. It's incredibly freeing and definitely my favourite part of getting older. (Please keep this in mind when you see me walking my dog in my pyjamas.)

Rhonda and I are heading to Crystal River Water Sports to learn the basic skills of being a mermaid. Our mermaid guru, the lovely Lauren – a young, maybe mid-twenties, woman – seems shy and a little distant. She looks at us overly excited middle-aged women dicking about with manatee memorabilia and gives off a slight air of disdain at our silliness. In recent years, I've often noticed this look from younger women. What they don't realise is that, if they are lucky, this is their future.

As Lauren fits us out with suitably garish tails and equips us with masks and snorkels, she warms up a little, and her obsession with mermaids becomes apparent. Lauren tells us she's part of the Crystal River pod of mermaids and has dreamed of being a mermaid ever since she was tiny. Now she teaches others how to mermaid in the warm springs of Crystal River.

Once in the water, Lauren relaxes, and she seems to blossom as she ebbs and flows with the spring. It's obvious that she was born with gills, and when science catches up she can retire to the water to live her life fully as a mermaid.

Under a blazing Florida sun, our legs encased in shiny Lycra tails and powered by mono-fins, Rhonda and I dip and dive through the warm spring waters like frisky porpoises. For someone who can feel claustrophobic in a skinny jean, I take to wearing a tail easily, like a haddock to batter. Over the hours, we learn to duck-dive, flipping our tails out of the water to get down to deeper depths and also to wave to passing boats. We spin and blow mermaid kisses.

After my initial fear of drowning, it feels incredibly freeing to swim with a tail, and we both learn quickly as we dart around the warm springs. Soon enough, Lauren deems Rhonda and me ready to captivate our first sailor and lead him to a watery death. Exciting!

Like the mermaids, I want to live life on my own terms. I want to be the ruler of my sea. I think this is one of the reasons why I'm getting divorced. Disney's *The Little Mermaid* has been a popular fairytale with young girls since the dawn of time, or at least 1989 when it was first released. It tells the tale of a mermaid who falls in love with a prince and battles evil to live happily ever after as a human. Of course, it's a predictable love story designed to fool young girls into thinking that men are the answer.

However, Hans Christian Andersen's original fairytale is deliciously darker, much to my macabre delight. First published in 1837 as part of a collection of stories designed to scare the shit out of children, it does have the young mermaid fall in love with the prince after saving him from drowning. But in her quest for an immortal soul she makes a deal with the evil sea witch, and swaps her tail and her tongue for human legs and a painful life on land. A bit like marriage really (said the bitter divorcee).

Of course, the dickhead prince goes and falls in love with another woman, one who can actually speak and walk, and spurns the mute mermaid, causing riotous rage among her mermaid sisters. The evil sea witch suggests she murders the twat prince and bathes in his blood if she wants her tail back for a life under the sea. However, our fishy femme doesn't kill the git and instead throws herself into the sea and turns immediately to sea foam. Once again, a good woman sacrificing herself for a bloke.

Now we have the basic skills under our gills, it's time to meet our heroes, the mermaids of Weeki Wachee Springs. Waving goodbye to Lauren, who I swear has a tear in her eye, we hop in the Mustang, throw the roof back and hit the highway south with even louder German techno stoking up our fire.

One of the deepest natural springs in the US, it feeds the seven-mile-long Weeki Wachee River and pumps more than 100 million gallons of fresh water into the Gulf of Mexico every day. In 1947, Newton Perry, a former US naval officer, took over the springs and carved an underground auditorium out of limestone. While in the navy, Perry invented a unique way of breathing underwater using compressed oxygen. Seeing a buck to be made, he recruited local girls to dress up as mermaids and perform underwater shows in the spring by taking discreet puffs of air from the free-flowing oxygen pipes.

As someone who gets overly nostalgic about kitsch seaside attractions, I've been obsessed with the mermaids of Weeki Wachee Springs since Ariel was knee-high to a crayfish. Weeki Wachee was considered Florida's original theme park and the mermaids performed eight shows in the underwater theatre every day. In the Eighties, the park added the Buccaneer water park, daily critter shows and a river cruise experience, but it was always the mermaids who were the main attraction.

When it first opened in the late 1940s, the performers would stand at the side of the road in their sparkly costumes to entice passers-by to come and watch their shows – not unlike the sexy sirens luring sailors with their pearly charms. Swinging the Mustang off Route 19 and driving under the Weeki Wachee Springs sign, I feel giddy and a little sick with excitement.

There is a disappointing lack of land-based mermaids luring us into the park, but it doesn't dampen our anticipation. We arrive before the gates are opened to the public and join a line of ladies by the Siren Camp sign. Getting a place on the camp is harder than securing Glastonbury tickets. Camps, which are held one weekend a month, sell out in hours as legions of women from around the world, but mainly the States, sign up to be trained by the Legendary Sirens, the mermaids who performed at Weeki Wachee during its golden era in the Fifties, Sixties and Seventies.

There are eight of us altogether, ranging in age from early thirties to late sixties, including Tracy, a shy artist from Gainesville, Florida, whose parents visited Weeki Wachee in 1969. She's dreamed of coming ever since.

'I'm recently divorced, so now I can do whatever I like. And I wanna be a mermaid!'

I wasn't sure what to expect of my fellow mermaids. Part of me wanted a kind of Louis Theroux-style exposé of women experiencing a mermaid-themed midlife crisis. Women leaving their husbands and families in droves to run away with the Weeki Wachee mermaids in a shower of glitter. Or indulging their life-long fetish for scales and tails in the hope that they can live a life underwater. What I actually experience is real, honest American women in all their raw glory – and a tail.

The sirens have a rule. All attendees have to be over thirty to attend the camp. I like this. I assumed it was to purposefully exclude the nymph-like youths who would come purely for the Instagram clout, but no. When the camps first started, some younger women would come for the weekend and then trade on the fact that they were 'trained Weeki Wachee mermaids' to get work as performers.

Even though Rhonda and I are here to research a travel article, I think there's something rather brave and raw about women following their dreams. It's opening up a side of you that people rarely get to see. But there's also a strong sense of 'Fuck it. I'm here. I'm me. And I'm going to be a fucking mermaid,' which I particularly like.

It's the energy I really need right now. Just being here and around these wonderful women, I start to feel the rumblings of the former Tracey re-emerging. The woman I was before marriage, before kids, before responsibilities. And she's going to be a fucking mermaid.

Still using the same oxygen pipe technique, today's professional mermaids perform three shows a day, each lasting forty-five minutes. Our first task is to sit in the Newton Perry Underwater Mermaid Theater, surrounded by a hundred little girls dressed as Ariel, and watch the show to see what's required. As the dusty blue curtain rises, exposing the tank, we can hear the mermaids' signature tune:

'We're not like other women;
We don't have to clean an oven
And we never will grow old.
We've got the world by the tail!'

It reveals a trio of mermaids waving and blowing kisses at a rapturous audience. Like the children, I'm mesmerised by these mythical nymphs. They look ethereal as they dart and writhe through the spring, and I struggle to keep my emotions in check.

'I was seventeen and a week out of high school when I first became a mermaid,' says Vicki Smith, a sprightly 84-year old who reigned the Weeki waves between 1957 and 1962.

'We were like movie stars back then. I even performed for Elvis Presley.' She grins. 'But we were more famous than him at the time.'

But it was the actual feeling of swimming in the spring, the freedom of swimming with a fin, that was always the biggest draw for the mermaids:

'Being underwater is so quiet and serene. When it rains, it's like stars on the ceiling. It's like heaven for me,' says Vicki.

A natural spring, the water is a constant 74 degrees. We watch the mermaids perform their underwater ballet along with a supporting cast of sea life. The odd manatee and alligator have also been known to make a cameo appearance, although there is disappointment that they haven't turned up today, an equally thrilling and petrifying prospect.

'We couldn't hear underwater back then, so we had a special hand signal if an alligator swam into the spring,' Vicki says and chuckles. It's a fact I'd rather not know.

Over the weekend, the 'Formers' teach us how to be a Weeki Wachee mermaid. We swim in the spring between shows and learn how to perform underwater. Vicki and her pod of mermaids – Becky, Cheryl, Bev, Rita and Mirt – giggle and banter as they show us 'guppies' the ropes.

We all need older women as role models. Cher and Dolly Parton have always been my traditional go-tos, but after this weekend I look to Mermaid Vicki and Mermaid Becky and the rest of the Formers, each still fizzing with passion and vitality even in their most senior years. These are the real-life role models I want.

'This is my third camp,' says Phyllis, who in her sixties has fully committed to the lifestyle, with her abundance of mermaid-themed attire from towels to tiaras. 'It's just magical, that's what it is. There's something so magical about swimming with a tail.'

To outsiders, mermaiding is often seen as a trivial hobby. Childish even. What grown woman wants to dress up as a Disney character? But it's more than that:

'Swimming in the spring, being a mermaid is just freedom,' says Mermaid Vicki. 'Freedom in its purest form.'

After wriggling into my Lycra tail, I shuffle along the deck and slide into the cool clear spring like a sparkly aquamarine sea slug. I'm relieved to hear we're not allowed to breathe from the air pipes – it takes weeks of training and a scuba-diving qualification. Instead, we spend thirty minutes at a time in the water in our tails learning the basic underwater ballet moves, including mermaid spins, backward flips and, most importantly, how to smile and wave underwater.

During its heyday the Weeki Wachee mermaids did a full set of underwater tricks, including eating a banana and drinking a bottle of soda.

'Back then I could hold my breath for three and a half minutes,' says Mermaid Becky, who performed here between 1973 and 1985.

After a performance, the Currents (the mermaids who perform daily) come backstage and say hi. They are very young and very pretty, and I feel more like a manatee than ever. But as they chat with us and the elder mermaids, I can see their passion and their dedication to the mermaid lifestyle. They are a real sorority, proper sisters of the sea, and there's a respect between the generations. The young mermaids understand that without the elders, the mermaids who swam before them, they would not be performing at Weeki Wachee Springs today.

After our first swim, we sit together in the Sorority of the Sirens area, still in our swimsuits and towels, and warm up with mugs of hot tea and biscuits. The Formers talk about their

Weeki Wachee careers and their lives now, their post-mermaid careers, their families, their grandchildren.

Over the weekend, it becomes clear that female friendship is at the very core of mermaid life. Between swims, the trainee mermaids continue to gather around the Sirens area at the side of the spring and chat. Rachael, her mum Phyllis and best friend Jennifer have flown in from North Carolina, while Logan, a gorgeous tattooed burlesque dancer, has travelled down from Brooklyn.

It's listening to these tales of women's lives that makes it such a special experience. Best friends, mothers and daughters, a trio of women on their own, and Rhonda and me... We all have our tales to tell. I think about why I want to be a mermaid, and I murmur to Rhonda: 'No wonder it's called a "gossip of mermaids". I just want to hang out like this. With a bunch of great girls, dicking about in sexy shell bikinis, luring sailors to their doom. A life underwater and free of arseholes – that's living the dream!'

Sitting in our damp swimsuits, our 'performance' make-up streaked down our faces and hair crisping in the heat, we each explain what brings us to Weeki Wachee Springs and why we want to be mermaids. The women listen intently to each other, nodding and smiling in encouragement.

Rachael and Jennifer are young widows from North Carolina, who lost their husbands within months of each other and wanted to do something positive and bring some joy back into their lives. Phyllis is a pocket-rocket pensioner with bleached blonde hair and full mermaid attire, an aquatic addict on her third camp. She twitters and snips fondly with Rachael. Logan, the statuesque burlesque dancer, wants to learn the art for her work, and in her words 'jump on the mermaid bandwagon' before heading further south to relax on some 'big-ass beaches'.

Some people might see Siren Camp as just a bunch of over-the-hill ladies in fake nails and tails, pretending to be mermaids – and it kind of is, but in the very best way. There's a real vulnerability that comes with pursuing your dreams. I explain that I have teenage kids and I'm going through a divorce. I talk about how my need for freedom and release from my situation is overwhelming at times, and about how I struggle.

As I look around my sorority of sirens – a bunch of damp women in synthetic mermaid tails – I realise that life is all about sisterhood, innit? Look at the suffragettes. Look at the MeToo movement. Women need women. It's only other women who understand what life is like for us. I feel buoyed up.

As Mermaid Becky puts sun cream on my back, she gently whispers in my ear that I should get one of my moles checked out, and it brings a lump to my throat. I feel cared for among these women. I've known them for barely a few hours and already they are checking in on one another. The solidarity is palpable. That's the power of the Weeki Wachee mermaids.

After waving a reluctant goodbye to our mermaid sisters (although we've linked on social media and had invitations to visit them all in their various states, and promised to host them at home in the UK), Rhonda and I fling the roof back on the Mustang, whack up the tunes and head south towards St Petersburg and Anna Maria Island. Seven miles long, half a mile wide and fringed with coral-white beaches, Anna Maria Island is our last stop on our mermaid adventure and the final chance to lure some poor sailor in the Gulf of Mexico to his doom.

Crossing over the bridge past a group of barefoot surfers, we quickly realise that Anna Maria Island is our kind of town. Palm-fringed streets are lined with mid-century motels and dusky-pink clapboard homes, and, rather noticeably, there's an abundance of leatherback old charmers with pots of money and a house on the beach.

In search of a sugar daddy or a surfer, we head to the hottest spot in town, the Sandbar, where we dine with our toes in the sand as the sun sets. While we fail to lure a sailor, we do entrap a poor young waiter named Travis, who certainly wasn't expecting a pair of salty would-be cougars in his section that night. As he earnestly explains the farm-to-fork menu in his tight T-shirt and dreamy smile, my rheumy eyes fix on him in a manner that causes Rhonda to mutter, 'You bloody mervert.'

After dinner, I mention to Travis that we're having a nightcap next door in Bortell's Lounge and will buy him a drink. But while the young buck actually does rock up for his liquid tip, Rhonda and I are already deep in conversation with a couple of women at the bar. Hailing from West Virginia – 'You won't know it, it's shit' – they are here on holiday with their partners, who are standing at the bar silently watching baseball on the TV. Discontented with their company, the women turn to us, the sisterhood, and we bond over life, loves and thoughts about mermaids.

On our final morning, we wander down to the beach to say goodbye to the sea. I stare at Rhonda, lost in her own thoughts as she paddles in the shallows. I imagine she's kicking herself about not meeting Young Daniel, but there was just no way they could make it work.

I think about home. I've just spoken to my children, one of whom is having a particularly difficult time, and the reality of life and my responsibilities has come flooding back. I've had a taste of the delicious freedom I so desire, and now it's time to return home, but not beneath the waves. Not yet. Not yet.

CHAPTER 2

BUMBLING THROUGH

Rhonda

> '...*if we could be at home there*
> *back where we began*
> *where gravity does not pull us down, buoyant*
> *in the briny*
> *if we could truly*
> *be at home there*
> *feel the currents passing between*
> *the continents, see the coloured coral*
> *in all that vast and hidden space*
> *then we could be happy*
> *a mermaid.*'
> Anonymous poet, London

As our plane lumbers its way back up into the skies over Florida like one of the state's neon-pink flamingos, I gaze down at the Earth falling away and disappearing out of sight and I feel a weird emptiness.

I'm always happy to be going home to my kids. And I'm happy and endlessly grateful to have had these completely bonkers days with Tracey, diving deep into the surreal parallel universe of Old Florida — a place where we drank in bars along alligator-filled channels, amid men wearing Trump caps, debating whether the reptiles or the men were the most dangerous while we scarfed baskets of deep-fried pickles. And, of course, where we met

Darryl the crayfish minutes before tucking into a plate of his brethren.

A place where we flew on an airboat piloted by a delightfully butch lesbian into the Gulf of Mexico from Homosassa as a storm started to swirl overhead, and a place where, after being told not to swim too close to manatees out of respect for nature, I was virtually molested by an over-friendly lady one in a hot spring. Well at least I was getting *some* action, because god knows my love life was both a hot mess and a dusty desert.

West Florida was a place where we genuinely wondered if we should be fearing for our lives as we lost our way in the backwoods one day, driving past lawless-looking houses, huge American flags flapping in the front yards. When our route was blocked by sudden signs that were clearly home-made out of bits of decayed old fencing, announcing 'private roads' that were obviously no such thing, so that we half-expected wild-eyed rednecks to come running out from the trees with shotguns.

I'm sad because Tracey is sad. Things at home have preoccupied her for the last twenty-four hours, and I hate to see her so worried and also so disappointed to be ending this trip on a low.

And I'm sad because of Young Daniel. Of course, I didn't come to Florida thinking I would start a relationship. I'm not even looking for a relationship. So what am I even doing on Bumble?

A while ago, when the world opened up again after Covid, Tracey persuaded me to join a dating app. Mainly for the bants, she said.

I had a holy horror of online dating and, in fact, dating as a concept. I couldn't imagine anything worse than talking to strangers on my phone, or, shudder, meeting one in person to see if we wanted to get jiggy together. I'd never really gone on any dates in my life, and instead had mainly just slid into relationships with people I already knew like an out-of-control novice on an ice-skating rink.

At first, it was mildly entertaining, as Tracey and I traded screenshots of some of the specimens who liked us. It was also an eye-opener as to how brutal human beings can be – ghosting, unmatching in the middle of conversations, and, of course, sending unbidden dick pics or demanding candid photos.

Tracey's first foray into the world of post-separation dating had been via the medium of Hinge, a supposedly gentle dating app ideal for the perhaps trepidatious middle-aged woman dipping her toe back into the water.

'It was three months before I turned fifty. A friend suggested I bite the bullet and get on the apps quickly because "It's a barren wasteland the second you hit five-oh!", she told me.

'Shopping for men is fun,' Tracey assured me. 'It's like swiping through a digital Panini football sticker album, except the men are less attractive.'

She soon matched with a bloke, a divorcee and father of teenagers – another writer, who also lived in Brighton.

'I met him for coffee – I was nervous, but, weirdly, not as nervous as I thought I'd be, considering it was my first date for more than twenty-five years. But we got on well. Things progressed on WhatsApp. We chatted and chatted, sometimes into the early hours, and then one Sunday afternoon he suggested I go round to his for coffee the next morning. Coffee turned into sex. And that was that. For the first time in twenty-five years, I had sex with someone who wasn't my husband.

'It lasted a couple of months, in the form of quickies after the school run, and coffee was rarely involved, but it was great to get back in the saddle,' she said.

The Bearded Wanker sounded conceited, in my opinion. We called him BW because he sent her unsolicited videos of himself wanking, even when she was wiped out with Covid. It's an eternal mystery to women why men think they would want to see this kind of thing.

After a while BW told her he didn't see her as relationship material, just friends with benefits. She was 'too keen'.

I was livid. As was she.

'He was projecting. I told him that I'd just come out of a

twenty-five-year relationship and the very last thing I wanted was another one.'

It ended as quickly as it had begun.

Over time, I did come to see the worth of dating apps. Just as in the pre-app age, when, alone in Berlin, I'd once put a call out to my friends on Facebook for local contacts who might entertain me, and ended up spending a fun night out in the bars of Schöneberg with a lovely writer and his husband, I started using them as a tool for enriching my travels.

Whenever I was going somewhere by myself, and sometimes with Tracey, I changed my setting to Travel Mode and looked at people who liked me in the destination I was heading to – men, women and trans people, of all ages (within reason). Sometimes I liked one back and we chatted. Often it led nowhere. Most times, when I got to my destination, I found I was really very happy just to have time by myself and the freedom to amble around without worrying about whether another person was happy.

With Young Daniel it was different. Within twenty-four hours of setting my travel mode to Tampa, I'd been liked by around six hundred men and women in Florida. That's not because I'm a great catch, it's a measure of how ridiculous it all is. Most of the men wore baseball caps and seemed fully interchangeable. A lot were pictured swinging golf clubs, or delightedly dangling tarpon from their fists. It was both overwhelming and uninspiring.

But in among the many thumbnail pics to scroll through, one face jumped out at me. There was just something about his cheeky-sexy, unabashed grin that made me know I had to chat to him. I somehow felt I recognised him.

Our conversation took wings. Young Daniel was a science teacher, a long-term single dad turned empty-nester, and a sometime poet. We had an immediate connection via long, long text messages, which very quickly turned into voicemails and video messages from him that let me see that he was a) real b) incredibly cute and charismatic and *right* up my alley.

And that was before I'd even arrived in Florida. Alas, after Tracey and I landed and hotfooted it out of Tampa to meet the crayfish, mermaids and molesting manatees of the Gulf Coast, it quickly became apparent that, because of our packed schedule of activities and Young Daniel's teaching and prior commitments for the week, we probably wouldn't actually be able to meet. But we kept messaging and he gave me lots of tips about the places we were going to – tips that made our trip that much better (Rule #1 of travel being that nothing beats insider intel from a local).

But we didn't get together, and that's why, as we break through the clouds and leave Florida behind us like a fever dream, I'm struck by a sadness that seems incommensurate – as if I've missed out on something that was meant to be.

Fast forward just two months and I'm hugging Young Daniel outside King's Cross station in London. Letting go of each other, we laugh, then we hug again. Perhaps it's the sheer relief that, from just one glance, we know we like each other IRL too.

Dan called me yesterday evening and said he was flying into London today to get a connection back to Tampa. Before I'd unearthed him from the rubble of Bumble, he'd been planning a solo Europe trip for summer, and this was the endpoint of that. At one stage, when he reached Marseille, he asked me if I could maybe fly down to meet him there, to dance in the streets amid the crowds of partying locals, but I couldn't make it work logistically. Now he's returning to the States a bit early because of his dad's cancer, hence the call. As soon as he told me, I rejigged my deadlines for the week and looked up train times. It was now or never.

We spend eight straight hours together, and they pass at the crazed, vertiginous speed of a runaway train. I'm like a rabbit in his headlights. We walk around a London he's only briefly been to once before, and that was when he was four. I take him around Brick Lane with its street art and to Spitalfields Market for lunch, and to an unfathomably ancient pub. Then we walk past the Tower of London, across Tower Bridge and along the South Bank, stopping for a drink every so often. Young Daniel is dumbfounded by how old everything is here. We talk the whole time and we laugh, a lot – so much so that I (admittedly slave to a dodgy menopausal bladder) nearly pee myself several times.

Outside Tate Modern, we stop when Daniel spots a man feverishly typing on a manual typewriter perched on a tiny foldout table. It turns out he's a poet for hire and, for a sum of one's choice in the currency of one's choice, he writes a piece on any topic you suggest.

Young Daniel fishes out some dollars and asks him to write a poem about serendipity. After a few minutes of pounding away on the keys, the man hands us a poem about two people meeting and falling in love – and asking themselves if their encounter was something willed by the universe, or pure chance, the product of chaos. Daniel, I already know, believes there's no such thing as random – no coincidences.

Then it's my turn to pick a topic, and because I don't want to be a simp, as the kids say, with a romantic gesture, I think beyond Daniel to Florida and to Tracey, and I ask for a poem about mermaids in honour of our friendship and our road trip.

Waiting for the poem, Dan and I exchange a lingering glance loaded with questions. There's something special to this day, we both know it.

The man with the typewriter hands us an equally beautiful poem about mermaids.

About an hour later, Dan seals his place in my heart forever by buying a cheap metallic rose from a vendor on Hungerford Bridge to take back to a fierce female toilet attendant who just yelled at us for jumping the entry barriers to avoid paying, because we had no change. He feels guilty, he says, for disrespecting her by claiming we hadn't done it. His face as he apologises to her makes my legs wobble. I get a second rose and hold it to my heart.

Time starts running out for us. It starts to gallop. I feel sick. Dan calls the single room he'd booked near Gatwick to find out if he can arrive later than they stipulated. I look at last trains to Manchester, seeing how far I can push it before running to the station.

I already know Dan is a gin fan and before we part I lead him to a secret gin parlour behind a hidden door, where he goes into raptures over a tasting flight that includes a pungent truffle gin. His sheer delight in it all makes me so happy. But I have to sprint for my last train. There's no fighting it any more.

Out in the street, as I come over all sensible and mumsy, explaining to him which way to walk to get his Gatwick train, he shakes his head and laughs and leans in to kiss me. And I kiss him back, I keep kissing him, wondering why it didn't happen earlier in the day, why I didn't make it happen, wanting time to just stop right there. It's delicious. He's delicious.

I turn and run for the station, and everything I pass on the way, all the places I have known for most of my life, I see anew and more vividly as if through his eyes. I've shown him so much today, London through my eyes, yet I want to show him more, *everything*. But time has called itself on us.

'And love is a ghost that the others can't see, it's a danger'

On the train back to Manchester I listen to these lyrics from Agnes Obel's 'Familiar' and I start to get the horrible feeling that despite what I said to Daniel as we parted – that we will meet again some day – I won't ever see him again. And though we do exchange a few messages, I can already feel him pulling away, like someone going up in smoke in front of my eyes. Most tellingly, over the next few days he doesn't post anything on social media about his day in London, despite having taken photos. Everywhere else he went in Europe, he did.

Young Daniel is, to me, the very best kind of person: open, curious, intelligent, sexy, political. But he also, I sleuth out via social media after he's back home, seems to have a girlfriend – one he probably got together with not long before his trip to Europe but omitted to mention.

I'm sad but I try to be sanguine. He's fifteen years younger than me, he has a constraining job as a teacher and responsibilities as a single dad, he lives a nine-hour, seven-hundred-pound flight away from me. And yes, there's probably a pesky girlfriend on the scene.

I tell myself it was never going to be anything more than a day – but what a day it was. When a friend I tell about it dismisses it as sounding like a Richard Curtis movie, I retort: But don't we all need the odd Richard Curtis day in our lives? In fact, I think it should be obligatory. I'd actually like one a year, please.

Meeting Young Daniel also does me a huge favour by helping me define/refine what I do want from a man, because he was pretty much the right person in the wrong place and at the wrong time. Meeting him and thinking about what I liked so much about him inspires me to draw up a mental list of eight things I would want if I was to have a relationship. He scores seven and a half.

I apply the same checklist to my mental Rolodex of exes and am startled that so many of them score around the two or three mark. *What the fuck have I been doing all my life?* Have I been sleepwalking? And will I ever find anyone more well suited to me than Dan?

Young Daniel isn't my first Bumble date. My first was almost too ludicrous to talk about, for so many reasons. His age, twenty-nine, was really the very least of them.

It was all Tracey's fault, as per usual. Somehow she'd inveigled her way into getting us (her, me and four girlfriends) a few days at an €8-million villa in the middle of nowhere in Chianti for the purposes of belatedly celebrating her fiftieth birthday after lockdown cheated her of the Cher-themed party she'd planned for years.

Turning fifty was the catalyst for many of Tracey's wild decisions, it seemed. Months earlier she'd got her first tattoo and then tickets for Glastonbury. Midlife crisis, much? She announced she was also on the (to-my-mind) terrifying path to becoming a stand-up comedian.

'It's my present to me for my fiftieth birthday,' she announced, after booking herself on a ten-week beginners' course in Brighton.

I thought it was just a fad, a new hobby, and that was where it was going to end. Partly because personally I can't imagine anything worse. It seemed like a form of self-torture to me. Why would you put yourself through *that*?

Until one morning she messaged me she'd just done her first gig. She was high on adrenaline. I realised that she was serious about being a funny girl and that this was just the start of something big.

Where we stayed in Italy was a place so shockingly Tuscan (rolling vineyards, gnarled farmers on tractors, shimmering silvery olive groves) that we not only had to keep pinching ourselves, but even questioned if it was all fake – a kind of Italian *Westworld*. Or if we were all dreaming. Or drunk.

To be fair, we were drunk quite a lot of the time, Tracey strutting around the place in a black body stocking, silver ankle boots and a Cher wig that became more and more tangled as the nights went on, our karaoke blasting out even as dawn spread over the olive groves.

But I wasn't drunk the morning my phone rang as I was tucking into a late hangover breakfast cooked for us by our personal chefs and saw that someone was calling me via Bumble. I stared at my phone in horror. I didn't even know you could make calls through dating apps. That said, I was still new to the game at this point. This was a year pre-Daniel and I was still at the 'bants' stage.

The six of us girls were happy as clams, making day trips to Florence and San Gimignano, wine tasting at local vineyards, gorging ourselves senseless in hilltop restaurants and swimming in our pool with its laughably dreamy views. All of us women friends present were going through difficult things, including divorce, the ill health of parents and issues with our offspring, and there were a lot of deep and healing conversations as well as those moments of pure hedonism.

But those of us who were on dating apps hadn't been able to resist browsing the offerings of the surrounding countryside in our spare moments, cackling as we swiped right on one after another Italian menfolk as ludicrously gorgeous as the scenery, comparing our matches.

The man who called me over my hangover breakfast turned out to be a once-globetrotting sommelier who had come home in the pandemic to settle down and be near his parents, and had retrained as an electrician. He was also twenty-three years younger than me. It seemed unlikely that anything could evolve from such a match, but he was heartbreakingly good-looking and it seemed churlish not to at least chat and even, encouraged by the others, invite him round for a drink by the pool.

Ultimately, our attempts at a Tuscan idyll fell apart: Luca's work obligations and the things we womenfolk had planned together scotched our attempts at an actual hook-up. But when, from the airport, I sent him a flippant parting message to the effect that I would take him out to dinner next time I was in Florence, or that he was welcome in Manchester whenever he made it over to the UK, I was shocked but rather thrilled when he responded with screenshots of imminent flights.

Of course I hesitated. I'm not completely insane. And as I said, I'd never really been on a date, as such: I'd mainly known my men 'in real life' and then careered, often unthinkingly, into relationships from friendships. Just the idea of walking into a pub or restaurant and meeting a stranger gave me hives. But I played along with Luca's Manchester suggestion and tried to view it as a regular Bumble date. He could book a hotel, and we could go out for dinner, and if there was a spark we could take it from there.

When this second plan also fell through – Luca's work schedule combined with the flight schedules would give him less than twenty-four hours in my city – I found myself doing what I'd ardently promised myself I wouldn't: I said I'd think about booking a flight out to see him.

Think about it...

Rewind: perhaps I *am* insane. All I can say is that, at the time, we'd been cooped up in successive lockdowns for two years, I'd lost all my work, I'd been overseeing the homeschooling and mental health of my kids, and my marriage was irretrievably broken down but there were no financial means of separating.

I'd had a spectacularly ill-judged and disastrous affair with a much older married man, followed by an emotional affair with someone in another country I'd met just before the pandemic started and couldn't get to see in person. That had also ended in a bit of a car crash. My head was all over the place. I wasn't sleeping well due to a toxic combo of almost homicidal rage towards a variety of people and spiralling menopause symptoms.

When I flew out to Italy, I was your classic woman on the edge, in full midlife crisis mode.

Luca picked me up from his local train station and drove me to lunch in a place so beautiful and, again, so ridiculously Tuscan that I nearly puked. Having got up for the airport run at 3 am but also, out of sheer petrification at what I was doing, barely slept for days in the run-up (it had been eight weeks since we 'met'), I was delirious with tiredness too.

Luca chose from the menu for me, which I loved (sometimes it feels like such a treat not having to think and make decisions), and we topped off our sublime lunch and wine with shots of limoncello. Both quite drunk by this point, we headed to a viewpoint over vineyards unfurling as far as the eye could see and exchanged sticky-liqueur kisses like sickening fools in the most clichéd of romcoms.

As I hadn't wanted to agree to go to his place until I'd met him and ensured he wasn't just a very handsome serial killer, I'd booked myself a boutique hotel in the hills outside Siena. I invited him to come there with me, and there we swam in a shimmering pool with glorious views, drank the champagne I'd bought from duty free to celebrate his birthday (he turned thirty the day before, bless his little cotton socks), went to bed, and then had dinner in a candlelit courtyard shared by only two other couples, both in their seventies.

When one of them, Americans, saw fit to announce that they were celebrating their fiftieth wedding anniversary, I had to bite my tongue. If only they knew that this was the very first time Luca and I had met. And that I was easily old enough to be his mum. God knows, I hadn't asked and didn't really care to know, but his mother might even be younger than me. Awks.

The woman parading her half-century-long marriage then remarked on how cool it was that I was with a 'real-life Italian', and, before I could think better of it, I found myself blurting out, 'Oh yes, I rented him for the night.'

I glanced panic-stricken at Luca to see if he had understood. We were getting by, but his English really wasn't very good and my Italian is minimal. He didn't react. From the couple, on the other hand, there emanated an uneasy silence. Part of me relished their discomfort. But I felt bad for Luca. I'd been disrespectful.

In the night, I woke up and he wasn't beside me. I got up and found him in the second bedroom, awake. He said he couldn't sleep. I knew that I – *this* – wasn't what he had been expecting. Did he even know what he'd expected?

Regardless, the next day we tried to stay on at the lovely hotel, but found it was fully booked for the weekend. We talked about driving to another region, but Luca was indecisive about which one. He'd been like that from the start – hopelessly millennial, expecting me to make all the decisions and then quibbling about them. I was a bit tired of it all and couldn't be bothered to make a decision and then have him later turn it on me. It was his country, he knew the good places, and I wanted him to just take charge.

So we went to his house for the next two days. In some ways it was blissful. He cooked for me, made me cocktails, took me to bed. He smoked spliffs and I sunbathed in his yard with a book. We got takeout pizza and watched a movie together, me trying to absorb more Italian from the subtitles.

But there was still something awry. I knew, deep down, that Luca was cross with me. I knew I was not what he wanted. It was hard to understand each other, but from the things he said it seemed he wanted someone to look after, someone to *serve*, even.

And that wasn't me and he'd realised that. I'm an independent modern woman with an all-consuming career I love, and at that point I was fifty-three years of age. I had gone to Tuscany for some fun and yes, undoubtedly the ego boost of being bedded by a young hot Italian. Somewhere in the run-up to it all, the communication had failed. As I said, his English isn't great and my Italian is non-existent. There was a lot of Google Translate involved. But also, there are words, and then there are ineffable feelings and yearnings.

And it seemed Luca wanted me to be dominant even in bed – perhaps thought that's what older women do. But although, yes, we have the benefit of experience and knowing what we like, what I've been learning over these past few years of singledom is that I am, or at l least sometimes can be, a sub. As I did when I so happily let Luca order my lunch for me, it turns out that sometimes, just sometimes, I love giving up control. I find it relaxing in a life during which I've had so much responsibility and decision-making on my plate. But that's another story.

Anyway, I had a divorce to deal with and three teens to steer through exams, impending university and all manner of other things. I also travel a lot for work, while Luca was just starting a new job that meant he'd only have one day off a week for the next six months.

At one point he lost his temper with me, said I had a perfect life. He *wanted* it, he said. Which I kind of got, while thinking: I came to Tuscany to get laid, not to be attacked or made to feel ungrateful for my privilege and luck (which I recognise and am grateful for).

In a vile mood now myself, I told him I was going to the Palio the next day. By complete coincidence the world-famous horse race was on in nearby Siena while I was there, and there was no way I was going to miss out on it. Luca said he didn't want to come, and I didn't push it; he'd lived there all his life, it must be old hat to him (I later found out he'd never even been to it – something others travel from all around the world for).

The Palio turned out to be even more of a disaster than the date. I found it chaotic and cruel. I hated the remorseless whipping of the horses and the seemingly endless false starts that exhausted them. All this and, along with tens of thousands of other spectators, I was corralled into an enclosure in the centre of Siena's main square, Piazza del Campo, which was transformed into a boiling sea of lobster-red people beneath an unforgiving Tuscan sun.

But my real problem was that, although the race itself takes only ninety seconds, with the many false starts and then the time it takes to line the horses up again, it can actually drag on for several hours. I began to get antsy. Luca was coming to pick me up and we were going to dinner. He was already annoyed with me; I knew being late would really piss him off. But I was trapped here in this ridiculously beautiful piazza turned scene of bedlam.

Deciding I couldn't put up with the nonsense any longer, I headed over to one of the high wooden gates keeping people in the enclosure. I approached a member of staff and told them I felt faint and absolutely had to leave. They can't keep me here, I said to myself. The horses were being given another rest, it was demonically hot, and things had overrun by two hours. People had lives to get on with. It was against human rights.

All at once, two people arrived with a stretcher and slam-dunked me onto it, despite my protestations now that I didn't actually feel *that* ill after all. Then I was carried over to the other side of the square, with spectators ogling me as the stretcher-bearers jogged through them, yelling at them to make way. I was mortified. When we got to a medical area, I was force-fed water and told I wasn't going anywhere until the race was over.

By the time the whole saga was done, the race run and the gates opened, I was catastrophically late. I'd messaged Luca, but he'd already left home. By the time I barged my way through the exiting melee and found him in his car on the edge of the city, he was furious – said he couldn't understand how I could be so fucking dumb.

I told him that if the race is supposed to take ninety seconds, I couldn't be expected to know I'd still be stuck there two hours later. How was I supposed to know about all the false starts? He stayed cross. We didn't go for dinner.

I left the next day, feeling a bit broken. Luca clearly couldn't wait to see the back of me and that's never a pleasant feeling, even when you think someone has been behaving like a bit of a dick themselves. I told him that, given my flight was last thing that night, I was going to spend the day in Livorno – a rough port town I'd always fancied the sound of for its associations with the doomed lovers Modigliani and Jeanne Hébuterne, and with the equally tragedy-soaked Byron and the Shelleys. It was the perfect place to head after a failed romantic assignation.

Before my train even got to Livorno, texts were coming

through from Luca, asking how I was doing. And when I finally got back to Pisa airport that night, he said he wished he'd come with me – he'd never been to Livorno either. He also told me I was welcome back at his place whenever I 'needed a rest'. I stared at all these messages in bewilderment.

A few days later, he messaged me to say he was missing me. Then he went quiet for a long time, and after that a couple of years went by with him occasionally dropping me a message on Insta. The last time, a while back now, he told me he wanted to be my bitch, and I replied that I can't be like that with him – that that's not me. His conclusion: a) I over-complicate things and b) I'm 'too nice'.

Well, fine, maybe that's all true. We all need feedback. And false starts.

A less foolhardy woman than me would probably have deleted Bumble by this point, on the basis that her rational decision-making faculties were on the blink. Instead, just a week and a half later, I found myself loading my bike into the back of the car and driving an hour to West Yorkshire for a date with another much younger man. With this one, the conversation positively glittered. He also liked some seriously good music. There was no question of not meeting.

Anurag – a lovely name meaning attachment or devotion in Sanskrit – had come to Yorkshire from Mumbai, leaving his very young son behind. I didn't know the exact circumstances, only that the kid was with his mother. I didn't pry.

It wasn't really any of my business – partly because the minute I met the guy in a Heptonstall café, and despite the fact that he was very cool, quirky and also quite handsome, I knew there was no physical spark for me. Don't you just hate it when that happens?

But we did have an absolutely cracking date, cycling six hours through a mainly deserted Yorkshire valley, stopping at Sylvia Plath's grave and then for beer in one of Britain's most remote pubs – one where mute locals gawped slack-jawed at us when we walked in. All burly and brown and bearded and bright in a Hawaiian shirt and cycling helmet, Anurag wasn't what they were used to in those parts. Unlucky for them.

We talked about India, one of my own favourite countries, and we talked about places in the UK he should see (he'd never even been here before he relocated), and we had lots of belly laughs and planned another ride in the future. Beside a reservoir that felt like it was at the end of the world, I sensed he was about to try to kiss me but instead I turned back to my bike.

We'd stayed out so long, we ended up cycling back to Heptonstall in darkness and, sod's law being in operation, Anurag got a puncture as well. I had to ride ahead to get my car and go back for him and then drive him home. Despite all this faff, the mood stayed very light and fun. In fact, it was one of the best days ever. Just not a Dan day.

And so it went. In London, I had a date with a fashion lecturer in his early forties who said he was looking for something casual, only to reveal midway through that he was partnered and ENM. Which is fine, I have no problem whatsoever with polys – only I thought he should have been fully clear about that before. We had a long, entertaining evening that finished with a drunken canoodle in the street, but then I decided not to go any further, aware I shouldn't dabble with people with partners. Been there done that – the risks are too great.

In Malta, on a work trip to write about Pride celebrations in Valletta, I indulged myself after a sparse summer with a hook-up with a hot guy in his thirties, ordering him to my hotel suite like room service. I'd already checked him out because he listed himself on Bumble with his full name; googling him, I discovered he was well-known in football on the island. I could see his friends on Insta, and he told me his mum even worked in the hotel I was staying in.

Mikki was not a danger – or only in the make-believe way I wanted him to be. I let him indulge his dom fantasies and he let me give up control for a few hours, and it worked out well for both of us. The next night he asked if we could get together again, and maybe find another girl to join in this time, and I said I wasn't at all averse to the suggestion but that I was knackered and had an event to host in London the next day so would have to take a rain check. But we were both happy and I told him I'd let him know when I was out there next. He occasionally messages me to ask if I'm going back any time soon.

In Mumbai, I flirted with the idea of going out with someone who sang for Bollywood movies, until jet lag struck me down. I regret that I didn't – it could have been a blast and a fascinating take on the city. And while I was in India, I messaged Anurag and it turned out he was back there, for good – back in his son's life and back with his son's mother. And I was delighted for him that he'd sorted everything out, and, though we couldn't manage to meet, I told him I'd be in touch next time I was in India.

There are others I've never met and maybe never will, collected all around the world like 'mermaid's tears', another name for shiny pieces of sea glass. *Interesting* people I'd never normally have encountered in real life – a fireman in the wilds of southern Australia, for instance, who I matched with when I was out there with my youngest son, the summer post-Luca and post-Anurag. A sexy, naughty, dommy Sri Lankan pilot living in Kuwait, who wanted me to go to sex parties with him in Europe or Singapore. A nomadic polyamorous Brazilian who founded an eco-village in a remote valley. A man from Connecticut, uprooted indefinitely back to his home city of Chennai to help his family nurse his terminally ill father. All human life is there.

Almost all of them, again, are quite a bit younger than me. All are fascinating in their way. They fade in and out – disappear below the surface and then pop up again a few weeks or months later like mermen breaking the skin of the water. Perfect for a mermaid like me.

CHAPTER 3

LIFE-CHANGING ENCOUNTERS IN LAPLAND

Tracey

'It's *Chriiistmaaas!*' booms Noddy from the plane's cabin speakers.

All right Holder, give it a rest. The all-too familiar tune, which has been belching out of high-street stores since mid-September, is a little too much for my head right now. Normally a fan of all things festive, I'm struggling to match Slade's energy on this gloomy December morning at Gatwick Airport.

It's three weeks until Christmas and two weeks until I turn forty, and I'm taking one of my daughters to Lapland, along with eight thousand million other children.

Fuck my life.

On paper, I should be as smug as a talentless influencer on a freebie in the Maldives. I live in Brighton, I have an incredibly cool job where I get to travel the world, I have three gorgeous kids, a husband, plenty of friends. But in reality, I'm falling off a cliff. I'm so unhappy I could quite happily cut my own head off with a blunt spoon and fling it into the ether on a medieval trebuchet.

But first I have to meet bloody Santa.

One of the many (many) benefits of my career choice is the opportunity to bring my kids along for the ride. However, with only one place going, I have to make the Sophie's Choice of which of my twins to bring to Lapland. I sit the girls down and explain my predicament.

'Right, Mummy's got a trip that I'm allowed to take only one of you on. So we're gonna toss a coin to see who goes, okay? No fights.'

I toss the coin and N wins. L promptly bursts into tears and N, ever the charmer, says, 'It's okay, Mummy, L can go on this trip and I'll go on the next one.'

Phew. Crisis averted. So L gets to meet the big man with the beard in Lapland and N gets to lord it over her for the rest of time.

Our plane is packed with wide-eyed children, many on the verge of hysteria about meeting their toymaker. I'm equally a little hysterical, not least because of my delicate mental health. But also because it's where I meet Rhonda for the first time.

Rhonda Carrier was one of my first editors as a travel writer. We've been in touch via email for a couple of years, but this will be the first time we meet and I want to make a good impression. Unfortunately, my stupid head has other ideas.

Two weeks ago I moved to Brighton with my husband, six-year-old twin girls and boy aged nine – and I'm now dealing with the mental fallout of a new home, a new school, a new city, an increasingly absent husband and a spiralling marriage.

However, with a well-practised rictus grin on my face, I make a valiant attempt to be a normal functioning human being in front of Rhonda and the four other mums on the press trip.

As we land at a snowy Ivalo airport deep within the Arctic Circle, the festive excitement reaches fever pitch.

'Where are the penguins?' asks L, and a lengthy geography lesson ensues on the coach as we wind our way past frosty forests of fir trees and clusters of cute wood-panelled cottages crouched under blankets of snow.

There are five of us on the trip, each with our chosen child, and you can almost sense the underlying threat of 'You'd better behave yourself' behind every mother's gritted grin.

We're staying in Saariselkä, a small one-horse (or perhaps one-reindeer) town in the northern Inari region of Finnish Lapland, where according to legend the nearby Korvatunturi fell is the very place Santa Claus is from. It's 1 pm and the sky is a grubby, twilight grey with barely a hint of warmth on the horizon. In winter, the Arctic Circle gets roughly five hours of grey light a day, which for many of the indigenous Sámi population evokes a state of lethargy. But it doesn't, I notice, for L and the thousands of excitable children who visit each December.

With temperatures a nippy −10°C, we shuffle across the icy road to a ski shop, where we're fully kitted out in thermal snowsuits, boots and gloves, which means we can body-flop to the floor and snow-angel without fear of the cold. Which is what my girl does approximately every seven minutes.

Inside the hotel, the 'Now That's What I Call Christmas' album is playing on an eternal loop, which I fear does more damage to my mental health than the crippling depression. Our festive holiday reps, Jinglebell Jenny and Gingerbread Greg, are on hand to gee up the children into a pre-Christmas frenzy with games and dancing while we parents get into the festive spirit with mugs of complimentary *glögg*.

In saner times, I'm a sociable extrovert and am in my element on press trips, particularly when they are with a bunch of awesome, like-minded women like this.

I bloody love women. I think we are the most brilliant, genuine, tough-as-tits, beautiful sacks of skin on the planet. And I'm so proud to be one. But on this trip, thanks to my delicate mental health, I feel like I'm on the fringes of the group dynamic, partaking from its outer limits.

On our first evening in Saariselkä, as the kids are knocking about together having fun with the elves, the group bonds round the dinner table, drinking wine and swapping stories. I sit quietly on the edge, listening to their lives, willing myself to join in.

There's S, a bubbly force of nature who seems to juggle several careers including one as a moderator and sometime writer for

Mumsnet and one as a freelance PR. She's quite a bit younger than the rest of us but had had a novel published by her early twenties. She's there with her adorable nine-year-old son, who proudly takes the rest of the kids, who are all younger, under his wing.

Then there's B, who's half-British half-German and has relocated to the Continent with her husband and four kids, one of whom is a niece she adopted after her sister died far too young. I wonder at how much she must have on her plate. And quieter than them is J, a high-flying director of a creative agency.

With her gorgeous brown eyes and huge smile, S is immediately likeable, and I watch a little enviously as she and Rhonda bond at the speed of light. As the wine flows, so inevitably does the honesty. That's what almost invariably happens when women get together.

S talks about problems with her father and also about being raped in her teens – her first experience of sex. And from that it's not long before B reveals that her husband had an affair while she was pregnant *and* mourning the loss of her sister.

God, men can be shits, can't they?

Bolstered by the wine, which somewhat soothes my sad head, I confess that I'm not entirely happy in my marriage either and am in counselling, but add that I'm hopeful that our recent move to Brighton will help.

I've had a wobbly head at various points in my life – aged eight and in my teens and then my early twenties – but depression has been more of a regular visitor since I had the twins.

It was a quick pregnancy. Less than seven months in all, as I developed twin-to-twin transfusion syndrome (TTTS), a rare condition affecting the blood supply between identical twins in utero. If unmonitored, it can be fatal for one or both twins, and as a result I was having weekly scans at King's in London. At my last scan it had progressed too far and the girls had to be whipped out, rather dramatically, nine weeks early.

To add to the fun, there were no ICU beds for them, either in London or beyond. I was on the verge of being flown by helicopter to Dundee (a prospect I found rather exciting) to have them there, when two ICU incubators became available in a hospital in Portsmouth and we were whizzed down the A3 in the early hours of Thursday morning, me swearing like a navvy all the way.

At 8.50 and 8.52 that morning, I went from being a mother of one to three children in a matter of minutes, performing a rather impressive magic trick in the style of Siegfried & Roy, except with babies not tigers. Ta-dah!

After a flurry of visitors – big brother, grandparents, friends – over the first weekend, I was left alone in a hospital room while my teeny-tiny premature girls were wired up to monitors in intensive care.

My husband seemed to be treating it like a minibreak. His parents had come down to meet their new granddaughters and they were all staying in the local Holiday Inn. They disappeared off in the afternoon to make use of the indoor pool, steam room and sauna.

After the weekend, my husband headed off with the rest of his family and went back to work, and I was left alone with a bag of strong painkillers, *Hello!* magazine and a pair of leaky tits to process this incredible, scary and life-changing experience.

That night, I was in ICU staring at my tiny somewhat Jurassic-looking underweight babies with tears streaming down my face. The duty nurse – an absolute darling, aren't they all? – comforted and reassured me that they would be A-OK. But oddly, I don't think I was crying just for them. I was also crying for me. I felt completely and utterly alone in the world and now I had these three small humans to raise and protect. I'd never felt so overwhelmed in my life.

After a week in Portsmouth I was discharged and the girls were transferred back to our local hospital in London to spend another few weeks in special care. The girls were taken by ambulance in their incubators, one at a time, and my husband drove down to pick me up and take me back to London.

Of course, things took their time and we had to wait a while for the consultant to discharge me. He was getting antsy and pacing the ward, desperate to get back to the office. We didn't really speak about the situation, the enormity of what had just happened in the last week. I was still processing everything: the lack of beds, the midnight dash down the A3, the emergency Caesarean, being alone in hospital for a week. And the babies weren't out of the woods just yet. They still had a few more weeks in hospital before I could bring them home and adjust to life as a mother of three.

I looked at him, pacing, and I felt like an inconvenience.

When we eventually got back to London, he stated that he needed to get back to the office and asked if my mother could pick me up from here – Wimbledon. I had just, rather dramatically, given birth to two of his children and it felt like he couldn't dispatch me quickly enough. I said it was okay for him to drop me on the side of the street and I called my mother to come pick me up and take me to the hospital.

The next few weeks were like living in a weird bubble. At times I felt high with happiness that my babies were here, safe and thriving – look at me, a mother of three! At other times, I thought I would pass out with the pure fear of keeping them all alive.

At home, I dutifully expressed milk every four hours and then took my son to nursery, before hopping on the bus to King's College Hospital to deliver said milk and spend the day with my girls. I'd then pick up my son, and my husband would sometimes pop in to see the babies after work, returning home late. Those first few weeks, we barely saw each other, let alone talked it out.

The girls were finally discharged from hospital a few days before Christmas. That same day, my parents moved to Norfolk for their retirement. I felt incredibly lonely. My mum and dad, who were a fantastic help when my son was born, were now several hours away. And the mum friends I'd made through my first child were not there either; one by one, they had fallen away as their families grew and got busy.

The twins' first year was a blur. I have very little memory of it. Even now, I look at photos taken and I don't recognise myself. My husband was working twelve-hour days and I was left to muddle through bringing up a toddler and two tiny babies, along with trying to cling on to the threads of my career.

Thank God for the OG sisterhood. My friend Sharon would stop by once a week after work without fail, to help me get the nippers to bed, and then we'd share a bottle of wine and chat for an hour. We met in Hong Kong when she was my boss at Oscar's, a bar and restaurant in Lan Kwai Fong. Then bizarrely, in a time before mobile phones, the universe brought us back together when she walked into the bar I was working in at London Bridge. When I got pregnant with the twins, it was Sharon's gentle kindness and unwavering support that I needed.

But there was more drama to come. In that first year, I noticed the twins were developing at different rates. Although bright, sparky and full of energy, N struggled to sit up unaided, roll over or crawl like her sister. After I'd raised my concerns several times with the health visitor, we were finally sent for an MRI scan to see what the deal was.

Likely as a result of TTTS and the twins' rather urgent arrival, N was diagnosed with hemiplegic cerebral palsy at eighteen months of age. The consultant told us the result of her MRI in his office, my husband and I each holding a twin as we were informed that one of our babies had suffered brain damage.

I burst into tears. Hugging her close, I thought I might vomit over the consultant. He, however, could barely look at me, let alone comfort me, as the consultant explained that he could not predict the outcome – she may or may not walk, she may or may not live an independent life.

We drove home in silence. I felt completely numb, tears still streaming down my face. And while I understood that he was in complete shock as well – of course he was – the fact that he could barely look at me, let alone hug, touch or comfort me, screamed so much about our relationship.

In a daze, I went up the road to pick up my son from my friend N's house, and promptly broke down in more tears. I explained what the consultant had said and N gave me a huge hug. She'd been through a similar experience when her oldest daughter – who was just five – had been diagnosed with cancer around eighteen months. She was now out the other side, just, but it was her incredible support that got me through those first days and weeks.

Yet at home it felt like I was dealing with this bombshell on my own, attending every consultant, paediatric and physio appointment going while being given very little assurance.

The good news is that my darling girl actually went on to take her first steps the summer she turned four, started horse-riding at five, and at the grand age of seven took to the ski slopes for the first time. She is a stone-cold legend.

But it was not until fourteen years later, when I was knee-deep in therapy, that I eventually processed that first year, the abandonment I felt after having the twins, and N's diagnosis.

Back in Lapland and the big day has arrived. L is so delirious with excitement about meeting the big man that I fear she may vomit her breakfast berry pancakes directly into his beard.

A clutch of snow-draped log cabins, twinkling cottages and traditional *kotus* (Sami teepee-style tents), Santa's Village looks like it has sprung up from nowhere. With L holding my sheepskinned paw, we pad along a candlelit path to a twinkling white crossroads, where we join the line for 'Santa's log cabin' and our meeting with the big man himself. Sadly, Dasher,

Donner, Blitzen and the gang are nowhere to be seen. Instead we cuddle up in a fur-lined sleigh and are pulled through the snowy pine forest by an elf on a snowmobile.

Within minutes we arrive at a small clearing at the edge of the woods. Santa's cabin is pure fairytale; a tiny wooden door, red curtains at the window and a soft amber glow beaming from within. Outside, a roaring bonfire is being tended to by an elf named Whisper. I discreetly hand her our ticket (which has L's name and age on) and we patiently wait our turn.

Being a jaded hag, I was fully expecting the resort to be a Santa machine, churning kids through the experience a dozen at a time. But as we sit here alone on this quiet Arctic morning, watching as the grimy sun desperately tries to buoy itself over the snowy horizon, I feel a flutter of belief myself.

L nervously knocks on the wooden door and we're welcomed into the cosy cabin by two cheery elves. A twinkling Christmas tree overflows with gifts, reindeer skin rugs cover the wooden floor and knitted stockings hang over the fireplace. And there he is. Resplendent in red and as rotund as a Christmas pudding, with a creamy curly beard longer than L is tall. He is magnificent.

L stares in disbelief and I feel that heart-squeeze you get when you make someone's dream come true. Quietly, Santa asks her in his gentle Lappish tones what she would like for Christmas. My pink-cheeked girl shyly chews her nail, quite unable to take in this momentous occasion.

Somehow I resist the urge to push my small daughter out of the way, sit on his knee and demand a divorce for Christmas.

Why the move to Brighton? Well, because it's the love of my life.

Having grown up just outside of the city, I have delicious hazy memories of sticky 1970s summers streaking on the beach, squealing down the helter-skelter on the pier, and trundling along the prom on Volk's Electric Railway, high on candyfloss and peppermint rock. And I wanted my kids to have that too.

Well, not the candyfloss and rock, obviously. Because, you know, teeth.

Because we had more children than we could house, we had to sell our two-up two-down in South London and move into rented accommodation. Sadly, also in South London. I wanted to move straight to Brighton but my husband was not ready to leave the Smoke yet. It was around this time that my mental health started to slip and slide like a greased yam.

I felt very unsettled. My husband was an estate agent, an industry known for its long and unsocial hours. It felt like we hardly saw him. I was desperately unhappy and becoming more and more reclusive. I managed to avoid everyone I knew. I would take my son to school late so I didn't have to meet other parents in the playground. I'd mute my phone to avoid calls, instead spending hours walking the twins around the local graveyard, desperate for silence and solace.

I didn't tell anyone I was struggling. I felt incredibly unhappy in my marriage. I felt unheard, unseen, unloved, undesired. I was lonely and lost and I didn't know what to do.

My sorry state came to a head one Saturday evening. He arrived home after work to me still in my dressing gown bawling my eyes out. The children were playing in another room when I announced, dramatically, 'I'm working out how I can leave you.'

Come Monday, I was diagnosed with depression.

The pills helped. As did the twins starting nursery. I love my kids, of course I do, but I also love my work as a journalist. It makes me feel like me. An actual whole human person, not just a long sausage skin with a pair of nipples and questionable hair.

Now with a few hours to myself every day, I was able to get back into the swing of work and start putting out the feelers for getting back into travel. As part of this, I did a travel writing workshop with Dea Birkett, then a columnist for the *Guardian*'s travel section, who also has three children, including twins. Although I was getting some commissions here and there, I was still very much in the regionals and in-flight magazines orbit, and I wanted to crack the nationals.

One Saturday, I found myself sitting round a table on the South Bank with Dea and maybe twenty other writers, learning the tricks of the travel writing trade. The main reason I chose Dea's course was because she offered the opportunity to pitch a travel editor face to face. Which was utterly horrifying, now I come to think of it.

With this in mind, I brought with me a story I thought might work. It was about the rise of overnight nannies in Ibiza, so party parents like us could go clubbing. It was a story that was right up my *strasse,* and that, if I was lucky, would result in a lovely trip to the White Isle too – a place I'd been going to since I was sixteen.

I pitched it to the travel editor of the *Observer*, who subsequently commissioned it. We went to Ibiza as a family the following spring and had a wild old time, and the resulting feature was the springboard to my career as a proper travel writer.

And Dea's workshop was also where I met Rhonda's boss, who ran a popular family travel website. He liked my ideas and the cut of my jib and suggested I contact Rhonda about writing for them…

The Ibiza feature came out on a Sunday, when we were staying with one of my oldest friends. I got up early to pick up a few copies from the newsagent and was excited to see they had used one of my favourite pictures, of L standing in front of the Pacha Beetle.

Giddy with pride, I showed it to my husband, who announced in front of my friends that he had actually been on the holiday so knew what had happened. And that was it. The proudest moment of my career to date and he couldn't even be bothered to read it.

Leaping forward three years, when the Lapland commission came in I dutifully checked with my husband that it was okay to go.

But as long as someone looked after the kids, he never really took much interest in my career – unless he was enjoying the perks.

Luckily, the kids adore both sets of grandparents. Without their support my career wouldn't have got off the starting blocks. I saw my trips as an opportunity for the kids to have quality time with them, and they all relished having a closer relationship with their grandchildren.

I think having time away does parents the world of good. In my case, the kids could spend time with their father and grandparents. And when I could take one or more of them with me, I had the headspace to appreciate them away from the routine of day-to-day life.

While I was more than happy to do the school run, attend assemblies and run from pillar to post delivering each one to ballet, gym or football, I also really liked my own space and got noticeably antsy if I went too long without a breather. My work trips usually lasted a few days and were every six or eight weeks or so. I also made sure that each of the kids, and my husband and I, had a couple of solo weekends away together a year.

With this Lapland trip, however, I hadn't told L where we were going for fear of N rescinding her original offer. Naturally, maternal guilt meant that I actually spent the fee I earned for writing the piece paying for the other two, their father and my mother to go to Lapland UK, a snowy pop-up Lapland theme park in Berkshire, so they could have their own Santa experience.

Moving to Brighton was a new start. I promised myself I'd draw a line under the London episode and also try to put the hurt and the abandonment I felt in the early years of the twins' life behind me. From now on, I would only look forward in our relationship.

Easier said than done.

My husband was still working in London. His long hours made commuting untenable, so now he was spending three nights a week there. I think he liked this freedom. He stayed with two different friends, came home late on a Wednesday night to leave early on a Thursday morning, and then saw the kids at the weekend. On both days, if they were lucky.

I was enjoying the space from us, too. We were in a routine here in Brighton. Now they were all at school full time, I could work. I was making new friends. Brighton life suited me and it suited the kids.

On one Friday night, I was invited to join some of the mums from the twins' class for drinks. I had a lovely time. They were a great bunch of interesting, fun women. However, what I struggled to comprehend was the fact that everyone seemed really happy, I mean *really happy*, in their relationships.

Odd.

When we lived in London, many of the women I knew were just as unsatisfied in their marriages as I was. I assumed it was the normal status quo. Friday afternoon play dates would segue into wine nights and that familiar grumble about our significant others. I'd seen the idea of divorce bandied about, affairs contemplated. I saw erudite, successful women who felt unsupported, undesired, unseen.

The longer I was in Brighton, the more I started to realise that feeling unheard and unhappy in a relationship was not the norm. There was another way to live. And this realisation was where it all started to unravel.

The loneliness I felt in my marriage was debilitating. I looked at him sometimes and tried to find the bloke I met and fell in love with all those years ago. But I couldn't see him. I started looking at and unpicking other people's relationships – why did theirs work and mine didn't?

Every time I brought up that I was feeling unhappy, I was shot down. My hormones were to blame. Or my depression. Whatever it was, it was my fault. Eventually I gave in to the sadness. I'd up the dose of antidepressants, I'd have another glass of wine. I'd push on through, suffering in silence, because that's what marriage was, wasn't it?

Looking back, I think I got married too green. He was my first proper relationship. My first love. I hadn't had nearly enough experience of relationships to know what was right or what was wrong. Or even what I wanted from one. Maybe I said yes when he proposed because I worried that no one else would ever ask me. Maybe I didn't know what I could have had.

While he was working away, I found friendship, kindness and support in an unlikely place. Next door.

Sometimes someone comes into your life and you just feel blessed. I don't use that word often, or at all really, because a) I'm not religious and b) I'm not a lifestyle influencer.

But when a small Colombian woman turns up on your doorstep on the day you move in, with a pound of rum cake and a glorious smile, you know you've been blessed by the God of Good Neighbours.

I simply adore P. She has a heart made of the purest gold and she loves all and everyone with it. A proud Mormon, she will pray for me and my family at the drop of a hat. And she does. Often.

She's been a constant source of joy and support since I moved to Brighton. Whether it's bringing over plates of her heavenly empanadas or concocting a magic spell to ward off, ahem, dark energies, she brings nothing but joy to my life. And a little bit of white witchery, but more of that to come…

Still giddy from our Santa experience, on our second afternoon in Lapland, we're driven up into the Arctic hinterland for a snowmobile tour. While the nippers huddle under rugs as they are pulled behind in a sleigh, we mums get to power up these bad boys and snow-scoot through the desolate, monochromatic landscape towards the Russian border, like a frosty Thelma and Louise.

As we battle the elements, I realise that the Sámi women of this region must be proper nails. Fierce, independent and spiritual, they are the absolute warriors of the Arctic. In the early days, it seems, Sámi women ran the show. They weren't just herding reindeer – as well as their husbands and children – they were also the traders and the decision-makers in the community. And many were also shamans, because they had such powerful connections to the spirit world. In traditional Sámi culture, women were properly respected.

And then along came pesky Christianity and colonialism, which brought a whole new bag of patriarchy. Suddenly, women who once held more economic and spiritual power than men were pushed into the background. It was only in the 1970s, when women reindeer herders started to demand the same rights as the men, that Sámi women started to rise up again and regain their power. Now they are activists, writers, artists and political leaders, and they are demanding their voices be heard.

On our final afternoon in Lapland, we go dog-sledding. Despite it being only 3 pm, it's as dark as night, the eerie atmosphere enhanced by packs of blue-eyed huskies baying like the Hound of the Baskervilles. After a short lesson, L reluctantly climbs into the sled while, as the driver, I'm entrusted with both her life and our team of huskies. Luckily the dogs know their stuff, and speed us through the icy fields with obvious glee.

While this is far from L's favourite part of the trip, I find it utterly thrilling, and I start to feel the faint but familiar flutter of my mojo coming back. At last.

On our last night, we stay up late chatting, drinking wine and scanning the skies for the green ribbons of the aurora borealis. L is getting tired and ratty, reluctant to leave the party, and my patience is wearing thin. S, ever the darling, sweeps her up for a cuddle and a chat and soothes her.

Despite my low mood, I know how lucky we are that the stars have aligned this week in Lapland and I've met these women. I know I will have pangs of regret that I wasn't my best self, that my poorly head has not been as buoyant as I'd have liked it to be, but even so this bunch of great, supportive women are carrying me along with them, no sister left behind, and I know I want them in my life for ever.

CHAPTER 4

IBIZA NIGHTS

Rhonda

'Going on holiday with your girlfriends is like having an affair, only you don't end up with cum all over your face.'

Lying in our cabana sharing hair-of-the-dog jugs of sangria and picking at cheese-laden nachos after a big night out in Ibiza Town, my friends and I try not to spit out our wine. Cackling, we all agree that that's *exactly* what this feels like: illicit, almost too good to be true. I must have done really very marvellous things in a past life, I think, to get to hang out in the Mediterranean sunshine with these epic women. To get these four days stolen from real life.

Spool back five years...

It's 4 am and S and I are in Eden in San Antonio, drenched in sweat and glitter, draped around each other, only now starting to flag after hours on the dance floor. Since we first met in Finnish Lapland, along with Tracey and the others, we've been close, getting together for a day or two in London, in Bath, in Manchester, sometimes with our kids, sometimes without, and often sharing our innermost thoughts, our secret fears and regrets and our wildest longings, with each other.

S is twelve years younger than me, so in some ways I feel protective of her – big-sisterly. She's been through a lot and to me feels both tough as a nut and incredibly fragile at the same time.

Now, pausing on the dance floor, she glances at her phone and her face falls.

'What is it?'

'It's D,' she replies. Her husband. He's hacked into her emails and texts and found flirtatious messages between her and a man she recently met through work. In fact, D reveals he has been spying on her for a while and he's livid.

I know from messages S sent me just before we flew out here that she hasn't been happy lately. She says D hasn't touched her in seven months and she doesn't know why. There have been issues with his work too; him getting 'let go' from a couple of jobs in succession, leaving her struggling to support them and their two boys. He's always been a bit rubbish when it comes to joint providing. Hence, she says, this flirtation. It's nothing more than that. She's been confused and lonely and this other man has crept into her life and made it known he wants her.

We're in Ibiza to celebrate my fiftieth birthday. Having never been a massive clubber apart from a couple of raver years with my uni boyfriend, a medic and wannabe DJ, I'd not been attracted by the White Isle. It seemed lairy, downmarket. But now I found myself drawn to the idea of it for this big threshold birthday, as somewhere for girlfriends to dance and feel free and unencumbered by responsibilities. Weightless, if only for a few days. Untethered.

And so here I am with S and twelve other girlfriends, touching down at Ibiza Airport at eleven on a Friday night. We are an odd, mismatched bunch, featuring incredible women from different places and eras of my life. A friend who came all the way from New York is someone I met at baby yoga when my eldest son was six months old. And then as well as S, who lives in the south-west, there's a friend who lives in Barcelona and a gaggle of northern mates. Many of them are meeting for the first time.

Some are fellow writers; some I met as mums of my kids' friends and first got to know in those long hours in the schoolyard at pick-up each day, or in the local park, chatting to one another as our children played together. These were friendships of circumstance that often became deeper over wines in back gardens while our kids rampaged around or smashed into one another on trampolines.

I'm happy but also gutted, because Tracey wouldn't join us on this trip. I don't know her that well at this point, but unlike me she's an old Ibiza hand, so I thought she would love to. I also thought she would show us the ropes and stop us making tits of ourselves by going to uncool places.

Tracey first came to the island when she was sixteen, on her first holiday without parents, with some girlfriends – something I find astonishing. I had to be home by 10 pm when I was sixteen (I complied, but it was easy to be slyly drunk even by 10 pm, if you hung around with older boys with cars and off-licence access).

Tracey can't believe it either, that her parents allowed her to come to this den of iniquity then, with a handful of sixth-form friends.

'I think it cost £57,' she told me. 'For a week! We stayed in San Antonio in an apartment block that was condemned a few weeks later. I was nervous about being allowed to buy booze, so on the first night we went out for food and I ordered an Irish coffee to test the waters. From then on it was carnage.'

They didn't really know about clubs, she went on. This was 1988 or 1989. Instead they took up residence at the Wigan Pier Fun Pub ('cringe'), drinking Malibu and pineapple, or vodka and Coke, snogging boys from Huddersfield. 'Or was it Middlesborough? – Northern scallies anyway.'

'One friend gave a boy a blowjob in the street,' she says with a cackle. 'And everyone copped off. I think mine was a Spanish boy called Angel.'

She calls this the 'booze and boys' trip, one spent in proper Spanish discos. When she came back, around a decade later, after travelling round the world and meeting the man who would become her husband, it was for a 'cheap-as-chips, booze-led' holiday with him and two friends – this time costing a princely £97. They stayed in San An again, this time in a trashy 18–30s-style hotel. Her memories from this trip range from performing topless karaoke to raging rows with her future husband ('unsurprisingly').

In her early thirties, she returned for a 'caning it in Ibiza holiday' with some friends who were veterans of the island from the likes of hen dos – things Tracey had missed out on, as she'd got married and had a child younger than most of them. Now it was time for the clubs – Pacha, Space, Bora Bora… The side of Ibiza that I was just about to encounter.

Hearing about all this gave me retrospective FOMO for all I'd missed out on more than thirty years before, and after that all the other kinds of girl time of which I'd been cheated. Cheap Mediterranean holidays with girlfriends, flats shared with other females… I hadn't really thought about it before, but I'd been in back-to-back (or overlapping) relationships more or less since the age of sixteen. Hence, I'd mainly travelled with boyfriends and lived with men. I'd been deprived of something fun and formative, it seemed to me now. Brainwashed by society to put men first.

Recently, a couple of girls' minibreaks, to Valencia with about ten other school mums, and to Budapest with a handful of female writer friends, had given me a taste for what I'd missed. Hence this first Ibiza trip.

But Tracey was having a bad time, she told me, in her 'car-crash marriage'. Her husband wasn't working, he was having a midlife career change that had come to very little, and she was even more unhappy at home, to the extent that she had recently started on Prozac. While it was kicking in, she felt erratic and worried she would bring everyone down.

I tried to persuade her that a few nights in Ibiza would be the perfect pick-me-up, but, despite being devastated to miss it, she was insistent she'd spoil it for the rest of us.

Wayward Women

★

When we arrive in Ibiza for the first time, just short of midnight, we minibus it to our hotel, check in and neck vodka and tonics as we shower, style our hair, try on and reject outfits, swap clothes and pose for the obligatory mirror selfies, worrying if we look like mutton clothed as lamb, if we're over- or under-dressed, before deciding we *really do not care*. Let's do this.

At 2 am, the thirteen of us – a flurry of bouncy or sleeked-back hair, short dresses or playsuits or cut-off denim shorts, cowboy boots or trainers – finally bustle out of our apart-hotel and throw ourselves in taxis up to Pikes, the legendary lost-in-the-hills hotel and club where Freddie Mercury celebrated his fortieth birthday – the one with the pool where Wham! filmed their 'Club Tropicana' video.

With a 'No Filming, No Sportswear, No Glitter, No Flip Flops, No Under 27s, No Cunts' rule on the door, Pikes is a haven away from the superclub hangars such as Pacha. Its spaces are intimate, with little alcoves to hole up in with mates, and the music is ecstatic. Inevitably, a few cunts do slip in, but mostly people are there to lose themselves to great tunes.

This is our first night, and, while we quickly realise we'll have to ward off some male attention, we meet some interesting people too. Gorgeous P is pursued by a sexy, roguish yachtsman we nickname The Pirate, who wants to whisk her away on his boat, and we also befriend a local DJ who gets us guest-list tickets for clubs for subsequent nights. We drink and dance 'til dawn and it's heavenly.

The next morning things are not quite so rosy, but we force down a late breakfast and crash out in cabanas around the pool. Bleary, I watch as S jumps into the water and starts talking to one of my Manchester friends, Z, a highly-strung singer from Central Europe via California. Her screenwriter husband is as volatile as she is and their marriage is eye-wateringly turbulent. Once they argued in the street in front of their house and he ripped off his shirt like the Incredible Hulk and beat his chest with his fists like a silverback. All is far from well in their world.

Within seconds, S and Z are talking like the oldest of friends, like women often do, and, from the snatches of conversation I hear, I understand they are confessing their marital woes to each other.

And indeed, for much of the rest of the three days Z can most often be seen stalking around the lobby of the hotel in a bikini and a sequin-studded trilby she's bought in a seafront tat shop, mobile clamped to her ear, as her husband hurls abuse down the line at her. It seems he's not happy she's here. Surprise, surprise! – he did the same a few months ago when we were on a short writing retreat in her native Prague. She got no writing done and the rest of us were disrupted too.

We beg her to not answer the phone to him any more, to insist that he rings only if there is an emergency, but she can't seem to get a handle on the situation, or maybe doesn't really want to, and the rest of us can only look on appalled.

But between them, S and Z seem to create a domino effect of tumbling women that leads me to look back on this trip as my 'Armageddon holiday'. Not all, but some of us, begin to unburden ourselves. P reveals she hasn't slept with her live-in boyfriend in two years. H's boyfriend can't/won't support himself and leans on her too hard financially and emotionally even as she combines a full-time professorship with care for her elderly widowed mother.

And it's as I listen to all this, these conversations over those three days in Ibiza – to the deep dissatisfactions of these awesome, talented, strong, caring women (most of them mums, and fantastic, hands-on ones at that) – that I realise how unhappy I am too.

Suddenly I acknowledge to myself that I've been putting a brave face on it. I've been defending the indefensible for the sake of peace and harmony and the kids. I've lost faith in my marriage. In fact, I'm not sure I ever had it. Not since the kids arrived and it became clear what I was up against.

I'm not sure that the phrase 'weaponised incompetence' exists at this time, but if it had, a good handful of us would have nodded vehemently, sadly, knowingly. And agreed that it was a huge part of the everyday sexism that we all experienced – an undervaluing of our time and of both our physical and emotional energy.

And some of us would have nodded sadly, too, thinking about the many ways men control women, through money, through moods and atmospheres, through aggressive body language, through the intimation of physical violence – and, of course, sometimes through physical violence itself.

And now, sitting here in Ibiza, I'm not sure how I've fooled myself. There had been a short period when my husband was going over to work, for a week or two at a time, in Los Angeles. And during that time I was overwhelmed, for sure, but I was *much* happier, because I wasn't resentful about doing so much yet still more being asked of me.

When I was alone, I just had to get on with it, and I was regimented, getting up at 5 am and getting everything done, like an automaton marching through the day. When he was at home, a large part of my energy went on being angry and frustrated, moaning and shouting and being told I was a bore and a nag, before being badgered for sex.

Los Angeles aside, I was the sole or main money-earner for the vast majority of time when the kids were growing up, often working in the evenings after doing the school pick-up and then dinner and bath and storytime. For a long time, I was either working or looking after the kids or sleeping or doing housework. I had no personal life.

And in Ibiza, inside this bubble of short-lived freedom, I realise I've been defending my domestic set-up to my family and friends because I'm ashamed of what I've allowed to happen. I also realise I've been hoping my husband would get a job away from home, and that then I'd tell him that we weren't coming with him because the boys were settled in school and their friendships, and that that was how we'd separate. Slowly and naturally and without drama.

But back to Ibiza, and, painful conversations about relationships aside, I watch delightedly as new friendships come into being between my friends, including some friendships that will develop and be independent of me. I feel I have gifted these awesome women to one another, and that gives me the most profound joy.

Walking home from Eden along the seafront, barefoot, footsore, twirling our shoes from our fingers, S and I wave over at M from New York, who has run off to ride some all-night dodgems in pure childish glee. Light is glimmering over the water, spilling us back into daytime and reality.

Unbeknown to me, but perhaps already known to her, S is going to leave D when she gets home. He's told her he won't fetch her from the airport after she lands; she's spent out from this trip and doesn't have the funds for a £70 taxi and there is no public transport. He's punishing her for the unhappiness he's caused her by his neglect. She's had enough. She's doing this.

Behind us walk P and C, and one of them makes a little video of S and I walking along chatting as the sun rises before us – a video that a few years from now, unearthed forgotten from the depths of someone's phone, will become like a holy relic of something precious we can't ever get back.

We return the following year – just six of us this time, because taking thirteen was like herding wild cats and also engendered a lot of politicking and girlish bickering: who bought who a drink and didn't return the favour, whose room was a proper shithole and *how the hell can you live like that?*, and did we have to go to clubs with such sticky floors, and other such nonsense. Ibiza wasn't for everyone.

We're now, as we see it, the hardcore — the ones who can all mainly agree on what we want to do and where we want to go.

It's like being sixteen again. Four nights in a row, we go out dancing and carousing 'til dawn, then we sit out on our balcony in our dresses still clinging to us with sweat, shuck off the shoes we've somehow danced more than twenty kilometres worth of steps in, peel off the huge false eyelashes we wear for their sheer ludicrousness, and watch the sun come up over the Med over a few beers.

When we've come down enough from all our merrymaking to contemplate bed, we sleep a few hours before heading back poolside to start the whole cycle again, ignoring all but the most urgent messages from home, debating which bar to hit up for tonight's sunset views and the best tunes.

This is girlfriend time — perhaps the most precious and nourishing time of all once your children have flown the nest or are barely ever home, lost in their own social whirls. And it's also the most hard-won time — getting a long weekend when we can all be away at the same time is the devil's own work, between all our family and career commitments. And with teen dramas and work stress and parental illness on our respective plates this past year, at times it's seemed it may never come to pass.

But we're here now, and, with no domestic mundanities claiming our attention, we can finally be — if only for a few days — who we really are, with the people who really get us as only women can get one another.

In Ibiza we go deep, confessing the most painful but also the most joyous of intimacies, crying and laughing, often at the same time. We share space, a bathroom without a lock, beds. We walk around naked without shame at our differences, our ageing bodies — that are not what they were but still do the job very nicely thank you. That are healthy and give us pleasure.

We share eyeshadows and pots of glitter and we trade clothes. We help one another to do our hair, we vote on our outfits.

We remind each other how beautiful we are, still, in spite of or perhaps because of everything we have been through. When we're in bars and clubs, we look out for one another, wade in when things on the dance floor get a bit too frisky.

There are trying moments, though. One voluptuously gorgeous friend won't come out clubbing because she feels 'too fat' next to the rest of us. She doesn't confess this 'til afterwards and it makes me so sad. Aren't we over all this by now?

On the other hand, the hotel room is where the real magic happens, the biggest love. Coming home at dawn, we keep dancing around, this time in our jammies, slinking to Grace Jones' 'La Vie en Rose' and Massive Attack's 'Unfinished Sympathy'.

There are moments of such tenderness. Divorcee T rolling over and asking me to check her moles because she lives alone and has no one to look out for her, for instance. And moments of pure daftness, like when someone balances tiny sponge cakes on T's nipples where she lies in bed and we all giggle like ten year olds.

But although I don't yet know why, S is not in a great place this second year. I know she's been struggling financially after leaving D and can't really afford to be here; she's made it happen because it and we mean so much to her, but she can barely stretch to drinks and meals out.

She's also struggling for time, between parenting her sons, her work for a national charity working to end violence against women and girls (following two MAs and an internship at the UN), her PhD in gender norms, consent and coercion among young people (on the basis of which she's been offered a brilliant lectureship) and writing fiction. So she has to spend some of her holiday time in the room working.

I'm in awe at her willpower. S kicks the ass out of life and has unbelievable energy for changing the world for other people, as well as becoming her best and most fulfilled self.

But there's something else going on. She's super-nervous in clubs this year, and that's odd, because she knows what Ibiza is like. It's predatory as hell, with men constantly on the prowl, trying to catch women's eyes. Men trying to dance with you, touch you. There's a lot of alcohol and a lot of drugs. The atmosphere is frisky, licentious. Clothing is often minimal.

But here's the thing: as women who have come to Ibiza to dance to some of the best DJs in the world, you stick together on the dance floor, you don't encourage it, and you look after one another. That means dancing close, telling men to back off where necessary.

Many's the time I've slung an arm round one of my girls and even kissed them on the mouth, and, if a man still doesn't get the message that he's not welcome, I'll lean in and tell him, 'We're together. She's my girlfriend.'

It normally works, although most of them will ask for a threesome before accepting defeat and heading off to find new prey.

This second year, S leaves a couple of clubs early and suddenly, and I'm confused. Later, after going back to the UK, she sends me a message. Earlier in the year, she tells me, she was raped in her home by someone she met via Tinder. This followed the rape she suffered when she was much younger, as well as a horrible period during her mid-teens of what she describes as being 'pimped out' by her dad, who tried to get her to go out on dates with his mates of the same age as him. She'd also, in her late teens working as a tour rep in the Med, been beaten up by the brother of a local boy she dated, after she left him – the family felt she had disgraced them.

Sometimes I wonder how S has survived, and how she has retained her ebullience and sheer joy in living and her ability to care. For despite her busyness and her ambition, she always finds time for others – her sons, her mum, her friends, her dog. And she is *the most incredible* friend.

One night during this second holiday, we go back to our favourite restaurant, in Talamanca Bay, and, with fishing boats bouncing about on the twinkling water behind her, I tell S something about myself that many people would judge and even hate me for. And S just absorbs what I'm saying with such empathy and acceptance and love in her eyes that I feel fully seen and understood.

I will never, ever forget how S looked at me that night.

Having been married to someone similar to my own husband, S knows why the situation I describe to her has arisen. But she doesn't have to say that. She doesn't try to give me advice. She just lets me talk, sponges up my pain. She's my shock-absorber. It's everything.

After S and my other friends leave, I go to the airport to pick up a hire car and drive down to the Parque Natural de ses Salines. As a travel writer, I'm ashamed to have seen barely anything of Ibiza beyond pool cabanas and nightclubs. It feels odd just flying in and seeing only small pockets of the island, and one side of something that is much more multi-layered and multi-textured than people often think.

The party scene in Ibiza only really started in the 1960s, on the back of the hippy incursion. The island's music scene is said to have begun at Pikes hotel, but its real transformation into a party destination came with the opening of Pacha in 1973, while Space, which opened in 1989, was one of the birthplaces of electronic music. Before that, Ibiza had a long and compelling history involving Neolithic peoples, Carthaginians, Romans, Byzantines, Moors, Pisans, Catalans and Germanic Majorcans, to name just a few.

It's also heart-stoppingly beautiful, with two national parks. Of those, Ses Salines is spectacular and in parts otherworldly: a place of shimmering salt flats, pale dunes and fragrant pine forests. But it's not untouristy in parts. When I get to the Playa de ses Salines, I find hip beach clubs and lots of fellow clubbers splayed on the beach recovering from the excesses of the night before. I'm knackered from partying too, so I just lie on the sand and pass out in the sun beating down on me.

Then I get up and go for a stroll. The further along I get from the car park, the more nudists I see, until I get to a point where everyone is naked but me. This doesn't bother me at all, but then things start getting weird and *very* Ibiza.

Where the beach gives way to rocks as I move towards the end of the headland, I see a man on a fold-out sunlounger openly giving it some, his fist bunched round his cock. Being British, I look away, embarrassed, and carry on walking. A little further one, another one is at it, and making even less of a secret about it – standing loud and proud on a rock, he's openly jerking off into the sea.

I message my friends who've gone home. **You don't know what you are missing at Ses Salines. Remarkable views on this side of the island LOL.**

Then I notice the boats, and, although I couldn't swear on it, it seems to me that there's a little line of them, backed up to the rocky inlets, and that people are sitting in the back of them watching the wankers. Is this some kind of open-air, free sex show?

Only, I think, in Ibiza.

People are oversexed in Ibiza. Nights out are supercharged and bawdy. There are absurdly beautiful people at every turn of the head, many of them wearing hardly any clothes. It's hard not to feel horny all the time. As well as men hitting on you, you often get attention from couples looking for a third. Often the woman is attractive but the man much less so.

And then on the other side of this gleaming, hyper-sexual coin of Ibiza, there's the spiritual aspect of things. And that's how, that same evening, I find myself sitting staring at Es Vedrà. This rock rising 400 metres out of the glimmering Med just west of the island is claimed by some to be the third-most magnetic spot on Earth, by others to be the birthplace of the Phoenician goddess Tanit (a mother goddess of spirituality and the moon), and by still others to be home to the sirens of Greek mythology, who sang songs that shipwrecked sailors and brought them to their deaths. Of course, being mermaid-mad and murderous towards (certain) men, I would like it to be the latter.

Having driven down winding country lanes to Cala d'Hort beach, in the nature reserve of the same name, club music playing on my car radio, I'm very happily alone for an evening. I'm also looking forward to a big catch-up sleep.

There are relatively few people on this beach facing Es Vedrà. The sun sets slowly. Water beats against the shore, spray flying up. In front of me, a just-married couple wade in the water in their wedding attire as a child takes photos on a phone.

I watch impassively, trying to feel something. Envy, perhaps, at their happiness. But I don't. I feel only the flatness of someone who is probably not going to be married for too much longer. Of someone for whom marriage – both my own and those of other people – has come to seem like a trap.

I sit and try to process everything that's happened since I first came to Ibiza just a year ago. A lot has changed. I am a completely different person.

On the face of things, I have spiralled out of control, and I have no idea where I am going and what is to come. I try to work out if I should be scared about that.

The next day, after little of the sleep I've hoped for, I drive back to the airport, to fetch my lover – the real reason I've stayed in Ibiza. This was the terrible thing I told S about in the restaurant. The terrible and glorious thing.

M and I are nearly a year in at this point, and in that time I have run away from him twice – literally, run away from him though the streets. M's wife doesn't know about me, and my husband doesn't know about him. But more of all that anon.

M is waiting for me at the airport, and I drive him across Ibiza, stopping in hip inland Santa Gertrudis for lunch. We are relaxed and happy – oddly, since the last time we were together I bolted from the hotel room where we were staying on Clapham Common.

M feels kind of like my dad, only we also have an intense sexual relationship. So it's weird and really not very healthy. But I can't seem to escape the dynamic or the pull he exerts on me, and hence here we are a month later spending three illicit days together.

On the drive over the hump of Ibiza and back down along through lush green scenery to the north-eastern tip of the island, the rocky corner where the coastal village of Portinatx lies, his hand on my thigh as I drive, I tell M about some of the unsavoury things that happened before he arrived. The pool party P and I ended up at after falling out of a club at 7 am, and the lurid offers we'd had from some of the (much younger) men there; the wanking at Ses Salines.

M takes it all dispassionately. He's, unbelievably (he easily looks fifteen years younger), seventy. He's been married for nearly fifty years, and he's lived a very staid life (albeit one punctuated by many or at least several affairs). Also, he knows he can't be judgemental about me because I will just tell him to fuck off, as I already have so many times. He doesn't decide if we carry on or not; he's already told me that he wants this to go on for ever, but only in its current format. On our second night together, he told me his life 'will never change'.

And my wildness, as he perceives it (I am really not that wild), is also what attracts M. I am the opposite of what he says he has at home – which is, in his words, a child-woman who has barely worked in her life, who doesn't like and won't have sex, who has 'collapsed' each time he has tried to leave her, refusing to eat and becoming skeletal even beyond her naturally doll-like frame. I love other women, but I struggle to understand this one – or at least the version of her I get from him. I do understand they may not be the same thing.

The conversation segues into the topic of what happens when people repress their real nature, about the unhealthiness of that. We discuss one of my friends I've been here in Ibiza with, about how her self-control masks an innate wildness. We talk about how the truth will always come out — agree that one day my friend won't be able to keep it all in any more. There'll be an eruption.

But M doesn't seem to find the conversation loaded or show any acknowledgement that what we are really talking about is him. He is not, deep down, who he is most of the time. Business owner and caring boss, devoted husband, father and grandfather. He *is* those people, but he is also not. Hence being here with me.

M is a wild seventy-year-old boy I share a bed with once a month, and he's also a pipe-and-slippers husband who cooks thoughtful meals for his wife as she sits immersed in *Holby City*.

Yet as we talk in the car, I'm aware that I'm purposely painting him a less-than-desirable picture of myself as some kind of midlife wild child — certainly not the kind of woman an elderly man would start a new life with. What am I trying to prove to him? And what am I trying to prove to myself? And is it okay that he's not shocked or annoyed, or does it mean he doesn't give a fuck what I do?

Whatever is going on in both our heads, we each already know that these three days together are going to change us both. They can't not. The question is: how much? Enough? And in what way? What is going to become of us, and this situation?

Sitting down to breakfast with M that first morning in the hotel feels weird. It's not as if we haven't sat across the table from each other for plenty of meals before now, but it was always dinners and lunches. I can tell that, for him as for me, there's something symbolic about this. The couples all around us in this adults-only hotel are probably just that: couples, *real* couples. Husbands and wives. Or official in some way.

Afterwards we drive a few minutes to the Cala d'en Serra. As we walk down from the rough track where we parked, there's an old concrete hotel that was abandoned mid-build, and down by the sands are some stone fishermen's huts and a tiny ramshackle beer bar with a hand-painted sign saying 'Lost in Paradise'. It feels so far from the world and our respective responsibilities.

We take a seat. M orders Caesar salad and a beer, I'm happy with a Bloody Mary. We sit there for hours. The day passes like a dream. We spend time on the beach, in the Med, just floating around, wrapped round each other like octopi, lost to time and the world. I don't think of anything but here and now. This rarely happens to me.

Then I remember how, not long after we got together, M told me about a song he said made him think of me and cry, about wanting someone to just lie with and forget the world. Snow Patrol, it turned out to be.

We go back into the sea. He starts to swim out and I make to follow him but can't. A couple of weeks ago, a large, very sturdy dog ran into me at speed while I was playing with my own dog in the local nature reserve. My knee twisted and swelled up. I was worried I wasn't going to be able to dance in Ibiza.

I did dance. How I danced! But yesterday, not long after M and I got to the hotel, we walked out onto a kind of rocky plateau and I, in my flip-flops, slipped and fell into a rock pool, bashing my knee again. And now I find I can't swim.

I stop where I can still stand and watch M carry on out into the cool, deep-green bay. More than anything else I want to follow him, be out there with him in the water flashing in the sunlight, my arms round his neck, my body against his. But I know I can't make it. The pain is too much. And so I just stay there, looking out at the bobbing of his head as he gets further and further away from me, until it seems to merge with the water and I'm not even sure there's anyone there. Wondering what he is thinking. M, my M. Always out of reach. Never mine.

Afterwards, long afterwards, I write that this was, 'The perfect day, the only one we would ever have.'

The restaurant is very Richard Curtis movie, with a terrace lit only by lanterns and tables where every seat faces the little bay.

I often choose to sit side by side with M anyway. I feel a kind of possessiveness towards him. But not the possessiveness of a wife, I think. The possessiveness of a daughter, and maybe sometimes even the possessiveness of a mother. I feel like both of those things to him, and more. It's complicated.

I'm keeping an eye on him. We're high. Back on our terrace, swaddled in bathrobes after shattering sex, I ground up some Ecstasy and mixed it into beer. I took more than him, but I have experience with it. When it became clear that he wasn't going to keel over and die, I gave him more to catch up. We've had one and a half each. Too much.

I'm wearing what I jokingly call my 'Turkish wedding dress' – an ivory ankle-length affair I bought for beach holidays, with a sort of lacy top layer over a silky slip dress. As we left the hotel room, I felt like an illicit bride.

There's no one else on the terrace, or if there is I don't see them. We're in our own little world, unreachable. The owner comes over every so often. Two bottles of rosé disappear too quickly. The food we order remains largely untouched. M keeps telling me how pretty I look. The view of the bay is ridiculously, almost obscenely beautiful. It's like a night from a dream.

Hours go by in minutes. I have no idea what we talk about. The owner doesn't seem to mind that we linger until the small hours, even though nobody else is around and we're keeping him from closing up. He doesn't seem to mind when M asks for the bill twice more after paying it. 'We've all been there,' he deadpans. This is Ibiza, after all. Anything goes.

I ask the owner the name of the restaurant. It's something that M went off to book when we got back from the equally dreamlike afternoon at the beach – providing him, I'm sure, with a moment to dutifully call his wife. The wife who thinks he is on a golfing retreat with his mates.

It's Los Enamorados, the restaurateur tells us. The Lovers. I shake my head. This is insanity. It can't go on. And yet how to stop it?

WAYWARD WOMEN

★

On the way back to the room I take three drunken, blurry, grainy photos of M and me under the waning gibbous moon. When I'm taking them, it's true that some dark part of me is thinking: 'evidence'. But I know it's not evidence I'll ever use, much as I want to (and I know I *will* want to and will carry on wanting to for ever).

The sex is a mad thing beyond our control, seemingly outside of us. At one point of this long sleepless night, M tells me that he and his best friend have wondered if he's the love of my life. I don't say yes or no, but a voice inside me says, 'I fucking hope not.' Because if he is, then where the hell do I go from here? What will the rest of my life be?

I try to ask him the same but he deflects, saying he's 'never known such intensity'. I ask him if he loves his wife. He deflects some more, saying there are 'different kinds of love'.

Well hey, thanks for telling me something I don't know, Mr Condescension.

I tell him I would marry him, but, even as I'm saying it, I'm thinking: 'What the fuck am I talking about? Of course I wouldn't.'

He says we wouldn't need to be married, we could just be together. And I know he's right: why on earth marry? Look where our marriages have brought us to. This room, these drugs. This conversation.

He tells me he would push his wife over a cliff if he could get away with it. I hate us for having this exchange, while relishing it too. I don't hate his wife, though. I would like to understand her. I would like to take her out for a drink and talk to her, woman to woman. Ask her why she clung to something so inadequate, so demeaning. Why *she* didn't want more.

He starts talking about brickwork. It comes out of nowhere, one of those brain-farts that Ecstasy produces. I laugh. 'You're talking about your need for security,' I say.

I've understood this need for a while now. Nobody ever

stood up to M's physically abusive father, including his mother. Nobody ever confronted the man who beat his three tiny sons and continued the abuse into their teens.

And now, today, his father is ninety-five and M goes to see him often, to give him company and to take him out for lunch. He also cleans his shit up where he's mismanaged his colostomy bag – like my mum did my dad even after divorcing him (but that's yet another story).

M has so many demons, it's unreal.

He shakes his head at my amateur psycho-therapising about needing security. 'It's more like another brick in the wall,' he says.

But I can only shrug. If he's been in a prison, if he still lives there, it's one of his own making.

After dawn we finally get some sleep and when we awake it's nearly midday and time to check out. M seems okay. He's a horse when it comes to tiredness and drinking – and now drugs. He never seems to feel rough. Amazingly, considering he never drank until he was twenty-six, because of his hyper-religious upbringing.

But I, the demon drinker, feel like hell. I hate checking out of hotel rooms as it is, but doing so in this state is mind-bendingly horrible and I'm snarky with pain.

M comments that it's 'always like this' when we part, that 'there's a pattern'. Patronising me, again.

'It's not that,' I whine. 'I just feel like shit and I want to be home with my kids.'

It's true, too. It's been a whole week of intense, illicit pleasures and I need to be back on solid ground, to be who I need to be for my boys. Domesticity suddenly feels very appealing.

We lie on loungers on the beach and I fall asleep with my head on M's shoulder, from time to time babbling in my comedown, and then suddenly it's time to drive us back up the winding green hills and across the island and into reality. Back through the curtain. We say our goodbyes at a petrol station on the outskirts of Ibiza Town, where I leave him to kill time before his flight back to London.

I drop off my car and check in. At my departure gate, a couple in the queue in front of me loudly discuss their desire to separate and never see each other again. Back at Manchester Airport, another couple argue beside the baggage carousel. Everywhere I look, unhappy couples.

All of this, the hedonism of Ibiza – at least the girlfriends aspect of it – was going to be annual, but the pandemic put paid to that. And by the time we do come back, S is dead, floored suddenly at age forty-two by an undetectable heart defect rarely seen in women as young as her – especially fit women who surf, kick-box, wall-climb and eschew drugs, as S did.

S is dead, leaving two much-adored teen sons behind. And leaving us behind too. None of us will ever recover.

At her funeral, more than half the mourners have to stand outside the sizeable crematorium, she was that loved.

The following year we take S's spirit back to Ibiza. It's down to four of us this time. We sit with her ghost in our favourite restaurant with the boats bouncing in the moon-washed bay and drink to her, go to the same clubs, stay in the same hotel. We feel her walk among us; we know she approves of us coming back here and having fun.

We are carrying the flame for her and for our friendship, just as we did at her wake when we got drunk and cried and danced with her other friends and made them into our own lasting friends. S would have been overjoyed by that, just as I was overjoyed when she made those new friendships within my Manchester group.

We are now older and wiser, more considered and serious – and sadder too, of course. Then the next moment we're tittering like schoolgirls at the shallowest of frivolities and most puerile of jokes. We gossip about others around the pool, rate their tattoos, their six-packs, their boob jobs. A DJ is playing over by the bar and our limbs, toasted by the sun, start twitching, ready for another night on the dance floor. S is right beside us and always will be, all a-glitter, diaphanous, dazzling us with that smile of hers.

I finally get to go to Ibiza with Tracey – ironically, hilariously, to write about the non-party side of the island. And we do have a brilliant, wholesome time, hiking down to hidden coves like the one I went to with M, perving after yoni candles at a hippy market, catching the ferry to stay a couple of nights on the neighbouring island of Formentera with its pine forests and crashing waves and low-key beach bars.

Of course, we being we, and this being Ibiza, when we get back to the island we do blow the lid. It would be rude not to.

We go to Pikes, the old favourite, and let loose on the dance floor. The atmosphere is mostly loving, loved up, harmlessly flirtatious; it's all just play and we all know it. If anyone goes too far, they're dispatched. For every inappropriate person, there are several who will intervene and protect.

Tracey, who will be on stage doing a comedy gig back in the UK the following night, has to basically drag me out by the hair at 3 am from where I'm shimmying with a bunch of 28-year-old lads from Crewe. But I'm back in Ibiza, and at Pikes, just a couple of months later, with just one of the original crew, my darling P. It's a holiday that has turned into work, albeit hardly very onerous work – reviewing several very chic hotels and restaurants for a stylish women's mag.

P formed a very close relationship with S after meeting her at Ibiza #1, a friendship that was independent of me. Coming back, we feel, as always, that S would approve.

One night, we go back yet again to our favourite Talamanca Bay restaurant, and this time I cry. By this point in the trip, I'm overtired. Of eight nights, we are out all but one, and until dawn. We taxi from hotel to restaurant to club and often to a second or even third club in the same night. We meet glorious people – a taxi driver cum fisherman who gives us brilliant insider foodie recommendations and invites us out fishing on his boat next time we come. Wonderful servers in restaurants, passionate about the food they deliver to us as we swoon at our table. Sublime chefs. Fantastic DJs. There is no day or night when we don't encounter fantastic people – and that is what travel is really all about.

In clubs we pretend to be a couple, to ward men off. There is no single night when some random men aren't trying to take us back to their hotel or villa, or inviting themselves back to our hotel for a threesome. Most are total sharks, but the odd one is adorable.

In one club I dance the last filthy two tunes of the night with a Spanish chef, D, who is working on Formentera, and as we stand out in the light of morning, his arm slung round my shoulder, talking to me in a charmingly garbled English I cannot hope to understand, I do contemplate taking the first ferry back with him as he suggests. Only the fear I won't get back in time for my flight home stops me. And I do have to go home. None of this is real. There's no life without could-have-beens.

But I'll always have that dance to look back on. And D and I stay in touch – we Zoom each other from time to time, and maybe some day, somewhere, we'll have another filthy dance.

As we dress up to go out and preen and pout in front of mirrors, P and I jokingly call ourselves sexy vultures, although we are hardly predatory. But the truth is, there's something empowering about glamming up – about the feeling of potency and control you have on the dance floor, knowing you are still desirable even and perhaps in some ways especially at our age.

But again, it's never really about men. We don't dress for them, we don't dance for them, and we don't bring them home with us, tempting as it sometimes is. On the other hand, when two younger women approach us in the Portaloo outside Pikes to compliment each of us in turn, we are thrilled. We are 'vintage

Pikes bitches', they proclaim, and I have rarely been so flattered. Because they have no ulterior motive. They are simply women making other women feel good about themselves. And that is gold.

Women hold one another up, and not only when we are drunk and footsore. In bad times, and also in the good.

CHAPTER 5

HONG KONG – THE RETURN

Tracey

The grimy grey apartment building sandwiched between dried fish shops looks, feels and *smells* immediately familiar: the narrow vertical windows, the air-conditioning units clinging precariously to the facade, and our thirteenth-floor apartment that we called Wing Lok Sai Gai – the place where it all began more than two decades ago.

Feeling like all the air has been punched out of me, I flop down on the kerb and sob.

After a few minutes, I pull myself together and look at my phone. I should call him. Text him a photo. But I can't. I don't think I can bear to. Weirdly, I didn't want to share the moment with him. Instead, I just sit with my sadness, fat tears falling down my face, and let the reality of it all sink in. A twenty-year tale and this is how and where it ends.

People have been travelling the world to find themselves since the dawn of time. So when I headed east in 1995 in search of my own spiritual enlightenment, I was rather dismayed to find the 'real me' was actually a loud, drunk, wild-haired woman who danced on Carnegie's bar in Wan Chai to Chaka Khan's 'I'm Every Woman' after a jug of Long Island Iced Tea.

Dammit. I was hoping for Enya.

Although I was twenty-three and officially 'cooked' in adult terms, I didn't feel it. I felt like one of those inflatable air dancers you get outside car dealerships; you know, tall, empty and just flailing about in the wind with a grin on my face. After four years living away from home in Southampton, two at uni and two temping, rather than grow up and decide what I wanted to do or be, I chose to go travelling.

A friend suggested Hong Kong as a first stop. It was a British colony, so it was easy to find work and earn money there, at least for the next two years before it would be handed back to China. It was also teeming with backpackers who liked to party, hard. Within the month, I'd left my temping job and bought a one-way ticket to Hong Kong on the loose promise of some bar work when I got there.

Waving goodbye to my family and friends, I boarded a cheapo Olympic Airways flight on which I chatted to a lovely young missionary named David who was making the most of the free booze before he answered the call of God in Kowloon.

Twelve hours and many gins later, my hangover kicked in as we flew into Kai Tak, aka the world's most terrifying airport, where you could almost stroke the laundry hanging from the apartment buildings as you came in over Kowloon to land. I touched down in Hong Kong crying tears of real fear – not realising that this tiny nation in the South China Sea would become one of the big loves of my life.

Hong Kong is where I found myself. It's where I fell in love for the first time. It's where I got arrested for the first – and hopefully the last – time. And it's where I found my tribe of lifelong friends.

It was the mid-Nineties and Hong Kong was a backpackers' paradise. Hostels, happy hours, free drinks for ladies' nights, booze cruises on red-sailed junk boats, Carwash club nights, twenty-four-hour bars… Hong Kong was like a cross between an 18–30s holiday and Disneyland for party people. It was easy to find work without a permit and there were plenty of opportunities for young people to earn good cash and travel around the rest of Asia and beyond.

With little more than a couple of hundred quid to my name, I arrived one sweaty August afternoon and immediately fell in love with its chaos. I was relatively untravelled and it was also my first time in Asia, so in those first few days I felt like I'd landed on a different planet. A sea of futuristic skyscrapers sat shoulder to shoulder with scabby apartment blocks dripping in neon signs. I'd wander past eighteen-storey buildings held up only by bamboo scaffolding and rope (and hope), which looked as if they would collapse if I sneezed within three feet of them.

On the street were tiny bird-like hawkers pushing giant wooden wagons piled high with knock-off Calvin Klein and Lacoste T-shirts, which I bought by the dozen. Steamy food stands sold strings of boiled intestines doused in chilli sauce, chicken feet or actual duck heads. I'd never seen so many people or smelt such funky scents, some of which I never, ever wish to smell again.

The sights and scents of Hong Kong shouldn't have been the surprise they were. I'd done my research before I arrived. However, it was not from *Lonely Planet* or the *Rough Guide to Asia*. No. I read *The World of Suzie Wong* by Richard Mason, a beautifully written time capsule of a novel set in 1950s Hong Kong, telling the tale of Robert Lomax, a young businessman who heads there after national service to try his luck as an artist. He moves into the Nam Kok Hotel in Wan Chai, which he soon discovers is a brothel, and meets and falls in love with Suzie, their most prized prostitute.

Mason's vivid depiction of Hong Kong – the Star Ferry, Nathan Road, the narrow double-decker trams, the seedy streets of Wan Chai – was the Hong Kong I was expecting. My naval dad had been stationed here in the Sixties, and he loved to regale me with his many (but I suspect not all) tales about his time in Hong Kong. Sweaty nights spent in the tattoo parlours of Kowloon, drunk sailors falling out of knocking shops in Tsim Sha Tsui, bouncing around the seedy bars of Wan Chai…

I landed expecting rosy lantern-lit streets scented with opium and salubrious neon-clad bars teeming with sailors and gorgeous hookers. It was not that far off the mark.

For the first week or so, I stayed at a friend's family home in the New Territories, the rural area north of Kowloon and close to the border of China, where monkeys played in the garden. I was largely left alone, and found my feet by hopping on a bus and exploring the streets of Mong Kok, Kowloon and Hong Kong Island.

I found modern-day Hong Kong just as charming as Wong's Wan Chai. It's the perfect combination of East and West, old and new. At first glimpse, the spiky silver skyline of Hong Kong Island looked as if it had been beamed down from space, but when I took a closer look I found Cantonese heritage threaded through its streets like woven silk. Dusty temples smouldering with incense rubbed shoulders with vertiginous twenty-first-century skyscrapers, cramped street markets selling everything from braised intestines to fist-sized rocks of jade, glitzy gin clubs and neon-lit 'girlie' bars. And a Marks and Spencer.

As great as it was to explore that first week, I felt like I was in limbo. I needed to work and meet people. I was in my early twenties and far from home, and I wanted to have some fun. On one jaunt into town, I wandered into Joe Bananas, an American bar and diner in Central, and promptly got a job as a waitress. What they didn't tell me was that I'd mostly be wearing a poncho and sombrero, selling tequila shots from a leather holster at their Mexican brunch. *Olé*.

Central was quite a schlep from Sha Tin and the New Territories and during that first week I would sit on a bus for hours travelling to and from work. Every day, the bus would stop outside the Pentecostal Tabernacle Mission in Kowloon and I'd wonder if David, my plane pal, was happy there.

I was fascinated by the love hotels that lined the streets of

Mong Kok. Scrappy motels with cheap neon signs advertising their rooms by the hour. Looking at the number of them, I saw that Hong Kong's sex industry was still booming, and it drew me back to the world of Suzie Wong.

'No money, no talk' was Suzie and her 'yum yum' girls' motto. It seems the hooker scene in Hong Kong had not really changed since Suzie's era. Prostitution was legal here; however, organised prostitution – soliciting or running a brothel – was not, so local sex workers offered private escort services or worked in massage parlours or nightclubs to garner their business.

In the Nineties, most Hong Kong sex workers came from Thailand, the Philippines and mainland China; the latter were referred to as *bak-gu* – 'northern girls' – and were considered more affordable and willing to provide, ahem, a wider range of services.

Compensated dating, where girls and young women offer 'companionship' to businessmen in return for gifts and money, was also a thing. Girls could demand around HK$1,000 an hour for their time, and some reported that certain men just wanted to spend an hour complaining about their life rather than doing anything sexual.

Fascinatingly, I discovered that Rhonda had lived in Hong Kong a few years before me, at the tender age of eighteen, and had experienced some of this kind of thing for herself.

'I didn't know what I wanted to do after A levels,' she told me. 'I'd been to Hong Kong with my parents a few years earlier and loved it. So I took a short typing course and then hopped on a plane to Hong Kong.

'Unfortunately my typing was execrable, so the first job the temping agency sent me to was as an interpreter for a French businessman. He was short and bald, probably late fifties. The interview was cursory; it was basically just a short chat during which he told me he needed me to accompany him all over East Asia for work and that I'd be staying in nice hotels, which sounded pretty cool to me – I'd get to see more of the region and get paid for it.'

Afterwards he took me to lunch and then to a fancy mall, where he kept pointing out expensive clothes he wanted to buy me, at which point I started to wonder what was going down. I said I didn't need any new clothes. Back at his hotel, he went up on tiptoe to try to kiss me and told me that my job would involve more than just translating. I legged it. But when I mentioned it to the temping agency, they seemed unshocked. I guess it wasn't that unusual.

'There was another guy, Charles. He was Hong Kong Chinese. I can't remember where I first met him but we went out for dinner in swanky restaurants a few times and I found him quite pleasant to chat to. He never made any kind of move on me or even really seemed to flirt, so I didn't see the harm. I guessed it was some kind of companionship thing, or just plain interest in spending time with a foreign woman. I thought he may actually be gay. And then one night he told me he was an erotic photographer and asked me if I was of a mind to go back to his studio and pose for some shots. I politely declined and he was fine about it, didn't push it, and that was the end of that.

'After that I was a bit more wary. By this time I was teaching English to young kids, businessmen and, in the evenings, late teenagers – and after work I'd go out clubbing with the latter, so I made some wonderful Chinese friends and had a ball after the initial weirdnesses. Hong Kong will always have a special place in my heart too, although I still wonder about my sanity at moving out there alone at that age.'

Unlike savvy Suzie and her 'yum yum' girls, I was still, like Rhonda, a little wet behind the ears. On one lengthy bus journey back from Kowloon, I sat on the top deck next to a young local man, probably in his mid-twenties. It was a hot and humid day and I was wearing shorts, and this young chap put his pinky finger in the crook of my knee for the entire journey. Silently staring ahead, I just sat there, not knowing what to do.

Now, I know what you're thinking. For fuck's sake, Trace! You smack his hand away, call him a prick and move. But I didn't. I stayed put and in my head went through every permutation as to why this would be acceptable behaviour. I naively wondered if it was a cultural thing. And if so, I reasoned that if I made a fuss he might get aggressive or, worse, lose face – a big thing in Chinese culture. So I just sat there and silently let a strange man finger my knee-hole, like a weirdo.

It was immediately after that odd experience that I decided to leave the New Territories. I'd met a brilliant girl at work called Sharon, from Bristol, who was living cheaply in a hostel on Nathan Road in Kowloon.

Like the notorious Chungking Mansion next door, Mirador Mansion was a microcosm of Hong Kong life. The ground floor was crammed with fashion shops, gadget stalls and shuttered lock-ups, tiny cubbyholes manned by old women selling cooking utensils, and vast Indian and Nepalese canteens, which were cheap as chips and always busy. On the higher floors were private apartments and hostels, including the New Garden Hostel on the thirteenth floor. My new home.

For the first week I slept on a mattress on the balcony, which, weirdly, I found quite acceptable. *Like a proper backpacker*, I'd think to myself as the streets roared below. It was here that I met Ann. Lovely Ann from London. A good ten years older than me, she'd recently arrived from Japan, where she'd worked as a hostess – 'not an escort' – in a Tokyo bar. A former model in the UK, Ann had left to go travelling and found herself immersed in Asia. She still lives in Hong Kong, on Lamma Island, with her dogs.

On Ann's advice, I upgraded my day job to waitressing the more lucrative nights at LA Café in Admiralty. And it was here that I met my crew. And through them, my husband to be.

During my first few split shifts working at LA Café, I'd spend the interim three hours alone wandering around Pacific Place shopping centre listening to my Walkman, reading Jilly Cooper and just spending time in my head. Looking back, I loved the feeling of anonymity during those split-shift hours. I never felt lonely, I just felt at peace, which is strange when you consider I was 6,000 miles from home and living on a balcony.

I think it was the complete freedom from obligation that I enjoyed the most. Even now, being alone in a strange country is still the most free I ever feel.

I was soon invited to hang out with some of the other split-shift crew in Pomeroy's Bar: Nicola from Aberdeen, who'd just spent six months travelling around India, Claire from Darlington, for whom Hong Kong was the first stop; Lady Miss Em, Emily, who was about to head off to Vietnam; Sarah from Manchester. Just great women. We'd drink beer and chat and while away the afternoon before our next shift. Sometimes the lads – Richard, Chris, Scott – would join us, but mostly it was just us girls.

Arriving in Hong Kong and being thrown into the incestuous backpacking/expat community, you'd think I'd have gone mad for the men. But no. Weirdly, it wasn't them I was interested in. It was the women I met. I was fascinated by them. Mesmerised by their energy.

Many of them had travelled before coming to Hong Kong; some were at the start of their journey. They had different stories, different lives, but all had the wondrous energy of brilliant, fascinating women. And I wanted to be like them.

Like Suzie Wong, Hong Kong is where I found my sisterhood.

It was on these split-shift afternoons that I really bonded with these women, particularly Claire and Lady Miss Em, who lived in a flat on Wing Lok Street in Sheung Wan. It would have anywhere between eight and thirteen residents at any one time, and hosted some of the most legendary parties on Hong Kong Island. I was desperate to move in.

I eventually did move in a few months later, when Miss Em left for Vietnam and a space opened up sharing a hallway with Sue. The flat was headed up by our luxury 'landlady', a gorgeous boy from Newcastle who we affectionately called Rita – aka Richard, another waiter at LA Café. The facilities were limited. In the bathroom we had a house Breville sandwich toaster on which my future husband would cook his famous hot dog and plastic cheese toasties at 4 am, and a ginormous fridge that only ever seemed to contain cans of San Miguel.

I vividly remember Claire climbing the stairs to our top-floor flat in the steamy heat of summer, removing clothes on every floor until she'd walk through the door in little more than a pair of pants. Meanwhile, Nicky, another housemate who I would later work with at Oscar's, would swan around in the nude drinking cans of San Miguel for breakfast because we'd run out of water.

Living with this marvellous bunch of people, my tribe, was one of the happiest times of my life. And the thing they all had in common was that they were truly being themselves.

The night I got together with A came as a surprise to me. Not least because I was in full drag at Carwash, an Eighties-themed night in a bar near Central. We snogged like loons in front of a kebab shop.

I fell hard. I hadn't had much – if any – experience of relationships and I wasn't sure what to expect. Or how to behave. This was all new to me.

We had a fun few months. We lived in each other's pockets, working together, living together, socialising all the time. It was a whirlwind romance and I loved it. I was having regular sex for the first time, although it wasn't always easy in a shared flat of thirteen – sometimes we'd head up to the rooftop, where everyone hung their laundry, and I'd wake up at dawn under someone's freshly washed sheets.

Now I think back to those times and find it hard to imagine how two people who felt that way could end up like this.

It was after a minor shoplifting incident resulting in handcuffs that I really felt the power of my urban family and my sisterhood. I should explain.

After a day of drinking at the dragon boat races in Stanley, I stole a Snickers bar from the 7-Eleven by putting it down my shorts – only for it to slide out at speed in front of a policeman.

Now, you'd think I would have complied with the police officer's simple request to see my ID and confirm my name. Unfortunately, I'm a professional dickhead and can't resist showing off in front of my friends. So I said my name was Elle Macpherson, after the Australian supermodel, who was currently in town.

While I might be six foot tall and blonde, that is very much where our likeness ended. Not least because I had hoisin sauce smeared down my *Fame!* T-shirt.

I was promptly arrested and thrown into the back of a police van, along with my friend Sue, who wanted to come along for the ride. Still not seeing the seriousness of the matter, Sue and I decided that we would re-enact the plot of *Mission Impossible*, and rolled about the van pretending to shoot each other with finger guns. Hilarious, not.

The situation stopped being quite so hilarious when we got to the police station. They did actually drop Sue off at the bar she requested, such was her charm, while I was locked in a cell until I would 'comply'.

I was questioned about the crime by actual detectives, who produced a 10" x 6" colour photograph of said Snickers bar and asked if I had stolen it. I confirmed I had, in fact, stolen the Snickers bar and asked if I could have it back, as I was a little peckish.

I had my fingerprints taken – they refused my offer of a tit-print. However, the big issue was the failure to provide my ID. Everyone in Hong Kong had to have an ID card, which I did, in the pocket of my bag. But, of course, I felt the gag was more important than the truth.

This changed when the detective decided to handcuff me and threatened to chain me to a table to stop me waltzing around the station like a queen. I quickly fessed up and produced my ID card to confirm that I was not, in fact, the ethereally beautiful Australian supermodel Elle Macpherson, I was merely Tracey Clark, a very drunk British waitress with a penchant for stolen chocolate.

Just like on *The Bill*, I was allowed one phone call. I called the only number I knew off by heart, that of our flat, and woke dear Claire up. It was three in the morning and she came – in her pyjamas and Deirdre Barlow-style glasses, which usually never saw the light of day – and paid my HK$500 bail, and I was released, pending a court case.

That's female friendship for you – a willingness to look shit in public to bail you out of jail.

All this happened while A was away on a diving trip in the Philippines. When he landed back in Hong Kong, the word had got out that I was basically Lizzie Borden. Luckily, he found it funny, even when I went to court and admitted my crime and was bound over by the peace until I left the country.

And that was the beginning and perhaps the end of my criminal career. Although, it's not to say that I haven't considered crimes *many* times in the subsequent years.

By now it was time to follow my original plan to go to Australia, so I bought a one-way ticket to Sydney and said 'Mañana, bitches', and that was it. I said farewell to Hong Kong, my tribe, and my first love, who promised to catch me up in Oz.

Well, of course, the following twenty years, three kids and impending divorce suggests that was not quite it.

'I was working as a waitress in a cocktail bar, when I met you…'
Human League

Twenty-one years later, I'm buckled in my seat about to take off, the space next to me empty, when the tears finally come. And they don't stop until I am somewhere over Greece. My husband should be sitting next to me, travelling back to the place where we began.

After Hong Kong, we travelled the world for two more years and then moved to London. It wasn't long after that my ovaries started pinging. I wanted babies. And I thought I wanted his babies. He agreed. But two decades and three children later, our relationship unravelled at a hefty pace.

We had a difficult time for several years, but over the previous twelve months, illness, grief and surprise debt had left our marriage on a knife-edge. Then I got this opportunity to return to Hong Kong to research a story, and I asked him to come with me. It was our special place and I hoped it would restore what we once had and get our relationship back on track.

We'd tried everything – marriage counselling, my own therapy, antidepressants – but the connection was gone and contempt was starting to set in on both sides. For me, this was the last-chance saloon for our marriage. But he said no. Although all our costs would be covered, apart from his flight, he was adamant that we couldn't afford it and stubbornly refused to reconsider.

Returning more than twenty years later, Hong Kong feels familiar yet entirely different. As do I. I have changed a lot in the absent years. I have grown.

Instead of the scuzzy two-bedroom flat we lived in, I stay at the Kerry, a beautiful five-star hotel by Shangri-La overlooking Victoria Harbour. From my suite, I can see the green-and-white Star Ferries bumbling back and forth. Over the next few days, I swing from being angry at his absence to frustrated at his obstinance and then inconsolably sad at what this means for our marriage.

I walk through Lan Kwai Fong, Central's party district and the scene of so many amazing nights back in the day. It still feels familiar, yet there are few bars remaining from my time. Every moment of recognition comes with a pang of regret that I'm seeing it on my own. In Sheung Wan, where we lived, the pungent scent of dried-fish shops slaps me in the face, just like it always did. Outside our flat on Wing Lok Street, I feel so overcome with emotion that I have to sit on the kerb to recover.

Sandwiched between Old Town Central and Sai Ying Pun, Sheung Wan has benefited from plenty of gentrification over the years I was away. One of Hong Kong's oldest districts, it still has dozens of stores on Wing Lok Street and De Voeux Road flogging sacks of dried scallops and fat puffs of fish maw (dried bladders). But although parts of Sheung Wan are still marvellously malodorous, it hasn't put the hipsters off moving in with their cold-drip coffee shops and craft microbreweries. I briefly think that I could easily move back.

Luckily, my packed itinerary helps balance the tsunami of memories Hong Kong unleashes – boozy nights dancing on bars in Wan Chai, lazy Sundays on Lamma Island, beach-hopping in Stanley. Instead I browse art galleries in the South Island Cultural District, see the parades at the bun festival on Cheung Chau, and dine in fancy restaurants on Lee Tung Avenue in Wanchai.

Over the five days, my poor head runs the full gamut of emotions. I was worried that my memories of Hong Kong would be tainted by my marriage ending, but, although there are indeed moments of sadness, ultimately it's quite the opposite. Hong Kong was the catalyst to the latter half of my life and was incredibly formative of who I am today. It also reaped a twenty-year relationship, three beautiful children and many lifelong friends.

On the last afternoon, I take the Star Ferry from Tsim Sha Tsui over to Central, a journey I've made hundreds of times. On deck, looking out as the late-afternoon sky bounces off the skyscrapers, I remember who I was back then and decide that I owe it to myself to be happy.

When I return home, things have definitely shifted in me. It's through his lack of interest in this important trip and saving us that I finally know the marriage is over – although it will take me another few years to actually end it.

On occasion, I still feel sad about what could have been. But that trip – and others afterwards – gave me the space to see the relationship from a distance. Even if A had come to Hong Kong, our marriage might still have ended. I feel like I've come full circle and can move forward with no regrets.

And best of all, I still have all these wonderful women, and Richard – my Hong Kong tribe – firmly in my life. Despite being scattered across the country, we meet up two or three times a year, we chat on WhatsApp, have the odd phone call, tag one another on Instagram. They are always there, always supporting me, always championing me – and lately, always holding my hand as I navigate my way through this new stage of life. My tribe.

CHAPTER 6

THE AFFAIR

Rhonda

> *'Fuck the pain away.'*
> Peaches

There remain fifteen Muslim countries in which women can lawfully be stoned to death for marital infidelity, including Iran. Outside Islam, other countries that criminalise marital infidelity are the Philippines and the USA (at least, in several states).

It's been this way throughout history. In ancient Mesopotamia, adulterers were drowned. In other civilisations, including ancient India and ancient Egypt, they had their noses amputated. In the Greco-Roman world, husbands could have sex with an enslaved person or an unmarried woman, but a father was permitted to kill an adulterous daughter and sometimes an adulterous partner. Among the Aztecs, adulterous wives were either stoned to death or, occasionally, impaled. Some Native American cultures mutilated unfaithful wives to prevent them being attractive to other men.

The Bible prescribes capital punishment for adultery between a man and a married woman, but, again, a married man gets off scot-free if the woman he beds is unmarried. In the Middle Ages, many Germanic tribes allowed the husband to 'take the law in his own hands' when it came to unfaithful wives, and in medieval Vienna adulterers were impaled.

Other religions have looked at things with a more kindly

eye. Hinduism has a wide range of opinions on the matter. Some texts accept marital infidelity as par for the course, some consider it a minor offence requiring penance, and some see it as severe – indeed, in the case of some castes, both the man and the woman are seen as deserving of the death penalty

Among exponents of the first position, the Vedic texts, including the *Rigveda*, *Atharvaveda* and *The Upanishads*, acknowledge that physical love is a basic fact of human existence, recommending only that extramarital sex be avoided during certain ritual occasions. The *Kamasutra* even devotes fifteen sutras to the reasons for which a man is allowed to seduce a married woman.

For Buddhists, adultery is not a sin but a cause of unhappiness. Stemming from greed in a previous life, it in turn has karmic consequences that carry forward to subsequent lives, in the chain of misery that is samsara: birth, mundane existence and death. And then repeat – unless/until, that is, one 'blows out' the desires, as one would a candle, and understands impermanence and the non-self reality that is the state of nirvana.

It was Bonfire Night when I began the affair. I didn't just fall into it. I initiated it. I set my life on fire and stood back and watched the flames take hold, dance, flicker and spread.

The night before that, I sat in a London bar with Tracey, on the eve of a big travel event, and told her I was going to spend the following night in a hotel with a much older man I had recently met on a press trip. A married man.

I didn't know Tracey hugely well at this time, but I did know from her honesty about her own marriage – which she'd been open about right from the start, when we met in Finland – that she wouldn't judge me.

Judge me?! Reader, she chuckled bawdily and said, 'Go for it.'

Okay...

Thinking I still owed her some sort of explanation, but probably really only needing to justify it to myself, I told her how fed up I'd become, how exhausted I was by being the sole provider for the vast majority of the time and lying awake worrying about the bills. And by also doing so much of the emotional labour, the day-to-day remembering, organising, fretting. Life had become so heavy.

Tracey listened, nodding, seemingly absorbing my pain. I felt understood.

Both of us knew I was doing a stupid, harmful thing that would probably have terrible consequences, but I think we both also knew that this was by now also unstoppable.

Sometimes it seems that my capacity for self destruction is unlimited – or perhaps rather my capacity for blowing things up before I've admitted to myself they no longer serve me. But perhaps sometimes we need to destroy ourselves.

Looking back now, I wonder if Tracey and I both had the same word in our brain: *payback*. Payback for being leaned on too hard.

Or as another wise close girlfriend, T, said when I told her I felt I was about to 'fall into an affair', as if I was tripping on a paving stone: I was 'socking it' to my husband.

They saw me, the other women.

I, and they, had finally recognised how very angry and hurt I was. That doesn't make what I did right. Nothing ever will. But regret it? I'm not sure I do.

Everything in this book is how I remember it. Reality is of course subjective. According to some psychologists, a whole 60 per cent of memory is false to some degree. We fill in the gaps. But even in the present moment of any experience, we are only taking in very limited fragments of a kaleidoscopic whole, depending on which sense we are foregrounding.

This is my story. Others will have their own versions, and I accept those as much as I accept my own. But nothing I say is a lie.

'I too am not a bit tamed – I too am untranslatable; I
sound my barbaric yawp over the roofs of the world.'

I watched my husband read the Walt Whitman poem I'd chosen for my father's funeral to the handful of mourners. I couldn't think about standing up and speaking in front of everyone. All I could think about were those four days and nights beside the hospital bed, the screams, the fading away of him, until he no longer knew who he was, and claimed not to know anybody by my name.

Then there were the two weeks driving backwards and forwards between Manchester and Leicester, setting out at five in the morning because that was when grief woke me, like an alarm clock. Not eating, just drinking coffee from a flask by my side as I wound through the empty lanes of the Peak District, swerving to avoid the night's roadkill smeared across the asphalt. So much blood and wastage.

Weeks of still being Mum and breadwinner (it turned out that that never let up, whatever else was going on in my life) while camping out at my brother's house as we struggled to clear out everything my father had so obsessively collected and hoarded over the years, while obsessively neglecting his body.

Those things included the last of the many cigarettes he'd smoked over a surprisingly long lifetime, beginning at the age of about thirteen. I did the maths: eighty cigarettes a day works out at about 29,000 a year. Times that by around sixty years... *Fuuuuuuck.*

But had I colluded in the self-neglect, or at least turned a blind eye? The question clawed at me.

The times I'd come home as a teenager to find him passed out on the floor in front of the fireplace, sleeping the near-death sleep of a man who's just downed a large bottle of whisky to himself. That time I'd seen him trying to get into a cupboard, mistaking it for the living-room door. The times I heard him shouting out in the night, when I knew he was all alone, my mother removed from it all at her end of the house they still shared, having failed to get him to talk to anyone.

My father wasn't the first alcoholic in the family. Ancestral research revealed a family fortune that was 'pissed away' on my mother's side. And there was also my father's own mother, who I was once told had responded to her husband having a decades-long 'secret' mistress by drinking her way through the days and hiding her stash of empties at the back of their capacious pantry.

My father was stubborn. So stubborn that he — more than once — nearly died rather than see a doctor. The first time it was a ruptured bowel and septicaemia. He was rushed to hospital; we were told to expect the worst. Studying in Paris at that time, I readied myself for a last-minute flight home.

He survived. When he got home, the divorce papers my mum had drawn up before he was ill were waiting for him. Their marriage was finally over, she had told him that before he became ill, and this near-death experience changed nothing. But when his colostomy bag came apart, it was she who cleaned him up and helped him reattach it. It was she who cleaned up her ex-husband's shit, just like M did with his abusive dad.

They hurt us and still we care.

My father would never have wanted to die in hospital. He'd rather have put a gun in his mouth. And ultimately I was surprised that he didn't kill himself. He knew how sick he was, yet he hid it from his only friend, his cleaner G — the woman (married, my age) he loved at the end and whose name he remembered long after he had forgotten mine.

The one who left lipstick prints on his blueing forehead at the hospital after my brother and I left, and who wept like a widow at his funeral. The woman who I only met beside his bed as he lay dying yet who felt like a sister — of sorts. A sister and what else?

Even today, years and years later, I can't answer that question.

My father died of four things, according to the autopsy. But it was essentially a clusterfuck of problems caused by diabetes. And the diabetes had been brought on by decades of drinking and a terrible diet.

I sat, and slept, beside him in a hospital armchair. My brother, who had been estranged from my dad for some years, arrived and we kept vigil together. When Dad was unconscious for a spell, I'd get my laptop out and work, because I was so worried about losing money and also losing ongoing work. I felt shame about that, self-disgust, but I was the only real earner; there was never any reprieve, even here, now, with this.

For four days and nights, we tried to save him. Only I wasn't sure he wanted saving. I doubted it very much. He couldn't tell us anything. When he was able to look at us, his eyes tried to say something, flashed us a wild message, but it was impossible to decode it. Was he asking to feel better or to be allowed escape?

Finally, at some point when my brother was away from the hospital, perhaps fetching some fresh clothes, the staff took me aside, into a little room, and several of them clustered around me as witnesses while a consultant listed out loud all the drugs they were giving my father and the fact that none of them seemed to be having an effect.

'The Zithromax hasn't brought any improvement. Do you give us permission to stop the Zithromax?'

I nodded.

'The ciprofloxacin hasn't brought any improvement. Do you give us permission to stop the ciprofloxacin?'

Another nod.

'Do you give us permission…?'

'Do you give us permission…?'

I nodded, and nodded, and nodded again, until all the drugs were scratched from the list.

Die, Dad. Fly, Dad. S*ound your barbaric yawp.*

It began in a bar in a hotel like something out of *The Shining*, in the midst of the tea plantations and strawberry fields of central

Malaysia. I was drinking Campari and orange. It suited the hotel, the decor, the mood – like something out of time, lost in the past, left behind.

There was talk, along the five of us on this press trip, of another round, but I was ready for bed. Or that's what I thought. M glanced at me.

'*You're* having another one, obviously,' he said and something inside of me cracked open.

He's got me, I thought. *He knows I'm easily suggestible, the last person to leave any party, against my better judgement.*

But more than that, he was telling me what to do. And for some reason, while I was irked by that, I was also a little turned on.

I stayed for another drink, and another.

A karaoke bar in Penang. We'd murdered a couple of ABBA songs and moved on to Oasis, 'Wonderwall'.

'*Because maybe…*'.

We were already, without knowing it, out of our depth. Each of us waiting, perhaps, for someone to save us. Or perhaps that was only me.

The rest of the clientele were young gay men who sang like Celine Dion. I had to get drunk to do this. M commented on how quickly I was drinking: 'I've been watching you,' he said. That weird feeling again: irritation and at the same time arousal.

We'd spent quite a bit of time together that day, with the others or just the two of us. Walking around George Town, stopping for *teh tarik* poured from on high by the theatrical vendors, to watch a service inside a Hindu temple, to observe people burning paper offerings at small shrines.

At one point, I had turned from peering into a café serving civet poo coffee to see him on the other side of the street. Our eyes met. I headed over and we walked around together, photographing street art. Another of our group caught up with us and took a picture of the two of us sitting on a bench.

I later lose count of the number of times he sends me that photo, both of us astonished at the sight of two people who have no idea what is going to happen.

I also lose count of the number of times M will tell me how hard he had to resist the urge to put his arm round me at that moment. But years later I still remember the feeling of his shoulder against me. The solidity of it, but something else I can't define. Not something sexual. Something powerful and protective, sturdy and reassuring.

M, who often called me 'kiddo' – something that again both annoyed me and turned me on in some weird way, that made me feel like a daughter.

He called his wife 'petal', which absolutely gave me the ick. And behind her back, 'the little sparrow'. Or, sometimes, 'cuntface'.

A week after returning from Malaysia, the *Wonderwall* chorus a constant refrain in my head, I took my husband and sons to Naples. I was always the one who paid for holidays, as well as everything else, the majority of the time. There didn't seem to be an alternative and I wanted my kids to experience wonderful places, like I had and did.

This trip was not far from perfect. Divine food with lots of laughter. Sorties to Pompeii, Herculaneum, Vesuvius, Procida. But all the time I was thinking of M, finding reasons to WhatsApp him. Photos: me and my youngest son by a fountain, me in a gelato shop, erotic statues in the archaeological museum.

Feeling guilty because I wasn't focused on what was there in front of me.

Or I was. I was *loving* this time with my kids. In Herculaneum we looked at skeletons preserved by ash – mainly children and teens sent to shelter in boathouses and cooked alive by a pyroclastic cloud. At the top of Vesuvius we peered down into the innocuous-looking crater that had caused so much havoc and will cause havoc again.

'Noisy, chaotic, smelly, scruffy' is how I later described Naples in a piece I wrote for a national newspaper. Horns blasting, mopeds hurtling along pavements, rubbish going uncollected.

But more than anything else, Naples is *alive*. I sensed that the city's inhabitants take life by the scruff of the neck because they know that all of this could be blown away in a cloud of hot rock and gases. *Carpe diem.*

M sent me a few pictures. He was at the beach, in Dorset. He was wearing a coat, a woolly hat. The sun was shining, though. It was a brilliant day. One of the pictures was of his wife, smiling, in shades and a hat too. I took it as a message. *I'm still* very *married.*

Later, he'd write to me: 'You and I went off like a rocket.'

Tracey met him in the morning, at the travel event. She liked him. She already knew some of his staff, many of whom adored him. The problem is, on some levels, he *was* (is) a nice man. On another, he was a hopeless people-pleaser who put up with nearly anything. From his wife, and from me.

The evening after Bonfire Night and our first fireworks, eating in a Goan restaurant I'd been to with my student boyfriend decades before, I held my hands up: *I don't want to hear about it. Our marriages are irrelevant. We're keeping our personal lives out of this.*

But M seemed to feel the need to explain, and how could I not be curious? It was only afterwards that I fully understood that this was not an unburdening but a laying down of the ground rules.

Married at twenty-four and from an ultra-religious, conservative background, he had never been able to see his way out of what he described as 'the dysfunction' of a wife who refused sex. He 'dealt' with things by having affairs. Later, in couples' therapy, he discovered that she, the one who 'didn't like sex', had also had dalliances – with his boss, with a colleague's husband, with a neighbour. In his view this was out of a wish for attention. But she wanted to stay married to him.

Along the way, he'd had two serious relationships. Each time his wife found out, she staged a big collapse. Once he even left and the wife was looked after by their grown-up daughter, but after a year he 'felt aimless' and came back.

Over fish curry, he told me he was now 'happily married'. I asked how it was possible to be happily married after all he'd described and he shrugged. 'I can't explain.'

It was all quite mystifying and so far beyond my realm of experience that I didn't really feel anything much about it at all. Yet enough had been said, enough doors had been opened and left ajar, for things to play in my mind, and when I woke up beside him in the night I was troubled enough to decamp to the apartment's second bedroom while he slept on – a bedroom we'd not used but without which I'd never have been able to agree to come and spend two nights in his company.

He came and found me, asked what was wrong. I told him it was the women, the women he tried and failed to leave his wife for. One of them – he'd told me – had cried on the phone from her native New Orleans five years later, about what could have been.

I told him I couldn't stop thinking about that woman and her wasted time and her broken heart, and he told me it was 'all about context' and we went back to the other room and fucked.

All my sense of direction had gone; I didn't have a map to chart this terrain. And I was sad, too. I couldn't tell him, but I felt sorry for all he told me he'd put up with, because he seemed like such a lovely person who didn't deserve any of it.

Nor did I tell him, until later, that the apartment where we were staying, the window he had me up against, looked right down over the pub when I first talked to the man who would become my husband, eighteen years before. A pub called The Hope.

A few weeks later, en route to Belize, M sent me updates from his journey. Over the Atlantic, he told me, he struggled to sleep as he thought about 'taking me apart'. It was a phrase he returned to several times over the coming months. I didn't know what he meant but it somehow excited me. For some reason, it seemed I wanted to be dismantled.

Twelve months, it lasted, and then some – then the bloody aftermath. Twelve months of euphoria; twelve months, also, of one body blow after another.

My girlfriends were always there for me, and then some. But I think they were evolved enough, from their own heartbreaks and fuck-ups, to know to cheer me on when I was happy and to be angry for me when I was angry. In other words, not to try to tell me what to do. I was a grown woman and I needed to make my own way through this unholy mess I'd willingly stepped into.

In fact, when I was sad, I tried not to talk to them about M because I felt like such an idiot. I'd brought it on myself.

Of course they were looking out for me. In Manchester, I met with my closest friends every Thursday night in the pub, and, over cheese and two-for-one fishbowl-size glasses of gin awash with peppercorns, we'd talk about everything in our lives, including my weird, aged, golf-playing Tory lover. One time, they laughingly offered to meet me off the train back from London with a stretcher because I'd have been fucked so much I would barely be able to walk.

But most importantly, I knew that psychologically they would carry me, if needed. That they were already doing that.

Another close girlfriend, T, commanded me more than once to stop whinging about M kowtowing to his wife and '*just 'av it*' – accept it for what it was and enjoy it. T had been married to a man so bullying that she'd had the police round to their house no fewer than sixteen times. The cops had never done more than give her husband a warning; to stop him, she'd eventually gone behind the scenes at the police force and had somebody shady threaten to look into his business affairs and expose him for tax fraud unless he left her alone.

She was very cynical about men. Yet sometimes this hard-boiled woman, when I told her about M and me, cried for us and the fact we couldn't be together. Because we really loved each other, albeit in complicated ways.

Complicated, because I also really hated that man's guts.

Before I had kids, I knew nothing, of course, of motherhood – of how it impacts you, changes you, rewires your brain. It was not something I thought much about.

But looking back, there had been glimpses of the anger of other mothers – glimpses I largely buried as soon as they entered my consciousness. Perhaps we all have to do that, to countenance becoming mothers ourselves.

The anger of my own mother, at my father's unwillingness to get a handle on his alcoholism and save their marriage. And then that of her mother in turn, at things she'd experienced. Once, home from uni for a weekend, I'd sat in the courtyard of an inn with both my grandmothers. My grandfathers had both died two years before. For now my grandmothers were fine, if struggling to get around. They were always asking after each other, and finally one of them asked if I could get them together.

I sat smoking and listening to them talk. I felt like an intruder. They had so much to say, so much to remember and to rue. One had lost her first fiancé to a diving accident, then her first husband when the HMS *Hecla* was sunk at the start of World War Two. Left alone with a baby, she slept with him swaddled beside her on the bed, ready to grab him and run to an air-raid shelter. That was when she had her nervous breakdown, she said almost matter-of-factly.

They carried on talking. I carried on listening, puffing on cigarettes and trying to look impassive as I took in long-buried emotions and grievances. Sexual harassment, destructive jealousies, illegal and unsafe abortions.

I could *only* listen. I could not engage with the knottiness and politics of it all, of family lives that had seemed so ordinary and familiar. I was remembering how, in turn, my grandad had once told me that, sick of the violence his father inflicted on his mother, he and one of his brothers had, in their teens, conspired to kill him.

Families...

At the same time, there was no chance of my other grandmother ever opening up to us about her alcoholism brought on by my grandfather's long affair. And she never talked about my dad's sister, who had died of leukaemia aged six, and whose double I had been as a child, terrifying everyone.

She wasn't one to talk, and I suppose, in some part of myself, I was grateful for that. I was thinking that maybe there are some things we shouldn't talk about.

Should I be talking about all this or should I be letting it lie? Are women dangerous when they get together and talk? And is danger necessarily bad?

I think of Björk's song 'Jóga', about her best friend Johanna – about how their close relationship pushed the singer into a 'state of emergency' – and how beautiful it was to be in that heightened space, emotionally.

It was in Eden in the Lake District, in a remote cabin on a river, that I had sex with my husband of sixteen and a half years for the very last time. It was only later that the irony of the name occurred to me. Like that of The Hope pub in London.

We went with two of the boys and the dog; the eldest wanted to stay home and celebrate the end of his GCSEs with mates. I'd booked it more than a year before, at great expense to myself. Now it was the last thing I felt like doing, with my husband at least. But it was a school holiday and one son's birthday, and I would make it lovely for everyone.

There were walks and waterfalls and huge boulders and streams to carry the dog across and much skimming of stones across the water. There was fishing in the river. I tried very hard to be fully present, to immerse myself in it all, not to think about M. I knew how precious this time was.

The cabin had an outdoor hot tub. I spent time in it with the kids, but later, when they'd gone to try to catch more fish, I had a dip myself, naked. We were deep in a forest, no one would see.

Upstairs, from the bedroom window I couldn't see into because of the sunshine, my husband was watching me. He was also taking photographs of me.

When I found this out later, I was pissed off but not surprised. And my reaction was – pathetically, I know – to fuck him. It was only the second or third time since I'd started sleeping with M nearly seven months before.

Later my husband would hold this against me.

'But you do still fancy me, because you initiated it.'

And: 'How was I to know how unhappy you were, when you initiated sex sometimes?'

The truth is that, on the rare occasions when I 'initiated', it was a pre-emptive strike to counter the whiny claims that we had sex less than anyone else we knew (which, by the way, I knew to be completely untrue).

There was always a reason we 'should' have sex. *The kids were all out of the house... It was his birthday... It was my birthday... We were in a hotel... I was going away... He was going away... One of us had just got back from somewhere...*

It was never about desire. Or never about my desire. It was about marital entitlement.

The story of so many women's lives. This is not my story alone. That's why I'm telling it.

When I was offered a four-month stint editing a book, when our first son was six weeks old, I handed over the main childcare role to my husband, who suggested a deal whereby in his 'free' time (evenings and weekends) he wrote novels. I agreed.

But as time went on (and on), I wondered: where was *my* free time? Where was *my* creativity? I'd already won a prize for my first published short story, and my first novel had gone out with a thrusting young literary agent certain it too would garner awards. It didn't, because it never got published – but that's not the point. When was I to build on that start?

The questions were academic at the time. In fact, for a long time I didn't really ask them. I was a new mum. I was consumed by my baby. Weekdays I worked (my husband bringing the baby for me to be breastfed at my desk), while early mornings, evenings and weekends I was Mum.

We moved to an old cognac farm in the middle of France, for no real reason other than that we had equity to draw down on my London flat. Life in rural France was hard and I quickly became miserable. When I wasn't working or looking after our son, I was spending his naptimes scrubbing baby clothes by hand because we didn't have a washing machine or even an indoor bathroom.

The question of my missing free time and my stifled creativity bubbled under the surface, but then came more kids. We moved back to the UK, sold the collapsing farmhouse. The kids went to school and made friends and we became part of a community. My husband wrote one novella and one novel about a couple in a French farmhouse. Money trickled in from his books. People mistook the unhinged, filicidal female protagonists for me, apparently unaware of the difference between fiction and non-fiction.

I should have been shittier about the money situation. Of course I should have been shittier. There were ultimatums. Just not enough of them, or rather never any that were followed through. Why not? Because of the kids, of course. You don't want to turn their lives upside down. You put up and shut up. You learn the self-sacrifice that the only real love, the love of your children, demands of you, and in a strange way you embrace it.

I asked for this, you think. And you convince yourself it's true.

★

M always did a little skip of joy when we met. It was one of the things I loved most – how visibly happy I made him. And I felt them too, those stabs of happiness. I lived for that day when I woke up, once a month or so, and thought, 'It's *here*.'

But I was tired and frazzled too. I didn't sleep well for the anticipation, and the stress of living that clichéd double life bubbled away underneath. I still didn't feel guilty – or at least I told myself I didn't. Were they one and the same thing? I told myself that what had been expected of me in the past had led inexorably to this situation.

Ideally, I'd have addressed those things or said I wanted to split up, rather than falling into an affair. But the boys were of certain ages and stages in their schooling that made this a less-than-ideal time to tumble sideways out of my marriage. And then there were the money issues. Up-and-going was not easy. So for now it was: *Distract, distract, distract*.

M never understood that I never had any intention of leaving my three sons and my home. Manchester was not my native city but had become 'my place' – left-wing and radical. I think he always wanted to believe I was ready to leave everything for him. A preposterous idea.

It was in a boutique hotel in the Cotswolds that I realised I hated M as much as I loved him. It was also the first place where he tied me up, and with that the first time he made me come. These three things cannot be untangled.

I hadn't yet started to consciously think about all the disappointing males in my life, to put together the jigsaw puzzle of men who had let me down. But on the surface at least, M was the kind of man I always met in my dreams: go-getting, dynamic, sure of what he wanted. He had his own company and was used to being in charge and making decisions. He was all the things I had missed in my marriage.

I'd had these dreams sporadically over the years. And in my dreams this imaginary man blew my mind – literally, short-circuited me. I *had* to be with him. There was no choice. I never even knew what he looked like. But I woke up with a feeling of yearning and emptiness.

I told some of my closest girlfriends about this, and about how I feared meeting this person because he would blow everything to pieces. All of them mentioned similar dreams and visions – the fear, which must also be the hope, of meeting someone who will explode the life you have so carefully constructed. The wolf who with a huff and a puff will blow your house down.

But in a hotel room in London, when I lay with my head on M's chest and told him I didn't want to fix my marriage and he said how 'sad' that was, I wanted to stab him. I wanted to tell him it was *his* marriage that was sad. Instead, I just stared out of the window at the branches of a tree moving sluggishly in the summer breeze and wished I were dead.

One of my best, wisest and most bruised friends, T (the one who'd had to get the police on her husband), persuaded me that I needed to try hot yoga with her, that it would help me when I was struggling so much. So for ninety minutes once or twice a week, I sweated myself thoughtless with twenty strangers in a dimly lit room.

There were twenty-six postures, repeated twice each, for sixty and thirty seconds respectively, in forty-degree heat. I couldn't think of anything else but enduring what my body was doing, getting to the end of the session without passing out. When it was over, the towel I'd placed on my yoga mat was so wet I had to wring it out over the sink in the changing room.

There was a sense of atonement to it all, a sense of sweating out my impurities and suffering for the sins that had made me so unhappy. Not the 'sin' of adultery that would be thrown at me. But the sin of wanting something that I was told, from the get-go, I couldn't have. And for making the mistake of wanting to save someone who didn't want to be saved.

'My life will never change': M's words at dinner on our second night together.

After the drugged-up sexathon when he came to meet me in Ibiza, M wobbled violently. I told him it was the drugs, the comedown. He told me he felt as if he was in some kind of shock. The sex we'd had had made him feel like an animal. He wanted me to reassure him that he wasn't being a jerk, that I had 'taken him to *that place*.'

'We've taken each other to that place,' I replied. But I told him I in turn was worried he'd been building up a false image of me.

'Sex can be a kind of front, too,' I told him.

Meanwhile, I was spending time with my boys, and resting and unpacking, only to start packing for a flight to the US Midwest.

The Midwest, where, in a hotel in the Black Hills, another man would walk the corridors looking for me after I'd gone to bed. Where, in the same hotel, I would book a return flight to Cambodia just to stop myself thinking about whether that was a sane thing to do or not (it wasn't).

The Cambodian National Gallery, Phnom Penh. M walks ahead of me. Occasionally he holds back to comment on the intricacies of an ancient script or some other detail that has caught his eye, but then I let him walk on ahead again. I need distance.

It's our last day here together. This evening, we will fly home separately. We're here under false pretences – or at least I am. He flew his daughter out to go to a yoga retreat south of here; she's a bit younger than me and married but travelling alone, so coming here seems to be for M's own reassurance, mainly. Or perhaps just as an excuse to be away from his wife.

I'm ostensibly on a press trip. I have that kind of job where it's easy to come up with reasons to be on the other side of the world for five days.

A statue catches my attention, causing me to stop. Two bodies, entwined, seen from behind. Each lacks an arm, their head. The surviving arm of one of them is round the other's waist; the other has their arm raised and propped on the first's shoulder. Their torsos are naked.

I sense M behind me. I hear his voice in my ear, feel his breath on my neck.

'That's us,' he says.

I close my eyes, picture him and me in bed together, this morning, last night, on a handful of nights over this last wonderful, terrible year. Or two handfuls. A dozen at most.

And then I open my eyes and read the etiquette.

The Wrestlers, the statue is called.

'They're fighting, M,' I say, but he's already walking away and I don't know if he has heard me.

The Wrestlers from Koh Ker: not in love but at war. Or maybe both.

I think of them again as my plane takes off and banks over the Phnom Penh cityscape. M is down there, in the midst of all the glitter and shimmer, waiting for his daughter in the riverside restaurant where he and I ate fish *amok* served in a coconut shell and I put my hand up to stop him when he tried to talk about 'us', looking as if he was going to cry.

'I'm here, aren't I? That should be enough. If we talk about things, we will argue.'

I'd crossed half the world to sit here with him in that restaurant – another one, like the one in Ibiza, resembling something out of a Richard Curtis movie. I *will not* argue with him, I'd said to myself. I *will not* fly thirteen hours home in tears.

I'd had too many train journeys like that already – London to Manchester behind sunglasses, tears washing down my face as the rails rattled beneath me and home got nearer.

Getting back, pulling myself together, pretending I was 'just tired'. Lying on the bathroom floor, behind a locked door, feeling like a punctured balloon.

The Titanic, the restaurant was called. Its name hung over me as we sat amid the lanterns, already trying to hold on to the moment. We were sinking, I knew that. I'd known that since the beginning. And yet there we were, a year later, trying to keep the whole rotten ship of us afloat.

But in some ways it was easier to do that here than back in the UK, perhaps because we were so far removed from our lives that we could almost pretend they didn't exist. Almost, because there were still the phone calls home. His to his wife, mine to my kids.

But there was also the feeling that we were in a completely different world. We cycled the islands of the Mekong, visiting silk-weaving families and ginger farms. We rode a tuk-tuk out to ruined temples. We went to a former orchard housing mass graves where 8,895 bodies were found, victims of the totalitarian regime that ruled this country in the 1970s. At moments the personal seemed utterly impertinent.

But on the way back from Choeung Ek, from behind the masks we wore to protect us from the pollution as the tuk-tuk chugged back to the city in the darkness, I told M I'd met someone else – the man, an Austrian writer, who'd come looking for me in the hotel in the Midwest. Someone who was single, the same age or anyway just a few years younger, and just out of a seven-year relationship. Someone who was on my wavelength: someone left-wing.

M stayed quiet as I talked. His hands were up my skirt. Faster vehicles than ours flooded around us on either side, making us feel lost in some other time-frame. Were we ever going to get back to the city?

When we finally did, our tuk-tuk driver hugged us each in turn. We'd been out with him all day and he'd become fond of us, it seemed. At one point, we'd even said 'Hi' to his kids while he was WhatsApping home.

Back in the hotel room, M told me he 'felt weird'. It was what I knew already: he was okay with me staying with and even sleeping with my husband, because it meant I would be unhappy and carry on with our affair. If I left my husband and started another relationship, it was unlikely that M and I would carry on.

M was all about the status quo. I knew this by now.

Whereas I was all about planting bombs.

Another day, in our hotel room, he cried to some music by the band Yes. The song 'Soon', with lyrics about soothing an 'endless night' within.

We lay side by side, listening. He said he didn't know why he cried, but I thought he must.

Another night, when he was tired, I let him roll away from me – he always slept so far away, echoing how he told me it was in his own 'very big bed' in his 'sexless', 'touch-free' home – and I picked up my book. He commented on how cosy it was.

'Like an old married couple,' I replied. It was a dig, of course, but he didn't take it as such.

'If only,' he said.

'If only,' I echoed, but, again, it was a dig. Because that was a refrain of his, and I'd come to hate it.

I think of *The Wrestlers* as my plane takes off and I sweep the city with my eyes, looking for the place where the Titanic restaurant holds the ghosts of us, the place where M is waiting for his daughter now. And I tell myself that we're done. It's done.

Later, M tells me that these five days were the happiest of his life, and I sort of believe him, and I also do not give a single fuck.

CHAPTER 7

OFF THE RAILS

Tracey

It's a nippy Sunday night in January and two adult women in varying states of emotional decay are taking magic truffles in a dark corner of an Amsterdam bar. Standard behaviour from our heroines.

Bar Bukowski is chaos – sticky floors, Eurotrash blaring, strangers pressed shoulder to shoulder. Rhonda stumbles back from the toilets, pale and shaky.

'I just threw up in a urinal,' she whispers, eyes wide.

'Oh god. I'm on my own with this.' I laugh, too loud, feeling the psilocybin starting to pulsate through my veins, vaguely wondering why she was in the men's loos and then deciding not to ask.

Then:

'Rhonda, I think my marriage is over.'

The truffles are acting like a truth serum.

She stares at me and, for a moment, the noise fades. We are just two women, lost in the middle of Europe, trying to outrun the wreckage we've left behind.

It's January 2020, and Rhonda and I have been commissioned to write a handful of features for national newspapers about Interrailing as middle-aged women, for the fiftieth anniversary of the Interrail Pass.

For us that means dicking about Europe on lengthy train

journeys, eating crisps and obscenely huge German sausages, drinking beer and staring out of the window for hours on end, watching our beloved Europe roll by. It's our dream trip.

I'm forty-eight and it's my first time Interrailing. It was a teenage rite of passage back in the Eighties, when getting drunk in twenty-two countries in twenty-eight days was the ultimate challenge. But while my friends pissed it up across Europe by train, I spent the summer selling overpriced unicorn balloons on Brighton Pier. A choice I've long regretted.

The trip couldn't have come at a better time. I've just survived another Christmas – mine and A's nineteenth together. I limped through the day, trying not to drink too much to avoid any rows, all the while wondering if it might well be the last. But right now – as we gear up to scarf the truffles – I'm not going to allow myself to go there.

I'm also ignoring the massive neon-flashing sign from the universe that tomorrow is Blue Monday, the third Monday in January – famously, the busiest day of the year for divorce lawyers.

It was touch and go whether Rhonda would be able to come or not. Her world had imploded two days before our departure from London when her husband discovered she'd had an affair, although that was now very over. And to really put her (and to be fair, his) world in a spin, his dad died the next day. She agonised about wanting to do the right thing, but it was also paid work – her job. And she was the one feeding the family.

When I met her at St Pancras station, she looked emotionally beaten. After giving her a big hug and shaking a bag of beers and cheesy snacks from M&S, I told her that this was exactly what we needed right now – the safe and nurturing space of a lengthy rail journey.

'I had to bring all my notebooks,' Rhonda sighed. 'Half my rucksack is taken up by them. There's nothing in them but work and writing ideas. But he'll go through everything if I leave them. Honestly, I can understand he wants answers, but it feels as if my head is being raped. All my innermost thoughts laid bare.'

Six cities in seven days was the master plan, starting from London St Pancras on the 11.04 Eurostar to Amsterdam. We boarded excitedly, and the train hummed beneath us as we discussed the 'situation' over beers and crisps while speeding through the farmlands of France and Belgium.

This was the first time we'd really travelled together, one on one, without kids. By now we know each other's foibles – I snore like an oil tanker, she's an insomniac.

But we quickly found our own rhythm based on the fact that neither of us needed constant chatter or entertaining – although we always do both.

And with each of us quietly wrestling our own uncertainties, it felt like this trip was exactly what we needed: seven days, six cities, and the gentle, unspoken promise that maybe, by the end of it, we might find a little more clarity in our situations.

We have just seventeen hours in the Dutch capital, which for normal people would be plenty of time to enjoy a scenic canal cruise and a stroll around the Rembrandts of the Rijksmuseum, and maybe a little browse around the antiques shops in the Spiegelkwartier.

But being professionals, we're taking our midlife backpacking assignment seriously and spend it drinking beer, eating baskets of fried *bittenballen* and hooning magic truffles procured from a seedy shop in the red-light district, like we're seventeen again.

And like the kids we are at heart, we're travelling on a budget and staying in hostels – not in shared dorms, obviously. No one needs to see we nannas in our nighties. Luckily, Generator Amsterdam in Oosterpark is not your standard backpackers – it's more like a hip budget hotel and there are other older travellers to blend in with. That said, it does also have its own basement nightclub, and, despite 'the urinal incident', Rhonda and I find ourselves in there with some much younger people, writhing around to techno.

Some might say that taking psychedelic drugs and dancing to techno in a basement when you're verging on hysteria is a mistake, but I say fuck it. In Amsterdam, decisions are made.

At home, I live at a thousand miles an hour managing work, kids and a social life. I find it incredibly difficult to switch off, so, when I have some rare time to think, I go in hard.

On Blue Monday morning, despite the previous night's excesses, we somehow manage to drag ourselves out of bed and make it to the station in time for our early train to Berlin. There's something quietly triumphant about it – two haggard women clutching strong coffees and pastries, boarding a train that promises six uninterrupted hours in which to nurse our hangovers and post-truffle existential dread.

Spending six to eight hours on a train every day offers me plenty of time to marinate in my thoughts, however uncomfortable and murky they may feel. It's one of the reasons why I love my job so much. I need the travelling time to be alone in my own head, to process the life I'm leading.

I lean my forehead against the cool glass of the train window, and, letting the vibrations hum through me as the stark, orderly German landscape slips past in a blur of green fields and distant church spires, I allow my thoughts to wander and percolate.

I think of my kids back home – three teenagers, currently under the care of their doting grandparents – and imagine them sprawled across the sofa, phones in hand, barely noticing my absence. The house will be quieter, but I doubt they're giving me a second thought, and in a strange way that's a comfort.

Then my mind drifts to my husband. The silence that hung between us before I left felt heavier than my rucksack, his unspoken disapproval etched into the lines of his face.

We haven't been right for years but I don't know how to fix what's broken, or even if I want to. The thought of tearing our family apart sits in my chest like a stone. Deep down, I suspect I already know what I need to do, but the idea of being the one to smash it to pieces feels impossible.

Over the years, I've looked intently at my friends' relationships. I'd unpick them and watch how they interacted with each other. The happiest ones always spoke with warmth, respect, maybe some gentle teasing, but they were never derogatory, judgemental or snide. Interesting. My husband once dressed up as me for Halloween. A fact that says it all.

Feeling uncomfortable as to where my thoughts are going, I pull out my AirPods and open up Spotify on my phone and turn on a song by flamboyant Australian film director Baz Luhrmann. I've been playing his 1999 hit '(Everybody's Free) To Wear Sunscreen' to my children every single day for more than a decade. Narrated by Australian voiceover artist Lee Perry to the backing track of 'Everybody's Free (To Feel Good)' by Rozalla, it's by far my best parenting hack. However, I recently found out that its wise life rules were actually penned by Mary Schmich, a columnist for the *Chicago Tribune*, who wrote it as a hypothetical graduation speech in 1997.

'Of course it's bloody written by a woman!' says Rhonda. 'Lines about your hair looking like it's in its eighties when you're forty, if you do too much to it, or beauty mags making you feel ugly could only have been written by someone who has lived it.'

There's one verse in particular that really resonates with me, one that talks about the fact that you may marry or have children, and you may not, and what everybody thinks are choices they are actively making are in fact half chance.

And there it is. We're all playing a game of marriage roulette.

When I got married, I really did mean it. I meant the vows, I meant the for ever. I'm just not sure I do now. And this is why that line resonates with me so much. The success of any relationship *is* half chance. Yes, I know you have to work at it – but it does take two, and there's a half chance it won't work.

I think this should be printed as a disclaimer on all wedding cards.

Rhonda is in an equally contemplative mood, sitting across the table from me, her phone lying face down on the table between us, ignoring the relentless ping of notifications. I know her husband is bombarding her from every direction: WhatsApp, texts, emails, Instagram – each message a mixture of provocation and pleading, all clamouring for her attention.

As she gazes out of the window, her eyes tracking the blur of countryside, I can almost see the flicker of her thoughts cross her face – worry, guilt, resentment – before she catches herself and reaches for one of the half-dozen books she's packed for the journey.

Before we know it, we're pulling into Berlin Hauptbahnhof, our second stop.

As with Amsterdam, Rhonda and I are no strangers to Berlin, which takes the pressure off seeing the sights. Instead we wander slowly along the Berlin Wall Memorial on Bernauer Strasse, the twisted concrete remnants reminding us of the city's fractured past.

Eventually, we find one of East Berlin's old GDR-era *Kneipe* bars – a dim, wood-panelled hole-in-the-wall bar that smells of cigarette smoke and spilled beer, where we order a couple of cheap pints and some salty pretzels.

After three beers, we fleetingly consider trying our luck at Berghain, the notoriously exclusive S&M-inflected techno club that's nigh-on impossible to get into, but we thankfully come to our senses. Instead we chat over pork schnitzel and German goulash with *spaetzle*, and more pilsner, at Schwarzwaldstuben, a sweet little Swabian-Baden bistro on the corner of Tucholskystraße.

Over the next few days we bounce between Copenhagen, Frankfurt, Hamburg and Paris, our train journeys deliciously long yet speeding past too quickly for our liking, both of us now a little addicted to the rhythm of constant motion.

In Hamburg, we fling our bags into the hostel and hop on the U-Bahn to St Pauli and Reeperbahn, 'the most sinful mile in the world', which I fear is about to get even more so once these self-confessedly unhinged thirst hounds hit the bars. Hamburg is city number four and we're getting into the stride of our new hobo life.

Now we've had a few days on the rails processing all our mad thoughts and feelings, I ask Rhonda how she's feeling about the 'situation' and she confesses that she's pretty sure she does not want to fix her marriage.

'I think I'm done with not feeling myself any more.'

As we wander along Reeperbahn in the drizzle, we agree that many of the bars in the city's notorious red-light district look a little too seedy, even for us. While the January rain is casting a damp, almost cinematic veil over the strip, its flickering fizzing neon signs beckon sad punters into bars where you can *smell* the ever-present risk that you might pick up something that will take more than penicillin to get rid of.

But we find refuge, as is so often the way, amid other women. As we head off the main strip to the side streets, Große Freiheit, Hamburger Berg and Hans-Albers-Platz, we find the world's best bar, the Chug Club on Taubenstraße. A kitsch little speakeasy filled with glitterballs and candlelit tables, it's run by the glorious Betty Kupsa, who greets us warmly as we settle down at the bar with a flight of her 'chugs' – five miniature taster cocktails and a small beer palate cleanser. Listening to some smoky jazz, we chat easily with Betty and her all-women staff, only every so often stopping to high-five ourselves over our life choices.

Just weeks after Rhonda and I return from Interrailing, I have another trip, but sadly there are no lengthy train journeys or late-night *Kneipe* bars this time. Instead I am crossing the pond to New York with my husband and our son, who is about to turn eighteen.

Somehow, in the last few years, it has become a rite of passage among his friends to celebrate their eighteenth birthdays in New York. I have no idea who started this tradition – probably a particularly persuasive seventeen-year-old – but I lean into it. We surprise him at his birthday dinner by handing him an envelope with three tickets to New York in it, leaving the next day.

While I am excited to take my son to the coolest city in the world, a knot of anxiety twists in my stomach. The thought of spending several days in close quarters with my husband makes me nervous. I tell myself I just need to hold it together for my son's sake.

At the beginning of our relationship in Hong Kong and afterwards, when we travelled together, I wanted to spend every second of every day with him. We were on the same wavelength. I seemed to make most of the decisions about where to and where to stay, but it didn't matter. I saw it as him being easygoing.

When we'd travelled together as a family, particularly for my work, it was like he made a point of disengaging from me, as if he didn't want to acknowledge what I do for a living. When I went to Oslo with him and the kids for a family feature I was writing, he did greatly enjoy our guided tour of the city – but largely because he wandered off with the guide while I was left wrestling with our three small children, who were determined to kill each other on the ice.

I was furious. Afterwards I said, 'I hope you've made notes for my feature, as I haven't a clue what we've seen.'

Our New York trip starts off with a pint in Wetherspoons, the traditional way to start any trip, but I'm nervous. My husband's excessive drinking has been an issue in our marriage for many years, but it's getting worse. Now I'm no angel, that much is already clear. But I'm not the one hiding bags of empty wine bottles in the pantry or morning glasses of wine in the microwave.

In New York, I try my best. I try to be upbeat for my son's sake, but my husband of nineteen years seems to struggle to even talk to me. And after having had all that time to think on the rails, I realise that this probably really is the end and that by the time the twins turn eighteen in three years we will be no more.

It all comes to a head on Liberty Island, where I can't bear the situation any longer. I can't even remember the precise catalyst for my removing myself from his vicinity, but I know my heart needs space from him.

Back on Manhattan, I say to my son that I want to visit the New York Public Library and am going to walk there. I need to think. My poor boy, stuck between a rock and a hard place, just smiles and says, 'cool', pretending like the rest of us that none of this is actually happening.

It only takes me an hour and a half to march from Battery Park to the library, such is my rage. I only want to see it because it's where Carrie Bradshaw almost got married, and thinking about it I rage at Mr Big as much as at my husband.

But the long walk through Tribeca, Union Square and past the Empire State Building, where we actually liked each other the last time we visited nearly twenty years ago, is exactly what I need.

I spend the time mulling over why it has gone so wrong. What was it? What have I done? What has he done? Why couldn't we make this work?

But the simple truth is I don't like him any more. And I have the feeling he doesn't like me either. Contempt is setting in and it's an unrecoverable situation.

I limp through the last days of the trip, trying to keep my spirits up for my son's sake, although I fear he can see right through me. My husband, on the other hand, doesn't seem to give a shiny shit.

Two weeks after landing we go into lockdown.

★

Often I just lie in bed thinking about the great train journeys of my life and dreaming about more to come. It's been when travelling by train that I've caught glimpses of the true humanity of life.

In January 1995, at Varanasi railway station in northern India, I tried to board three trains and was chucked off each time, so it started to look like I lived there now. The first time was because a gentleman sadly took his life by jumping in front of the train as it pulled in. The second one decided to change routes and head north instead. The third one… Well, I was just trying my luck and decided to chance it, but got chucked off for having the wrong ticket.

I was trying to get to Pushkar in Rajasthan to meet my friend Zara, as we'd arranged in drunken excitement on Anjuna Beach in Goa two weeks before. We'd even written it in our diaries. But I'd been there for six hours and singularly failed to make it out of the station. Flumping down on my backpack, I burst into big hot tears. As I was the only Western woman in the station, it was a scene that attracted quite the crowd.

I looked up and maybe twenty or so men had gathered around me, not quite sure what to do with this dribbling Amazon. But such is the kindness of human spirit, the vibe was of concern rather than threat. Heads tilted to one side trying to make sense of this strange tall girl with hair like candyfloss, heaving and sobbing in front of them.

A couple of the older men looked at each other, as if to encourage each other to approach me. They stepped forward and one handed me a small paper cup of chai, the other a packet of sweet biscuits. These acts of kindness set me off again and a stream of snot flew down my tie-dye top.

Another chap had found someone who could speak a little English, and between sobs I explained I was trying to get to Pushkar to meet my friend but kept getting on the wrong train. Eventually, my gang of knights in shining armour gathered me up and got me on the right train. Only then did I realise that

I'd accidentally booked a third-class ticket rather than a second-class sleeper ticket for the twenty-hour journey, and I burst into floods of tears again.

In a similar vein, it was a kind guard who now took pity on me and moved me from my seat next to a boy holding a chicken to his guard's seat in the corridor, where I was able to sit and watch the world roll by: weary buffalos and cows roaming aimlessly, women in colourful saris toiling in the fields, children running barefoot alongside the train, men lying prone smoking and watching. Life in motion.

India was a journey and a half, both emotionally and physically, but the one thing I took from that experience is that kindness and humility is everywhere.

If there's one thing I love more than just any old long and scenic train journey, it's one during which I can fall asleep in a moving bed. As much as I love flying, if I could get everywhere by train, I would. Being gently lulled to sleep by the clickety-clack of a trundling train feels like being back in the womb.

Interrailing was just the start of many train journeys with Rhonda – and many to come, I hope. One of my favourites has been a night on the Caledonian Sleeper from Fort William to London, after conquering Munros in Glen Coe, where the landscape is both breathtaking and brutal.

Walking holidays in Scotland attract a certain breed: hardy, competitive and rather generous in age. I'm competitive but not exactly hardy, which is how I found myself crawling along a narrow ledge followed by a septuagenarian plastic surgeon from Philadelphia, who was a little bit too handsy with his assistance.

After three days of hiking – and avoiding Bruce the surgeon – we reached Fort William running on fumes. We'd booked a cabin on the Caledonian Sleeper down to London, and Rhonda was going to jump out at Crewe at 5 am.

Laughing in the face of the early-morning wake-up call to come, naturally we headed straight for the dining car, where we ate haggis and neeps washed down with wine and whisky as the ridiculous scenery of the Highlands bumbled by. Best of all was making friends with two American women with whom we almost caused a riot when I let slip, in a louder voice than I'd anticipated, that my roasted carrot was the size of a dildo, causing other passengers to complain and earning me a warning from the conductor.

After our brief sojourn in Berlin on our Interrailing trip, Rhonda refused to let go of the idea that we should try to get into Berghain. Of course, which sane travel editor could resist a story of two fifty-plus-year-old women trying to get into one of the world's most exclusive and hardcore nightclubs – one with a reputation for attracting some of the most deviant of clubbers, from naked ravers and rubber-clad gimps to men who lie under the urinals? Naturally, she secured a commission from a national newspaper.

Great, now the world could witness and revel in our humiliation.

That's how we found ourselves on a cheap coach to Brussels to catch the inaugural Good Night Train, a then-new overnight sleeper train that was leaving Brussels Zuid (Bruxelles Midi) station at 19.22 one June evening.

At the launch, we enjoyed our fair share of celebratory wines in the Pullman Hotel before hopping aboard the night train. I have to admit, I was expecting a shiny new route to have a shiny new train, but no. Being a Dutch-founded company, the Sleeper is all about reuse and recycling and as such employs rolling stock from a 1955 German train company.

Retro and clunky – I could see them giving local train enthusiasts the horn – the coaches are more than sixty years old. Their age is most apparent in the shared bathrooms, which could have come out of the gulags.

However, there was something very charming about the lack of services. There was no air conditioning (although the windows do open a notch), and, where I was expecting a glamorous dining car to schmooze around in, drinking negronis and chatting up ageing Poirot lookalikes, instead Abigail, our carriage host, brought beers, Pringles and cup-a-noodles to our cabin.

Luckily I'd procured (read: stolen) a bottle of wine from the launch event, and we had a little party in our private sleeper cabin. We slept pretty well and before we knew it we were waking up as we pulled into one of the outlying stations of Berlin.

With only thirty-six hours in Europe's clubbing capital, we had to seriously focus on getting into Berghain. Having heard reports that it was hard enough to get into when you were young and hip, we feared it was nigh-on impossible when you were the wrong side of fifty with a penchant for disco.

This was a fact we confirmed repeatedly, into the early glare of dawn. We started our night with a pair of kebabs eaten out on the street and then found ourselves at Monster Ronson's Ichiban Karaoke bar on Warschauer Strasse, rocking out to Fleetwood Mac with a live band to accompany our warblings. And to be honest, the night should have ended there.

We failed – a miserable three times – to get into Berghain. The first time we were looked up and down by a Daryl Oates lookalike in stone-bleached jeans and Princess Diana flick, hatred of us oozing from his every pore. It was 6 am when we finally admitted defeat.

After this simply filthy, hedonistic and frankly probably illegal thirty-six hours in naughty Berlin (things happened that night that are far too beyond the pale to report here; if I die before Rhonda, she will recount them at my funeral), my hangover was of desperate proportions and I was more than ready to snuggle down in the warm embrace of a private bunk on the Good Night Train back to Brussels.

Because we were travelling through the Schengen area, there were no passport checks along the way, thank god – the last thing I needed was to be woken by an angry border guard demanding to know why I don't actually look like my passport photo. Listen, mate, it was taken nearly ten years ago and I'm a middle-aged woman speeding through the menopause, so of course in the flesh I look like Nicolas Cage.

But back to that epic Interrailing trip, on the final day of which our Hamburg hangovers were soothed by the luxury of an eight-hour train journey to Paris, where our final night was spent in the Canal Saint-Martin district.

As we checked into our room on the eighth floor of Generator Paris, Rhonda burst out laughing as she opened the door to our private terrace only to be met by the ultimate symbol of romance – the Eiffel Tower glittering like a disco ball in the distance.

The irony of two unhappily married women bagging this ridiculously romantic view in the City of Love was not lost on us. But we decided to see it as confirmation of the fact that friendships are just as important as romantic love, or in fact more so.

CHAPTER 8

AFTER THE AFFAIR – RATTLESNAKES AND LIFEBUOYS

Rhonda

The US Midwest: the Notch Trail through a Badlands canyon, with a sign: **BEWARE, Rattlesnakes!** K takes a photo of me beside it, gurning, because I can never take myself seriously in photos.

Looking at it later, much later, I think of Joan Didion's *Play It As It Lays*, one of my favourite books. A book in which the venomous snakes are metaphors for male predators. And I think of the Lloyd Cole and the Commotions song *Rattlesnakes*, inspired by Didion, and its final line about a girl for whom love was the greatest disappointment in life.

Across the rail tracks of Europe, Tracey and I drank beer, ate crisps, read books and catnapped. We tried not to talk about our husbands or our imploding marriages. About the fact that my husband had just found out about my affair.

Instead, I read Nora Ephron's *Heartburn*, about a marital breakdown. Instead, I read Emma Forrest's *Your Voice in My Head*, about mental illness, obsession and a romantic breakdown. Instead, we chewed magic truffles in Amsterdam and got drunk in the bars of Copenhagen, Berlin, Hamburg and Paris.

Little did we know it was to be our last trip together for a very long time, and more or less the last trip for either of us for the best part of two years.

I'm not sure whether M and I would have started seeing each other again if history – Covid – hadn't happened. We didn't take advantage of any gaps between lockdowns to try to get together, but we were very much in contact.

The year 2020 had been catastrophic for me even before the coronavirus started to wreak its havoc. My husband found out about M at the end of January. Though the affair was already over, it was all still there in all its gory, porny tawdriness in my WhatsApp messages after he got hold of my phone. There was nothing I could say. I'd been a complete arsehole.

He was devastated but said, immediately, that it was 'all his fault'. He would make it better, he said.

I said I didn't want him to. The next day, his father died.

I ran away. Interrailing for a week with Tracey was planned, commissioned by major newspapers, and I decided I wasn't going to fuck up a painstakingly organised work trip because of an old guy who had, frankly, had zero interest in me.

Waiting for Tracey in London, I met M and, after I'd got some sex out of him, broke the news. He confessed he was obsessed with me but said that, if he left his wife, I'd quickly realise what a 'complete twat' he was and leave him, and he wouldn't be able to cope with that. He needed safety, he said, because of his childhood – his abusive father.

Clearly, I was not safety.

When I got home from Europe, I was given the chance to make everything right. But I was clear about the fact that I was beyond that and wanted out. I didn't believe things would change. I was sick of everything: of spending and spending, of not having space for my things in the house I had always paid for, of the lack of privacy, of the dust and chaos. I was out of love and tolerance. I would always be my kids' mother, but I was done mothering another adult.

I was also disgusted that, since the affair had been discovered, my every conversation, including those with girlfriends, had been read: my phone repeatedly hacked into, every notebook combed, all my innermost thoughts and feelings surveyed.

One of these conversations was with K, the Austrian travel writer I'd met in the Midwest.

K and I had kept in touch, fairly loosely, and he'd invited me to join him in various locations – on a boat in the Seychelles, in the Philippines, in Ireland. I'd never been able to make it due to commitments, but I was open to the idea of spending time with him.

K always made it clear to me that we'd of necessity be sharing a room. Would that be a problem? I brushed away the question. I felt it was understood that if there was nothing between us, no spark, we were adult enough to share quarters in a brotherly–sisterly way.

He kept asking, and it kept not happening, and we thought we had all the time in the world.

In February I went on a press trip to Tenerife, to the carnival, and danced in the streets with strangers dressed as pirates, nuns, Freddie Mercury, aliens. We wore different costumes every evening, coloured wigs. It was like being somebody else for the space of a night. I felt free of the burden of myself.

A German journalist, a cultural broadcaster, pursued me. In his sixties, married for thirty and more years ('too long'), he was another M. I was fond of him but resisted his advances. Afterwards, it came to me that his behaviour really had been very physical and predatory but that I hadn't ever pulled him up on it. I realised with a sense of shame that I wasn't very good at rebuffing men. Was my need to be adored that strong, my ego that weak?

We hiked trails, saw dolphins. A sandstorm from the Sahara swathed the island in an orange cloud so dense that one night the carnival was closed down by the police. There was an Armageddon feel to it all. My phone started pinging from home. One person in a hotel in southern Tenerife had been diagnosed with this new virus from China that everyone had been talking about. Was I anywhere near that? I wasn't, I reassured them. It seemed so laughable.

Within a month the UK and many other places were in their first lockdown.

My marriage had broken down and I didn't want to fix it. But how to get out of it? My work had evaporated, I was forced onto state grants, and the government had ordered us all to stay in our homes. All any of us could do was hold it together.

As part of my ongoing yoga practice, I discovered a subset of kundalini yoga informed by Kali, the destroyer-creator goddess and consort of Shiva. It was a yoga of anger but also of liberation – liberation from illusions, fears and self-destructive tendencies. A yoga of acceptance of the self. A yoga of self love.

Poses and rituals included *kaliasana*, the 'goddess squat', and lion's breath, a type of *pranayama* breathing to expel anger, fear and toxicity.

As I bent my body and my mind into new shapes, I spent a lot of time thinking about India, where I'd nearly drowned, aged twenty-four, at a beach in Kerala. More than half a lifetime later, physically and also mentally stuck, I decided I wanted, *needed*, to go back there – not so much to the place, which must have really changed, but to such a significant moment in my life. It felt as if communing with my younger self about how my life had come to this current impasse might somehow help me work out where I was going from here.

Rereading the diary I had kept during my six-month trip overland to and around India, I marvelled at how much had been forgotten, at the girl I'd left behind – for better and for worse. Who was she, and who was I now?

I refreshed my knowledge of Indian goddesses, too. Kali aside, I had a fondness for the Hindu Mother Earth goddess Bhūmi. A *matriot* (*not* a matriarch), a lover and protector of the Earth, she was usually depicted four-handed, holding a pomegranate, a water vessel, healing herbs and a bowl. Or sometimes she had two hands, one holding a *kumuda* or *utpala* (blue or night lotus, popular in Ayurvedic medicine), the other shaped in the *abhaya mudra* gesture of fearlessness (right hand upright, palm facing outwards).

Doing my Kali yoga, thinking about mother goddesses and the power of rage, I remembered the anger of my mother, the anger of my grandmothers. The spoken and the unspoken anger. Anger expressed in defiance of those who didn't want to hear it; anger repressed that should have been spoken aloud. Which was best? Keep it in or shout about injustice and pain?

Yoga, it turned out, was a way of dealing with anger not by negating it but by channelling it. Because the power of mother goddesses and their gentleness are really the same thing.

Hinduism turned out to have many mother goddesses. As well as Bhūmi, there was Shakti, who embodied all the energy in the universe. Daughter of Himavan, king of the Himalayas, Shakti has several embodiments, including Sati, first consort of Lord Shiva, who self-immolated at her father's funeral and in doing so gave her name to the practice of sati or suttee among widows. They also included Shiva's wife Parvati. These different incarnations are explained by the fact that the goddesses are all shapeshifters without any fixed attributes.

Like human women, the goddesses are always changing, always in flux. Like us, they are defined by their relationships with others and between their different selves, by their oscillation between compassion and fury, by their goodness and their capacity for harm. They are *complicated*.

Shakti is tender, loving power, but one which, in times of crisis, is unleashed in its true strength. This tendency is seen at its most fearful in the Shakti who is embodied by Kali, a goddess best known for wearing a garland of human skulls. But despite being fearsome, her power is productive and protective, for Kali destroys evil, and also brings healing and wholeness by bestowing moksha – liberation from the human ego and from ignorance.

★

Aside from yoga and looking at old photos and reading about Indian goddesses, I finished a novel I'd started eight years before but had had little time or mental energy for. I oversaw my youngest's schooling while worrying about the older ones too. One had left school without knowing he'd never go back and had not been able to sit his GCSEs or go to his prom; the other had dropped out of college and resits with the idea of travelling and 'finding himself' but had been halted by Covid.

I worried about them, I worried about myself, I worried about my husband, who was slowly going off the rails trying to persuade me that he was worthy of 'another chance'. I couldn't give it to him. I knew the marriage was over; it had to have been for me to even entertain the idea of 'straying' (like a dog).

M, faced with the threat of his wife being contacted by my husband, begged me to 'save' him. And there they were again – those lines from *Wonderwall* in my head, on repeat, along with a vision of the karaoke night in Penang, when we didn't know what terrible fire we were igniting.

And now I was incandescent. That he could view continuing the way he was living as being 'saved' floored me. I'd heard of codependency but I just couldn't understand his life choices, knowing the things I did.

> I know you find this hard to accept – perhaps because you're in a different league – but knowing about all this would break her mentally and physically – and in turn it would more than likely break me beyond full repair.

The thing about being the strong one, or one of the strong ones, is that everyone thinks you can look after yourself. You think that yourself. Your whole identity is built on it. But every so often, every once in a while, it would be nice to know there'd be someone to catch you if you did fall.

It would be nice to have the option of letting yourself fall.

Coronavirus ground on, compressing us all. I saw friends when I could, had mighty drinking blowouts with them every so often. And the drug of M – when we were not in contact – was replaced by the drug of the Austrian travel writer K. Since lockdown, our intermittent chat had been replaced by daily contact.

K's messages greeted me in the morning and sent me to bed at night. In between, we talked about everything. Coronavirus, of course, but politics, the environment, his work, my work. He started leaving long voice notes and wanted the same from me. He sent songs via Spotify, some of them romantic. We sent each other our travel and other writing, commented on and edited each other's work. We sent each other small gifts: mugs, socks, books. He painted a picture for me, of a café in Paris where he wanted to 'laugh and love' with me. 'Café Rhonda', I spotted in tiny writing, on 'Rue d'Amour'. (Retrospective barf!)

My girlfriends more or less unanimously posited the theory that I didn't fancy K but was using him as a distraction from the M situation – that he was another lifebuoy to cling to. I denied that, to them but most strenuously to myself. I spent ages looking at pictures of him, telling myself that yes I did fancy him. Er – hello?!

The Badlands terrain is deformed, difficult. In long-gone days, it stopped the pioneers in their tracks as they tried to move westwards. At sheer drops, small signs announce, 'Go no further', but there are no safety railings, nothing to stop one from falling were one to lose one's footing.

The first time I set eyes on K, we were back in the lobby of our hotel after visiting a Sioux potter. He was looking at me intently, so I smiled and introduced myself. He seemed a bit spiky. I turned away. It didn't matter. There were about twelve journalists in total; plenty of other people to talk to over the coming week.

It was only later, thinking of this moment when I turned away, that I understood the discomfort I'd been in – the discomfort of someone who feels they've been seen.

M was forever telling me he 'saw' me. I didn't buy it and eventually came to see it as part of his manipulation, his gaslighting even. We were so different. How *could* he understand me? I felt we were creatures from different planets, thrown together by chance, held together by some crazed chemistry.

M and I would never know each other, and perhaps that was the drug that kept us coming back for more. I already knew that, as a writer, I couldn't seem to be able to leave things alone – people or situations – until I understood them.

I was so tired, the entire Midwest trip felt a bit hazy, both as it happened and afterwards. I knew what was going on, though. I saw K's annoyance when we had to swap cars and were separated. I felt his eyes on me from far along the dinner table, and when I turned my head and met his gaze he didn't look away. I saw him hang back in the bar when he spotted me coming, before coming to sit down to talk to me even though he didn't have a drink.

His cool blue gaze was a constant over the next few days, but especially when, sitting beside me, he asked the kind of questions a man doesn't normally ask a woman he barely knows. A married woman.

'Are you happy?'

Each time he did, I forced myself to hold his gaze and replied that I would tell him when I'd had more to drink.

I was panicking. I couldn't countenance this attention and feeling of being seen – not with all the other things that were going on in my life.

Yet I didn't intend to hold back when I did tell him. And I didn't expect him to like what he heard. Maybe I needed him to stop liking me. Maybe I felt I had to make him hate me. When I told him about the affair, then he would *really* see me and leave me be. I was a car crash, and no one wants a car crash.

Wayward Women

★

K found his mother's body on the floor when he was seventeen; he was an only child and very close to her. During Covid, he saw his ex-girlfriend occasionally but otherwise had very little social contact. He was a loner and he was okay like that, mostly.

He also travelled more than me, because restrictions were lesser where he was. When the situation looked as if it may improve, we tried to make plans to get together. When I mentioned a possible trip to Montenegro, he said he'd drive the several thousand miles to meet me there, which seemed excessive. But it fell through anyway. Everything fell through. Just as before Covid, we held our nerve. Things *must* get better soon.

I felt somewhat responsible for him, and perhaps he did for me. Occasionally we Zoomed. Sometimes he told me he loved me. We talked about future plans. An overland trip to India. A trip around the Mediterranean coast to write a book. Meeting in the Sahara for his fiftieth birthday, which he aimed to spend at the same spot that his late father – an diplomat who'd then been based in North Africa – had.

But I started to see that he was also restless and fickle. He said he was going to write a memoir of one of his many walks on the Camino de Santiago, and laboured long over 3,000 words that I helped him out with and thought had real potential, before he dropped it. He talked about writing a novel and sent pictures of his desk loaded with writing guides and plot diagrams, then that went away too. He talked about wanting to be a conflict photographer again (previous girlfriends had discouraged him from carrying on) but made no move towards it. He talked about devoting a month to learning Spanish and then didn't. Wherever he went, he sent me pictures of the future writers' retreat he wanted the two of us to run.

Which was fine. We are all like that. I'm like that too. We can all dream, and Covid was a difficult time to make any changes, or at least big life changes. But it started to make me uneasy.

★

Big life changes…

The summer morning when I woke to blood in my PJs and had to face a two-hour coach journey down to London and the curse of a blazing hot day schlepping between courts at Wimbledon with what felt like a soft brick between my legs is still vivid in my mind. The day I 'became a woman'.

Does the menopause, then, mean the end of being a woman? Hardly. The sex, with M, was like nothing I'd experienced before. I still don't know why.

Chemistry, he said. Mind-blowing chemistry. But I do wonder about the HRT, about the oestrogen that I massaged into my inner thighs each morning and that worked in parallel with progesterone in my contraceptive coil to stop me feeling low-key rubbish. I'd never had the night sweats. But I'd had restless legs that prevented me from sleeping. I'd had vaginal dryness. I'd had the mood swings and the moments when I felt like murdering someone, especially if I drank caffeine on an empty stomach, setting my brain on fire. I'd had the memory lapses and the brain fog.

I wondered whether the HRT was making me horny. And about whether it was actually just dragging out the menopause by stopping me from diving deep into it. Scientific advice varies. Women's experiences and their narration of them vary. I could only do what made daily life bearable, without thinking of where all this would end.

It was early new year and the UK was still in lockdown when K told me he was going to do another Camino. I felt sick. He'd done seventeen before, in twenty years. Some with one of his previous girlfriends, some alone. On one, he met a girl on horseback and moved countries to be with her, but it didn't last very long.

I was uncomfortable, but I didn't try to dissuade him. We were not boyfriend and girlfriend, but what right would I have even if we were?

And so the months peeled away across the hamster-wheel monotony of lockdown, fruitless months were torn from wall calendars, and June arrived. He left.

I went down to Brighton to see Tracey, who was by now living in the same hell as me – estranged from her husband but still in the same house because her finances had been crushed by Covid.

The second day I was there, I saw M for the first time in a year and a half, and the last time ever. It had been impossible not to ask him, given that he lived not so far away. He said yes without hesitation, despite everything he'd been through with my husband threatening to contact his wife – his wife who continued to pretend she knew nothing.

The plan was to go for lunch, but my resolve fell apart immediately. But wasn't that the real plan, if I'm honest?

I'd stayed out drinking Tuaca shots with Tracey until 2 am, and at 4 am I was awake with palpitations and nothing to take to quell them, while Tracey snored on next to me in that charming way she has. At 7 am I texted M in a panic to bring me some beta blockers or anything to stop my anxiety. I knew from the long list of her ailments and medication he had once sent me (to demonstrate her fragile state) that his wife had plenty of those. I asked him to bring some to my hotel.

A few hours later and he almost fell into my room, taking my face between his hands, kissing me all over it.

'I love you, I love you, I love you.'

I felt like stone. I'd wanted this for so long. It was almost all I'd thought about for two and a half years and particularly during the pandemic. Hours and hours spent actively longing for this moment, to have this man back in my arms, to have that sex again.

We slept together, but I found it dismal – technically good, astounding even, but on some level a case of 'job done', 'over and out'. M was old, enmeshed in his warm and cosy and easy life. He smelt different – like an elderly man. He felt different. The eroticism had evaporated. I felt sad for him.

We went out for lunch, holding hands as we walked. We ate a seafood lunch on the beachfront, then, because it was too misty to go up the i360, headed to a coffee shop. At a loss as to what to say, I started talking to him about a memoir he had decided to write a few months before. It was about his fifty years in publishing and about how much it had changed for the better since 'the bad old days'. He'd sent me a few initial pages to see what I thought, but I'd found it hard to be honest about it.

The pages he sent were about a toxic masculine culture and rampant sexism at the newspaper where he had his first advertising sales job, but he sounded extremely judgemental about some of the behaviour, especially infidelity, by both men and women. Given how he and his wife had subsequently led their own lives, I told him, he was on very dodgy territory.

The other problem I had was that I didn't believe things had changed so much, and I told him I thought this was a very clear example of his over-optimistic view of life and his tendency to look for the best in people and situations.

I reminded him that, when he sent it to me, a young woman called Sarah Everard had just been murdered in London. The police exhorted women not to walk around alone, as if it was their fault that men (some men) couldn't control themselves. And to boot, Sarah had been killed by an off-duty policeman, and furthermore one whose previous behaviour should have raised alarm bells. Appalled, women tried to hold a vigil on Clapham Common and were manhandled by further police officers on the grounds they were breaking pandemic restrictions.

I wasn't sure, I said, that things were any better for women. I told him that he didn't know how we have to live, from a very young age. That he couldn't know what it's like not to be able to walk down the street without men commenting on your body, staring at your body, making lewd comments.

Four times in my life, I told him, I had been frightened for my life due to men – and in public and in daylight. Once I ran for my life and the other three times I had to call on others to help me. That was in my twenties and thirties, but things like that don't go away. Out walking my dog, I'm uneasy when a man appears alone, walking without a dog. It's a bodily reaction to past trauma. It's self-preservation.

I'd had a conversation – and one of my few arguments – with K about exactly this. He thought women demonise men. I couldn't make him see that our experience makes us *instinctively* afraid of men, even when our brains know that, in 99.9 per cent of cases or more, that man walking towards us, or behind us, that man looking at us on the tram, means us no harm. You can't control your physical response, when you've had to live the way we do.

When M left, I knew I'd never see him again and I couldn't even really feel sad about it. I just wanted to get to Tracey and other friends and drink and laugh and feel normal.

The next morning, while I was still lying in recovery mode in bed, M texted me: It feels so wrong that you're there and I'm here. He meant this hotel room, where the day before we had made love for the very last time. He talked about 'next time', about spending the night together. I shook my head. I'd already told him we were not restarting our affair.

Walking along the beach to meet Tracey for a morning sea swim, I recorded a long voicemail telling M about a conversation I'd had after he'd left, with a friend aged sixty or so who'd left his wife a couple of years before. He'd said that, when the physical stuff is gone and you find yourself looking at other people, you should do the honest thing and get out.

'I'm so admiring of that,' I said. 'And I've realised I can't have a man with no balls in my life. You forgive everyone – your wife, your dad, shit politicians, arseholes you've worked with. And try to make of it all a virtue.

'I won't be wasting another second thinking about you,' I concluded. But of course I knew it was not true. I would think about him, and often.

'I won't be wasting another second on this either,' he replied. 'Bye for now.'

Bye for *now*!

As K continued the France leg of his latest Camino, I read to him, thinking he'd be bored or lonely walking on his own so much, or in the evenings in the auberges where he stayed.

I voice-messaged him excerpts from *Together: 10 Choices for a Better Now* by Ece Temelkuran, my latest read. And from *The Tao of Pooh*. We were conscious that, by talking to each other, we were in some kind of echo chamber. We rarely disagreed on anything. We would both have liked to change the world for the better but didn't know where to start.

In Pamplona, he reminded me I'd not read to him in a couple of days and asked for more 'bedtime stories'. He sent me pictures of the hotel that Hemingway stayed in, since I'd mentioned I'd read *The Sun Also Rises*, and I told him if I were there I'd say, *To hell with the expense* and check us in. Before long he video-messaged me from his room. He was in the hotel. I was happy to have tipped him in that direction. I was happy for him, because he was so thrilled.

That day he messaged me fifteen or so times in some guise or other: texts, voice messages, pictures. I didn't mind. I was used to living vicariously through him by now – although of course I wished I were there too, with or without him.

I always went out of my way to reply, even when it was inconvenient. In Brighton, when he chased me for news, I replied even though I was out for lunch with M. Of course, I didn't mention I'd hooked up with M. It made no difference to K and me, especially given how I felt about M that day – that for me it was finally the end.

Within a week, things nosedived between us. K fell in with a group of other walkers and I began to get a funny feeling that my fear about him finding another Camino girlfriend was going to come true. That feeling was heightened over the next few days as he barely responded to messages, including direct questions. By the end of day three I was getting annoyed, and told him I wouldn't be in contact if he wasn't going to be – that it wasn't a one-way street.

The next morning, he left me a message saying that he'd been in a 'bubble' with his group and that, when it disbanded suddenly, he was left alone with a Danish girl and a French woman. He and the French woman were 'hugging a lot', he told me, but there was nothing to worry about. It didn't change the way he felt about me. It was just how she was with people. And it was so good to be touched after so long alone during the pandemic…

I understand, I told him. What else could I say? But I already know where this was headed and how powerless I was. I could only sit in horror and wait for his updates – and suck it up when he wasn't in contact. Our whole dynamic had changed.

Two days later, the nail in the coffin. I would always be his best friend, 'the beloved', he told me. I was unique. My take on the world and life itself was deep and unique. I had a Buddhist soul. Nothing could affect what may happen between us in the future…

But the French girl had cried on his shoulder about some traumatic event in her past, and she kept hugging him and kissing him on the cheek, and he thought they were going to sleep together. She had a boyfriend of eight years in France; that was partly why she was walking the Camino alone – because she had doubts about her relationship. He, K, thought he was 'a bit in love'. But he recognised it was partly the situation he was in love with, the setting… Again, it didn't mean anything when it came to him and me.

Once more, anything I could say was futile, but I was not going to let myself be sidelined for the last three weeks of his trip, hanging on for scraps of news while he romanced this lost girl.

And of course it threw his pursuit of me in the Midwest into a new light: he had a thing for rescuing sad women in unhappy relationships. He'd already told me he'd once had a fling with a married journalist he met on another press trip, one who couldn't leave her husband because of money.

The question he kept asking that time in the States. *Are you happy in your marriage?* His 'in'. His line. His angle.

The sex thing I could handle. He'd been so long without; without any physical affection. And I loved him in some way, and wanted him to be happy. But I hated how he'd always been so quick to react when I wasn't in contact with him for a few hours, yet felt it was fine for him to go off into a 'bubble' as soon as he met someone. It felt cruel and one-sided and controlling.

So I shouted at him, by text, and told him he'd taken advantage of my unhappiness at home to encourage a close friendship that he thought he could then turn off when it suited him. He accused me of being drunk.

I left him a very long voicemail, but this time a calm and measured one, telling him how I felt about him (the good and the bad things), about relationships, about life in general. He refused to listen to it, said I was destroying the friendship and that he would be in contact when he got home.

Friendship didn't work like that, I said. If he elected not to listen to a message filled with my heart and soul, then he had chosen.

I was crushed, yet two days later I started feeling, at the same time, a sensation of lightness and freedom and even joy. I wasn't physically attracted to him, I could finally admit to myself. There was zero chemistry between us. But I'd tried to persuade myself there would or could be, because we were 'soulmates'.

I also felt full clarity about my marriage. This was not about M or K. I still wanted to leave my husband, even now that I felt totally alone. And in some ways that was exciting. The future was wide open to me. I would meet exciting men, have great sex, travel. But most of all, I would be me.

For I had to acknowledge it to myself: I had never been me with my husband, and I wasn't me with either M or K. By being largely reduced to mother and breadwinner, I'd lost myself for at least sixteen years. And when I'd tried to reclaim myself, I looked in the wrong places. M: a Tory, a golfer. The madness of it. And me, the naughty girl playing up to his sexual fantasies, using sex as a weapon, thinking I could make him rise up at last against all the wrongs that had been done to him.

The futility and the imbecility of it.

And K: yes, a soulmate, but a soulmate for whom I had to self-censor, sometimes, quite often even, because he was also very different to me in spite of everything that brought us together. He'd never taken drugs, he didn't like to party. He was a one-to-one person, serious-minded, thoughtful, deep. All good things that sometimes applied to me too, but not all the time. That was only a part of me. There were parts of me I covered up for him.

And he *hated* it whenever I disagreed with him, and would go dark on me for a few days, sulking. And those days he went dark on me frightened me. I was always scared I was going to lose what I'd told myself was the most important friendship of my life, so I started not saying things that I knew he wouldn't agree with, started avoiding certain topics.

And then I lost the friendship anyway.

Two weeks later I went glamping with two of my boys, along with a girlfriend, E, and her own teen boys. I felt fully broken, but I was determined not to let it spoil the trip. We swam in the river with giant dragonflies spinning around us, marvelled at double rainbows, toasted marshmallows on a campfire, went to sleep stinking of smoke in yurts with insects crawling over us. As the boys did their thing, I sank into the friendship of another woman, one who had had marital troubles of her own and nearly walked into an affair.

One evening I did yoga in a yurt and the teacher read aloud a poem that made me cry: 'Shinto' by Jorge Luis Borges, about being laid low by sorrow but saved, at least in moments, by simple things: memories of fruits we have tasted, water we have drunk, people's faces…

When I came back outside, the Shinto deities that also feature in the poem – nature gods that live amid and in trees and rivers – made their presence felt as a huge branch ripped itself away from a trunk and smashed to the ground, narrowly missing me, saving me for something. I couldn't know what.

I was so very, very sad, but I was still alive to the beauty and potential of the world, and that was what would save me from all the ugly feelings swirling around inside.

As with M, there had been many red flags about K, over the months and years, and I had chosen to ignore them because I wanted one of these men to be the answer to my problems. Now I could see there was something very odd about K doing the same thing over and over – his repeated pilgrimages to find like-minded people. It felt like he fed off the intensity of people carrying sadness and trauma – perhaps that was understandable, given his own.

A month after our last contact, he messaged me to say he and the French girl ended up walking together all the way to Finisterra, 'really fell in love' and were going to try to 'work it out'. He felt 'understood', 'fulfilled'. He felt like the person he wanted to be. He was hurt that I wasn't happy he'd found this happiness. But he was calling to 'offer me the chance to continue our friendship'. He was sorry for how he blanked me, said he should have just called me.

I left him a long voicemail about what I'd been doing with the boys and about work and projects I was cooking up. He replied with some thoughts and advice. I immediately saw the pattern, the condescension. I'd used to think he was trying to better me; lately I'd known it as an undermining. He sent a picture of where he was in Turkey, said it reminded him a bit of the Badlands and that it made him really happy we were 'talking to each other like before'.

But for me it was different. It was broken.

★

That week I went abroad for the first time in 2021, to southern France, to see a novelist friend, F, who lives alone out there after her latest, second divorce. I needed to get away but the Covid-testing process was so complex and expensive and the uncertainty so great that I couldn't face taking the boys abroad with me. And I was so sad and desperate.

Meanwhile, K was on the Languedocienne motorway, heading west across the same area of southern France to see the French girl, messaging me. I pictured him on the Camino, looking at her the way he'd looked at me in the Midwest, asking her the same question he'd kept asking me: *Are you happy in your relationship?* Finding the chink, the way in.

Those lines from *Wonderwall* again. People looking for people to save, and people to save them…

I pictured him shining a spotlight on a confused and unhappy woman, making her feel special, telling her it was fated, that she was a gift from Brahma, that they'd found each other for a reason, against all the odds. All the things he'd said to me.

In my mind's eye, I saw him walking the corridors of the hotel in the Midwest after dinner on our penultimate night, when he'd come looking for me, and suddenly I saw this incident in its true light: it wasn't flattering, not proof of some overwhelming, irrefutable desire on his part. It was the action of a hunter.

And I saw again, too, the German writer, the married one in Tenerife, grabbing my backside in the street during the carnival, trying to follow me into the lift and up to my hotel room, forcing eye contact over wine, and at the end hugging me goodbye just a little too proprietorially, as if something *had* happened between us.

I thought of the rich Swiss divorcé who sat next to me on a plane home from Morocco during the pandemic and followed me around the arrivals hall trying to persuade me to share his taxi back to London, hanging around even after I'd told him I was travelling with a friend, asking me to come down from Manchester to meet him even after I'd reminded him that both of us were supposed to be self-isolating for two weeks.

I saw my friend's husband W, trying to hold hands with me or kiss me behind his wife's back at parties or on the street outside the pub. And sometimes succeeding because I was very drunk, and I was very weak and miserable, and because sometimes you just have a very big, very pathetic need to feel desired.

I thought about men who prey on women when they are unhappy and therefore weak – including the man who was texting S when we were on the dance floor in Eden, before she left Ibiza and left her husband.

I thought about my husband telling me that his therapist had upbraided him for his lack of respect for me, and given him a lecture on feminism.

And I thought about M once telling me that he knew my vagina better than I did myself – the presumption of that. Superficially he did maybe, but my vagina, and all its nerve endings, and how it feels, are something only I can know. Under his veneer of a kind of perverse paternity, M was all control and sometimes even mansplaining. *This is how your vagina is.*

I looked at the picture that K took of me in the Badlands, the day after we first met. The one where I'm standing next to a sign, fake-screaming.

BEWARE, Rattlesnakes!

I thought again of Didion. She wrote that she had been taught two lessons, one about life being a game of chance and the other that if you turned over a rock there was likely to be a rattlesnake there.

I thought that I'd been looking under rocks, mixing with the wrong kind of man. I'd never wanted someone to look after me, exactly – not financially. But I wanted somebody who had my back. And no man ever had, so what was the point of them?

★

F picks me up from the tiny middle-of-nowhere airport and drives me straight to a sun-drenched Mediterranean beach, where she tells me about the post-divorce relationship she threw herself into, and about how it turned out not to be right for her, but that she's glad they had been there for each other at that time. We also laugh as she tells me how she trained him to be good at sex for other women's sake.

'Before then he'd been like a bloody jackhammer.'

That makes me think more positively about K, about what we did give each other – it was very far from nothing.

F and I talk and talk, about husbands, about sex with men, about sex with women, about sex with ourselves, about difficulties with our sons, about books, about writing, about food, about love, about astrology, about LIFE.

We exchange reading matter. We eat, we drink, we dance, we swim in cool green rivers. One day we teach pool to two of her English-language students, and one day we take them canoeing down the Hérault. The boys, twins, fifteen and of Moroccan origin, shoot us sly glances in our bikinis. On one stop-off, they skim stones across the water. Time seems to slow down, fan out around me like the ripples as they spread. I feel held in the moment, landed in grace.

The boys fight with each other in French even though they have been forbidden from speaking it while they are with us. On the way home in the car, one twin falls asleep with his head on my shoulder. I feel the peace of trust and acceptance without any claim on me beyond the here and now.

I meet some of F's friends, including C, sixty-eight and twice-divorced too. A sculptor. Until recently she had been enjoying the carnal delights of a local mechanic, in his fifties and outwardly fit but also an alcoholic. She'd call him whenever she wanted him, or he'd turn up drunk on her doorstep and she'd either invite him in or send him away. It had all been on her terms; it had been her appetite that was fed. Now she was dabbling with an even younger plumber who was in a relationship but had a thing for older women. She'd noticed him skulking around the woodshed, giving her the come-hithers. She'd known him since he was a teenager. C is a stone-cold legend.

I meet several women, mostly single and happy after a lifetime of failed relationships, fulfilled in their lives. It makes me feel I am not wrong, to feel what I feel. To want more by actually wanting less. To return to something fundamental. To want to be me again.

I'm not a man hater like K sometimes seemed to think I was. But I have been cross with many, many men, and I've not hidden it. Or mostly not hidden it.

With my dad I did hide it. I hid it when he was an alcoholic passing out on the floor, I hid it when I went to his house and saw the sink full of vomit, hidden by a towel, I hid it in the hospital after he wrecked his body and made me see that, and made me hear his screams, and forced me to make the decision that he shouldn't be saved because in the doctors' opinion he'd only go home and do it all again and be back in hospital within three weeks.

But what to do about all this anger? My dad was dead, and he had died – and lived – the way he did, and there was no way to go back and make any of it better. My husband would never be the kind of dynamic, self-sufficient partner I needed (if I needed a partner at all). M was too old and scared and dutiful to want to change. And K would always have his Camino and his lost Camino girls, and that was his right (although accepting that didn't stop Tracey and I renaming him the 'Camino Casanova' on my WhatsApp contacts list, which he remains to this day).

What to do about the anger and the disappointment I feel for all the men who have turned out not to be who I thought they were, or who weren't who I wanted them to be, or a mixture of the two – if these are different things?

Where to go from here? I google flights to India.

CHAPTER 9
A SEA OPERA OF WOMEN
Tracey

It's 7 am on a Tuesday and I'm screaming into the icy-cold sea.

I've shuffled down the steps to the beach in a pair of old slippers, the epitome of glam. It's three below freezing and there's actual snow on the pebbles, but the sea looks calm, peaceful even, its alluring, slightly tropical grey-green hue belying its 8 degrees.

I'm not the only lunatic down here. I just waved to at least eight other ruddy-cheeked women crunching along the frosty shore in their DryRobes, the official uniform of the Brighton sea swimmer.

After I'd shrugged off my giant fleece-lined camouflage cape, I strode down to the water and slowly waded in. The sharp bite of the water as it lapped against my mottled thighs caused me to momentarily stop breathing. The cold waves nipping rather deliciously at my arse sent a frisson of excitement through my body. I like it when she's mean.

Then I edged in further, my neoprene-clad feet feeling their way along the pebbly floor, until I could resist it no more and bodyslammed into the water, a siren returning to her sea.

'FUUUUCCCCKKKK!' I scream as I surface. My face, brain and skin fizz with the cold and I can barely catch my breath. But my god, it feels good. Dopamine courses through my body like frozen vodka and I start laughing like a loon.

'FUCK. MOTHERFUCKER!' I shout at the horizon and immediately feel 100 per cent better.

A flurry of snow whips around my ears as I paddle a swift breaststroke to warm up. While my skin starts to numb, a grin spreads across my face as the rush of dopamine hits, making the pain worthwhile.

Snowflakes gently melting on my nose, I swim out further towards the horizon, a watery sun hovering just above it, and think of nothing bar being in the beautiful sea.

What if I never returned? I think. And I just keep swimming. Maybe I would sink gently under the waves and dissolve into nothingness. Tempting.

It's not the first time these dark thoughts have entered my mind when I'm swimming. There's something about the horizon that feels reachable and safe, as if it's the answer to all my problems.

Of course, I come to my senses just as I start to feel high – a sign I've been in the water for too long. Plus, I remember I've taken a lasagna out of the freezer.

As I emerge from the surf like a frosty, budget Ursula Andress, my skin pink with cold, my smile has returned. I look around to see similarly ecstatic women. Some of my fellow seabirds wear woolly hats, others are in wetsuits, but the majority swim in 'skins' (the fancy word for normal bathers). And judging by the pure joy radiating from every single woman on the beach, swimming in winter eases away all of life's problems. It's nature's heroin.

It's these cold dips every morning that save me during the first lockdown. I know all of us sea-swimming converts wang on about the physical and mental benefits of cold-water swimming – yada, yada, yada – but it's all true. I could – and would – arrive on the beach in the foulest mood. But shedding my clothes and wading into the water is to put out the red-hot poker fire in my brain, so that I emerge fresh, focused and fired up to tackle anything. It turns my entire day around.

Prior to lockdown – and despite living in Brighton for eight years – I'd barely swum in the sea. The only time I'd brave it was on Christmas Day, when it was compulsory for a show-off like me to don a Santa hat and a figgy pudding bikini and join in the mass festive dip.

Come March 2020, when the world shuts down and we all lose our freedom, I am trapped in a house and an unhappy marriage. Sadness seeps out of me like brake fluid. But on one frosty day in early April, I stand on the pebbles, throw off my clothes and fling myself into the English Channel, and I find exactly what I have been looking for. An escape.

I come out of the sea on that first day reluctant yet shivering, and I feel like I've been reborn. For the first time in months, maybe years, my head is clear, like a brisk briny hurricane has blown through it, cleansing unwanted thoughts.

I was born in Southend-on-Sea and grew up on the Sussex coast, so the sea has been a constant in my life. It was my first confidante and my keeper of secrets, and I felt safe whenever I was near it. Any time I had a problem, I'd work it out by looking out to sea. Like a wise old fisherman. Or a harpy.

One of my earliest memories is of being on Southend beach in a right old mood. I was four years old. I'd had an argument with my mum, probably about an ice cream or the lack of one, and I stomped off to sit on an upturned bucket and sulk. A stroppy little monster who felt the world didn't understand her.

Not much has changed. As a heartbroken teenager, a lost twenty year old and now a depressed wife and mother of three, it has always been the sea that I turned to. There's something about that vast space, whether the waves are raging or calm, that I feel is always there to protect me. I find deep comfort in just being near it.

Even now, in my fifties, I still strop off to stare at the sea when I'm overwhelmed by life or dismayed by humanity. It was one of the reasons I wanted to move back to the seaside in 2011.

Swimming changed lockdown for me. It gave me a control I didn't feel I had at home. In a matter of weeks, my career as a travel writer had fallen off a cliff. I had no income and no purpose, only uncertainty. I also had three teenage children all trying to make sense of their sudden incarceration with varying degrees of frustration, joy and sadness. Christ, it was awful.

Those first days of lockdown were like snow days at school. It was weirdly exciting. Fun, almost. We were all glued to the news, simultaneously refreshing Twitter and Facebook to see what everyone else made of it.

My husband now worked from home, something he used to sneer about. And as my work did not exist any more, he set himself up at my beloved desk and continued to act like he was the most important man in the world. Well, until 5 pm, when he'd crack open the wine in time for Boris's brief to the nation.

After we'd been locked down for a couple of weeks, I was starting to slip down the wine slide too. There was never a mention by my husband of the effect coronavirus and lockdown were having on my work. The travel industry had been decimated. My eighteen-year-long career as a travel writer, which I adored and was incredibly proud of, had ended abruptly.

My loss was not acknowledged, even by me. With thousands dying, families stricken with grief, I felt I didn't have the right to be sad that my fun career had fallen off a cliff, but I was bereft. It was like a secret lover had died and I wasn't allowed to grieve.

Although nothing was said, I could sense a quiet delight in my husband that what he saw as my gravy train had ended. There had always been an underlying aura of resentment about my work. How dare I enjoy it? How dare I get satisfaction and fulfilment from working? And how dare I get to travel and enjoy nice things? The fact that he would not acknowledge at all that it had ended screamed volumes about what he thought of me.

Desperate to escape, I chose to embrace my seaside location and spend my allotted outdoor time on the beach. I would wake up before dawn and one of my daughters, the dog and I would venture down to Brighton Beach to watch the sun rise. It was a way to pretend life was normal.

Two or three days into this new ritual, we were down on Hove Beach, on the right side of the West Pier. As my daughter threw pebbles for Miss Babs, our dog, I watched a woman, probably in her mid-sixties, march down the beach, fling off her clothes and wade into the calm sea. It was early April.

Standing there in my big coat and bobble hat, I was fascinated by this woman in her sensible black swimming costume, black rubber swimming hat and protective booties. She seemed to own the world as she strutted into the water with barely a grimace, and swam and swam and swam…

'We should do that,' I said to my daughter. And the next day, we came back down to the sea in our bathers and big coats and threw ourselves into the sea.

Now I'm in the sea all the bloody time. Christmas Day, get in the sea. Birthday, get in the sea. Screaming row? Get in the sea. Dark thoughts and uncontrollable sadness? Oh. Get. In. The. Sea. It's fair to say I'm addicted to it.

Swimming becomes one of the few things I can control during this time. When it all gets too much in the house, I grab a towel and head to the beach. There's something about being in the cold sea that brings clarity to your thoughts. It's calming and meditative, and, just like in space, no one can hear you scream. And if they can, they'll just assume it's Clive, Brighton's resident and rather vocal seal.

Sometimes I go in twice a day, desperate for the icy-cold water to strip away the thoughts in my head. It feels like I'm cheating the lockdown system by getting up early for a swim and having a later swim too. My bathers are barely dry before I'm pulling them on again and padding down the stones in a pair of old boots.

And the more I do it, the more it annoys my husband. Perhaps he feels like I'm cheating on him with Neptune. Maybe I am. Have you seen Neptune? Buff, bearded, often naked and wielding a trident. Oh yes.

And I'm not the only one who finds solace in the sea. Every morning pods of women – almost always women – congregate on the beach for their constitutional swim. You hear their squeals as they enter the water all along the beach. It's beautiful. I once heard it described as a sea opera, which I think is just perfect.

One morning, about 7 am, I am down on the beach for my cold-water kicks when I bump into an old friend. As a primary school teacher, she is also suffering the effects of lockdown, and finds being in the sea helps with her mental health. She has that rougy, joyous look about her.

'It's like a drug! Honestly, it's the best thing!'

We spend half an hour catching up and I confess I'm having a pretty shit time at home and swimming has become my solace. It feels good to share.

Jan suggests we meet up for a swim the following day and this time another friend, Jane, joins us. The following day, Tamsin does. Our early-morning swims quickly became a thing. We set up a WhatsApp group, The Brighton Bobbers, and at 7 am every day I meet up with this bunch of great women for a swim. It's the highlight of my day.

And again, we are not the only ones. Cold-water swimming has become a veritable cult, largely formed of marvellous middle-aged women. It's what gets me through 2020. Swimming saves my sanity, if not my marriage.

According to experts such as Dr Susanna Søberg, exposure to low temperatures boosts our immune system, strengthens our willpower and can encourage weight loss. The latter is an effect I've sadly not been party to, largely due to the milky coffees and almond croissants I have after every swim.

But being in the sea is like popping a delicious codeine for my mental health. It's helped reduce my stress and anxiety, and my depression has got so much better – I don't bite the steering wheel of my car in rage and frustration nearly as much as I used to.

In 2018 the *British Medical Journal* published a report about using cold-water swimming as a treatment for depression. Studies have found that immersing ourselves in cold water puts our bodies into fight-or-flight mode, which helps us adapt better to stress. Your body experiences a 'cold shock' when it enters cold water that triggers a cocktail of endorphins, dopamine and serotonin, all famously good for boosting mood and creating a natural feeling of happiness and calm. Do it a lot and it will continuously lower your cortisol, the stress hormone, making you more resilient to life – exactly what I need right now.

Now everyone has jumped on the bandwagon. Since lockdown, the popularity of cold-water swimming has gone stratospheric, with everyone from the Beckhams to Prue Leith evangelising about its benefits, and the former going as far as installing a 3,000-square-metre swimming lake on their Cotswolds estate.

But I'm no fair-weather paddler. I brandish my love of sea swimming like a badge of honour and have swum everywhere from the Atlantic to the Baltic Sea, the Pacific Ocean to a pond in Sussex. I will, if pushed, wear a bikini.

Of course, there's an element of competition. And I like it. I like the fact that it puts fire in the bellies of middle-aged women, if not ice on our toes. I never thought I was a competitive person but I am when it comes to showing off.

Rhonda and I have swum together all over the world, from the great Bay of Fundy on Canada's Atlantic coast, which has the highest tides in the world, to Loch Leven in Glen Coe in the Scottish Highlands, which was colder than a witch's nipple. We'd spent the day attempting to conquer Buachaille Etive Mòr with a bunch of hardy sexagenarians, and celebrated with a bracing dip in the loch with three of the women, who barely flinched in the six-degree waters.

And we've even been in the Antarctic Ocean, where we achieved an entirely new level of swearing when we did the polar plunge in the flooded volcanic caldera of Deception Island while chinstrap penguins waddled by. It was like being dipped in liquid nitrogen – transformative!

It's in the sea that I first meet author Josie Lloyd (networking in a bathing suit is *so* Brighton) while visiting my friend Teresa, who swims in a neighbouring pod in Hove. We're bobbing around having a lovely catch-up when she spots Josie, her friend and the author of one of my favourite books of the nineties, *Come Together*, which she wrote with her husband Emlyn Rees. We paddle over to say hello.

Like me, Josie has been swimming in the sea all year round since lockdown, and her book *Lifesaving for Beginners* is about her love of sea swimming. Set in Brighton, it opens at the legendary Christmas Day swim and celebrates the deep friendships women foster when they swim together.

'We moved to Brighton in 2007, and for a long time the sea, which was just at the end of the road, was just where we'd occasionally have a dip in the summer,' Josie tells me over coffee.

'In 2017, just after Christmas, I was diagnosed with breast cancer, completely out of the blue. We'd just had my sister's fiftieth, so I was half woman, half Prosecco. I went into the clinic and was led to the quiet room and told I had breast cancer.

'I ended up having the whole shebang, chemotherapy, radiotherapy and a mastectomy. I wrote a book called *The Cancer Ladies' Running Club*, which was all about the experience of running through cancer.'

After that was published in 2020, Lloyd wrote *Lifesaving for Beginners*, about a group of women – the Salty Sea-Gals – who bond over their shared passion for year-round sea swimming in Brighton.

'The number one rule of writing is always write what you know. We swam in the summer before lockdown and just carried on through the winter. It became a real lifeline. I work from home, which can be quite insular, and I'm an extrovert.'

Set during the pandemic, the story opens with Maddy, who moves to Brighton when her twenty-year marriage collapses after her husband's affair, in search of her estranged son, Jamie. It then entwines the lives of five women, each at a different stage of life.

At the helm of the Sea-Gals is Helga. At seventy-two she's determined to stay active despite her health challenges. Tor is a woman in her thirties grappling with her identity and sexuality, while Dominica is recently widowed and struggling to find her purpose. Claire is a busy mother learning to prioritise herself amid body image and menopausal challenges.

And while the book is threaded through with grief, loneliness, self-love and resilience, at its very core is female friendship – the sisterhood.

'There's a really special camaraderie that happens,' Josie continues.

'There's been quite a lot of sniping about the DryRobe brigade, there still is now, and I really wanted to write about that community of women that have meant so much to me. What's really empowering is that there are all these groups of women that have sprung up all around the country, swimming together. It's very egalitarian, there's no "you can't join our group". It's very open and I think that's really lovely.'

Josie is part of the Splashers and Bobbers pod of Hove.

'We're not so much swimmers!' she laughs. 'I would describe myself as a firm sea chatter. I scream a bit, chat a bit, get the glory and get out. I love it. I think it's such a lovely thing that's become part of our culture, particularly since lockdown. I've never not felt invigorated by it.

'This was especially important during lockdown, when we were all consumed with the news, the NHS. You couldn't escape it. But once you're in the water, all of that is gone, you are at one with the sea. It only takes a couple of seconds. I found that mental reset became completely invaluable to my sanity and still is.

'One of my favourite bits in the book is about Helga, one of the older women, which I borrowed from someone. When you're a girl, you are connected to the moon, your cycles are monthly, but when you go through the menopause you come back down to earth and are much more grounded and come into tune with the seasons.

'And it really resonated with me. Now I'm older, I'm not monthly, time is different for me now. I know how quickly time goes. I do feel I live seasonally. I think it's something intrinsic to all the women I swim with. We're all so much more in tune with the ground, the Earth, the elemental-ness of the swimming.'

I hear her. Swimming is easy mindfulness. When life is tough for me, it's the sea that sorts me out, because for those few minutes my busy brain has a break from thinking about everything. It's an immediate absence of thoughts.

'I remember going on a full moon swim during lockdown,' says Josie, 'and there was this great big pink moon rising up from the horizon and I just remember all these women in bobble hats dancing around and singing and whooping. It felt euphoric, like being at a festival.'

The existence of my Brighton Bobbers and so many other swimming groups around the country make me feel that sea swimming is the new Women's Institute. There's such a camaraderie between the women, plus big flasks of tea, warm hugs, endless support for anything – marital woes and grief, and even career and yes, baking advice.

Like the WI, these swimming groups really foster a deep friendship between women of all ages, and it's beautiful to see. And when women swim together, the unsaid rule is you've got each other's backs. The sea is always in charge, so there's a real trust that forms.

This is all the more amazing because it wasn't so long ago

that women were discouraged from swimming at all. It was mainly considered a sport for blokes, and it was only in the late nineteenth and early twentieth centuries that women started to swim together – and even then never in front of men.

There have been some incredible women who paved the way for the sea-swimming communities we have now.

In the eighteenth century, Brighton's legendary Martha Gunn, aka Queen of the Dippers, ran Brighton Beach. She set up bathing boxes for women so they could swim in the sea, and was not only the muscle who pushed these huge wooden beasts in and out of the water but also the force behind Brighton becoming the popular Regency-era resort it did.

A century or so later, along the coast came Mary Wheatland, another formidable woman who oversaw the bathing machines on Bognor Regis beach for more than fifty years. Known as 'The Bognor Mermaid', she not only ran the beach but also saved more than thirty lives off the coast of Bognor and regularly dived off Bognor Pier well into her seventies.

Another of my favourite tales of damp dames is from a diary entry by Fanny Burney, a British satirical novelist (pre-dating Jane Austen) and frequent visitor to Brighton. In November 1782, she wrote in her diary:

> We rose at six o'clock in the morn and by the pale blink o' the moon we went to the seaside where we had bespoken the bathing woman to be ready for us, and into the ocean we plunged. It was cold but pleasant. I have bathed so often as to lose my dread of the operation which now gives me nothing but animation and vigour.

Women swimming in the sea as a challenge is also not a new thing. We follow in the damp footsteps of some legends of the waves. Hailing from Brighton, the great Mercedes Gleitze was in 1927 the first British woman to swim the English Channel. It was her eighth attempt and she swam the twenty-one miles in fifteen hours fifteen minutes, fighting off jellyfish, bitterly cold temperatures and tempestuous tides.

A year earlier, American Olympic swimmer Gertrude 'Trudy' Ederle had bagged the 'first woman' accolade when she swam across the Channel from Cap Gris-Nez in France to Kingsdown in Kent in fourteen hours and thirty-four minutes. At the time, only five men had ever managed to complete the crossing, and the previous fastest time was sixteen hours and thirty-three minutes.

So when I pad down the pebbles in my chichi DryRobe, I think of the women who paved the way and will forever inspire me to get in the water, however cold.

Before I announced my intention to divorce to my parents, I'd mentally prepared by throwing myself into the sea. It was a chilly spring day in early April, almost a year to the day since I'd started swimming. The waves were a little feisty but I needed the sea's energy to deal with the disappointment and grief about to flood my life.

After finding my usual spot, I'd shimmied off my DryRobe and tiptoed down to the shallows. I pushed through the gentle waves until the sea reached the tops of my thighs, then I flung myself forward into the icy water with the obligatory loud swear (it's scientifically proven that swearing helps you adjust to the cold).

Finally, I was ready. A bracing dip in the English Channel infused me with enough confidence to break a mother's heart.

On one of my darkest moments during the period coming up to my eventual separation, I'd woken at dawn crippled with anxiety. I couldn't get over this feeling of overwhelm and the all-encompassing dread that I was stuck in this sadness for ever.

Some mornings I'd stagger down to the beach having barely slept. Despite our Covid incarceration, I wanted to be out of the house as much as I could. I had insomnia and all I could think about in those dark hours was how I was going to get myself out of this shitty situation, particularly with my three children to consider.

When he called me a 'sea-swimming wanker' to my friends over Zoom, it was just another bong in the death knell of our marriage.

I stared at him. He stared back. He didn't understand what it meant to me. And what it meant for him.

I got in my car and drove down to the beach. Sitting alone on the pebbles, I spent probably twenty minutes just staring into the water, tears in my eyes. Eventually, I shucked off my DryRobe and my scrappy old sweatshirt, pulled on my boots and mindlessly walked down to the shoreline. I didn't feel the cold at all. My only focus was to get in the sea and forget my situation. I was worried I might never get out.

The sea is a judgement-free space. In the sea, I can think, say and do anything I want. So I screamed so loudly it scared a flock of seagulls off the beach. I immediately felt better.

Now, post separation, I need the sea and my swimming community more than ever. Separation is never straightforward or easy, and for practical reasons I've had to live under the same roof as my ex. To reduce the number of fucks I give, I start my days in the cold embrace of the English Channel.

Like Josie's characters in *Lifesaving for Beginners*, swimming in the sea has saved me. The combination of the cold water and the support of other women, and particularly the act of screaming into the sea, has been a real boost to my self-esteem and confidence, which has taken quite a bashing over the past few years. I think: Bloody hell, if I can throw myself into Baltic-temperature waters on a frosty morning, I can do anything.

Even get divorced.

CHAPTER 10

RIPTIDES AND RESCUE MISSIONS

Rhonda

Please god, don't let this be my *Eat Pray Love* moment.

I'm walking down the steep hill towards Kovalam Beach, having finally made it back to India. I'm assailed by memories of being here thirty years ago, although everything looks very different. I'm sure it's not really, though; I'm sure I've misremembered just about everything, filled in the gaps.

I'm looking in vain for where I stayed when I was last here, with the boyfriend with whom I'd travelled overland to India in an old Sherpa van, and then by train and bus around India and Nepal, before concluding our trip here in the lush southern state of Kerala. I can't see it, although the buildings standing in the right kind of place are all old.

As I'm pondering the treacherousness of memory, I become aware that a moped has slowed right down beside me on its way down the hill. I turn my head and a man is going past slowly, grinning and waving.

'Hi!' he shouts. He carries on down the hill but halfway down he pulls up and just stays sitting astride his scooter, looking up at me, still smiling.

Oh god, here we go, I think.

I carry on down, I don't really have a choice. As I approach, I see he's pretty young, maybe mid-thirties. And I also see that he's really very cute. Dangerously so.

Not now, I think. *Not here*. I've come here for something else, to find *myself*, not love.

He introduces himself as Raj, a masseur who works at the hotel he's parked up in front of. I tell him I'm staying at an Ayurvedic resort a few miles away, and he says it's the sister resort to this one. We chat for a while – about what, I'm not sure, because my mind is taken up by what our faces are doing. We're more or less consuming each other with our eyes. We're both grinning so hard, we'd make the Cheshire Cat look dour. It's one of those strange cases of complete, electric captivation. It's wild.

But I can't do this, I think. I did not come to India to be spirited away by a young masseur. And so, feeling much more sensible than usual, after ten minutes or so I force myself to say I hope I'll see him around again, knowing I most likely won't, and I carry on down to the beach, more than a touch regretful, but resolute. I've got my new sensible head on. Or so I think.

January 1994. Dusk over the Indian Ocean, twelve of us clustered around a table on Kovalam Beach – Brits, Canadians, New Zealanders, all barefoot, hair crunchy with saltwater, swimwear still damp. Empty bottles of cheap rum amassing on the table. Marijuana smoke hanging over us, swordfish cooking on the grill after being carried from the shore by fishermen.

We were enjoying the easy camaraderie of young backpackers whose lives were intersecting for a moment in time. My boyfriend, L, laughed. 'Are you sure it wasn't eight people a year, not six?' he said to one of the Kiwi blondes.

We all laughed. We knew this was how urban myths evolved, and we also knew we were being flippant. But we didn't care. Nobody had a copy of *Lonely Planet*'s guide to India to hand, but the next evening I checked and read that three to four people a year drowned in riptides off Kovalam Beach, the configuration of which created dangerous undercurrents even when the sea wasn't rough.

I'd always been at home in the sea. As a child, I loved the aftermath of tropical storms: the waves that picked me up and tossed me around and threw me breathless onto the beach.

But the next day at Kovalam I didn't get far out before something changed. The water churned. The wave pattern had broken and something had taken its place, something less predictable, less readable. Although I wasn't at any great depth, the water suddenly took me, pulling me back and under. I gasped and saltwater gushed into my mouth. Everything fizzed and rushed in front of my eyes.

When I came back up, I tried to summon L. He smiled and waved from the beach.

'I'm not waving, I'm drowning,' I tried to scream. But another wave bowled my feet from under me and I went down again. I spun and spun, sand swirling around me. I felt myself losing strength and breath.

It happened again, and again, and again, until I thought: *This is it.*

And, I thought, *I'm only just starting my real life.*

But then the water stopped. The riptide vanished as quickly as it had appeared. I stumbled towards the beach and fell onto the sand, water pouring from my nose and mouth, my tits tumbling out of my bikini top, past L, who knew, now, that the *Lonely Planet* joke wasn't funny any more.

It never had been.

We'd been revealed to ourselves as blasé, idiot travellers – ill-informed, laughing at warnings, too stupid to find out what to do if you get caught in a riptide.

Kovalam has changed. Of course it's changed, just as I have. How could it not?

But though it's busier and more developed, it still has something of a backpacker/hippy vibe and an off-the-beaten-track feel, far from the crowds of Goa.

By an extremely weird turn of events, it's thirty years to the *exact* day when I nearly drowned. I was supposed to come in September, but my visa was turned down. When I rebooked my flights, I opted for what I thought was a random week in January...

But is anything really ever random?

I walk along the beach, eyeing the waves. Then I notice the lifeguard. There were no lifeguards here in 1994. He sees me looking, walks over and urges me, in faltering English, to go for a swim. I ask about the riptides but he assures me that it's safe here.

I'm still not sure. I carry on walking, thinking about friends who haven't made it as far as I have. Back in 1994, just after the riptide, I collected my mail from the Poste Restante, and one letter from home told me that one of my best childhood friends, Rosie, was dying of cancer aged just twenty-four. Within two weeks of my near-drowning, she was gone. The two events have always been linked in my mind. Why was I saved and she not?

And then of course we lost S, also too young at forty-two. After she died, I found out through a mutual friend on Facebook she'd been planning a solo trip to India – her first visit to this country. She never made it. Coming back like this has made me feel guilty that I've been able to. But I also feel like I am carrying her fierce, life-loving spirit with me like a talisman.

Coming here has something to do with facing my fears, for sure – including my fears of the sea. My near-drowning made me very nervous of ever going out of my depth in the water. But it's also about my fears of the future and of being safe. Nobody has ever made me feel safe. Is it all up to me to do that?

I sit on the sand. There are other lifeguards further along. A couple of lads with boards are hurling themselves into the surf. It's rough, but isn't that what thrilled me as a kid?

In 1994, post uni and before my first job, I had no idea what the future had in store, and I desperately wanted to know. What would I do with my life? Would L and I stay together? I had in mind to ask him to marry me when we go home, but then I didn't. And when he asked me, years later, I still loved him but I was *in love* with someone else. Or I thought I was.

Back here today, several boyfriends and one husband later, fifty-five and separated, I still have no idea what life has in store. But suddenly I understand that's actually the point, the not-knowing. I've come back rich in thirty years of experience – motherhood, career success, great friendships and some regrets too – but new pieces of me are waiting to be discovered, and that's scary but also thrilling. I don't need to be afraid, I need to embrace it.

I stand up, strip down to my bikini and run into the waves, laughing as I let them submerge me. When I turn round, the lifeguard is waving at me. I wonder if he's warning me of a riptide, but then I see him point at my bag on the sand. It has my phone in it, all my Indian currency. The tide is about to reach it. I start running towards the shore. At the last moment, the lifeguard kicks it out of the way of the water and saves me.

I burst out laughing. I am still that blasé, idiot traveller, it seems. Some things don't change.

'Accidents' abound surrounding the India trip: the rejected visa, the felicitous change of date, and the way I mistakenly booked myself into an Ayurvedic hospital thinking it was a spa hotel.

Somatheeram, it turns out, is famous: one of the original retreats set up in a region now famous for its Ayurveda. When I find out my mistake, I decide to run with it. The place looks really rather lovely, and I'm also curious as to what this ancient Indian medical system can do for my ailments, physical and spiritual. I've been on HRT for a few years, but I'm having issues unresolved by a series of prodding and pokings by gynaecologists, ultrasounds and biopsies, and I've told my GP I'm going to see if coming off HRT helps things without causing me to end up in jail for anger crimes.

And maybe, just maybe, Ayurveda can help me with my unhappiness too. Because I'm really very fed up with feeling like this.

When I arrive at Somatheeram, I'm fully delighted by my life choices. The most welcoming of staff check me in and guide me down to my own little thatched cottage on the edge of the resort, on a cliffside overlooking a vast wild beach dotted with fishing boats.

There's no TV, there's no WiFi except in reception. I panic a bit about being out of contact with my kids, but two of them are adults by now and one of them is not so far off. I have to get it out of my head that I have to be responsible for everyone 24/7, 365 days a year.

I head to the restaurant, where all meals are included throughout my stay. A few women are sitting around, individually, at tables, wearing dusky-pink bathrobes and bandage-like turbans round their hair to soak up the oils from the shirodhara treatments. I eat insanely delicious vegetarian food from the buffet and I feel like I've landed in heaven. I am exactly where I need to be. This was no accident.

Later in the day, I see doctors – actual doctors. But these are not ordinary doctors. Shereena and Sajna are two of the kindest, most empathetic, forgiving young women I have ever met. Together they work through the thirteen-page questionnaire I've just filled in – a mortifying process that reveals all my most intimate secrets. The state of my bowel movements. The fact that I have a high sex drive but never have sex (despite all the Bumbling, it's been a while by this point). And the fact that I take drugs sometimes, and not just a bit of weed. Shereena and Sajna laugh at me as I try to justify myself – drugs are no big deal, they say, just a different way of getting to the same place that yoga and meditation take you to.

After diagnosing that I'm in the last stages of menopause (hurrah!), they decide on my dominant and my unbalanced doshas (the doshas in Ayurveda are the three fundamental energies, and exist in different ratios in everyone's body) and from here dispense dietary advice as to what to choose from the buffet, and prescribe me herbs and a regime of daily massages.

Which sounds blissful. God knows I love a good pummelling. But after I trot off with my lovely masseuses ascribed to me for the duration of my stay, Shalini and Ashwini, I soon realise that this is other-level therapy. Each morning for the next few days, I undergo a two-hour ordeal that begins with me stripping fully off and perching like a naked waif on a wooden stool to be vigorously cleaned and part-massaged by Shalini, before both of these muscular goddesses lay into me from tip to toe. Every day I leave them feeling like I've been through several rounds in a wrestling ring.

'For sure I get younger men chasing after me. They can *smell* that your eggs aren't working any more!'

I can't help but bark out a laugh. I've been sitting alone with my back to a group of four women, eating my dinner under the stars, watching the lantern flicker on the table in front of me. Happily alone, I think: ready to dive deep into the solitude of this retreat and sort my head out.

But it was not meant to be. Hearing me LOL, the women invite me to join them at their table, and I am English and it feels rude to decline. So I pull up a chair and before I know it I've made wonderful new girlfriends, all around my own age, from Hawaii and from Sweden. One is here with her Indian husband, another is alone, and one is here with her ailing sister, for whom this will probably be the last ever holiday. They are yoga teachers, actresses, activists – kindred spirits.

Suddenly, the retreat becomes a sociable thing – we swim together, eat together, watch the *Gandhi* movie together, and talk talk talk about our lives as women. And other women float in and out of our orbit, from all over the world, and our talk and laughter is magical and restoring. I also learn that it's possible to have a good time with other people without the crutch of alcohol, which is not allowed here.

In my little thatched village, it's a different story. While being on one level wildly happy, and grateful I am here, I spend a lot of time sobbing violently. Part of it's the setting. On waking at dawn the first morning to some kind of ethereal music and chanting, I stumble to my window and realise that what I'm hearing are actually Christian prayers and hymns in Malayalam, radiating out over the village and beach from loudspeakers.

Heading outside into my little patch of garden, I stand and let it wash over me for as long as it lasts (more than an hour), oblivious to the mosquitoes munching on me, letting myself soak in it all. When it ceases, the sun makes its appearance, a fiery red life-giving ball rising from behind the hills.

It happens every day, and on the last morning, I can't help it, I have to see where it's coming from. And so I get up, wrap a shawl over my head, and walk down the cliff path to the village, where I find a bright-pink church filled with worshippers on their knees before a giant neon-lit Jesus. The beauty of it all, and the music, almost bring me to my knees myself.

Mopeds are all parked up outside, and people wander in and out through the open doors as the service goes on. I watch women coming out but stopping again to say fervent prayers in front of little shrines. They look so entreating, I feel humbled by their pain and desperation. I really am so fucking lucky that life has been so kind to me.

Yet I keep crying all through my stay. It's the women who are holding me and lifting me up, both the new friends and the doctors and masseuses who are helping me back to wholeness. It's the yoga, which I can do three times daily, along with *pranayama* and chakra meditation.

It's the sanctifying holiness of this spot – as well as the Catholic house of prayer and shrine on one side, there's an important Hindu temple on the other.

It's the jaw-dropping sunrises and sunsets, it's the sweet, shy smiles and greetings I get from everyone, from the resort's orange-clad army of lady gardeners to the sari-swathed women coming out of the church and the local youths playing football next to the beach at 6 am.

It's the full moon over my cottage one night, it's the strobe lights over the sea in celebration of the seventy-fifth anniversary of the Indian Constitution, it's the resident astrologer who tells that I'm going to live 'til I'm past ninety – and also that I'm going to meet a new man in April, and after a year or so live with him.

To which I want to reply: Do I *have* to?! I'm just getting used to being single and free for the first time in decades. I'm just starting to really *love* it.

Chakras are energy points located along the spine and ending in the brain, and they include the third eye or *ajna* on the forehead, between the eyebrows. This is the chakra of intuition, wisdom and our sixth sense. The Hindu deity Shiva (the one that the 'anger goddess' Kali was consort to) opened this chakra to shoot dead the love god Kama with his burning gaze, because he saw within Kama his own lust, lack and longing. It was a kind of murder by yoga – one with which I sometimes empathised.

I'd first learned about Shiva when I was in India aged twenty-four, at the Halebidu temple in Karnataka, not long before heading further south – to Kovalam and the beach where the sea nearly took me. Within the holy triumvirate of Hindu gods, Brahma creates the universe, Vishnu preserves it and Shiva destroys it. But, like his consort Kali, Shiva destroys precisely in order to re-create.

Anicca, anitya, panta rhei. Everything changes.

And like Kali, Shiva is dual. Sometimes he is ascetic, sometimes he is led by unbridled passion and an untamed energy. This energy comes from that third eye, as does wisdom and insight.

Indeed, Shiva only achieves balance through his relationship with his wife Parvati (of whom Kali is an incarnation – remember, like real women, Hindu goddesses are all shapeshifters). Marriage allows him to be both an ascetic and a lover. Marriage saves him.

I still don't know where it came from, asking M to tie me up that time in the Cotswolds. Sex with him was the most intense I'd ever had and yet, until then, I didn't ever come with him. There was something in me that wouldn't let go. Was it guilt? Was it the fear of vulnerability, of letting down my guard? Or was I just struggling to maintain some vestiges of control as the shell was peeled off me?

Because it was all about control, me and M. He and I engaged in a battle of wills that lasted more than two years. It was a battle about what life is for and how it should be lived. It was also a battle about forgiveness, about who deserves to be forgiven, about what can and should be forgiven. I'm not, it turns out, a very forgiving person. I still don't know if that's a good or a bad thing.

When we were together, M still went out of his way to look after his 96-year-old father – the man who never apologised for his abuse of his sons. That was in addition to protecting his own fragile wife – the woman he said put him in therapy and who preferred to see him on medication for clinical depression rather than make him happy or allow him to seek happiness elsewhere.

But M now felt 'content'. He needed me to understand that, and I couldn't. I just couldn't accept that marriage, however feeble, saved him.

I'd seen a depiction of Shiva and Parvati's marriage in Hampi, once the world's second-largest medieval-era city after Beijing. And in other temples in Karnataka – Shravanabelagola, Chennakeshava, Halebidu – I'd clocked many carvings depicting *maithuna:* shagging, basically.

As far as I could understand it from what I read, *maithuna* was the actual intercourse part of Tantric sex, but Tantra itself was less about pleasure than about moksha or liberation. A term used by Hindus, Buddhists, Jains and Sikhs, moksha covers various forms of emancipation, enlightenment and release: freedom from the cycle of death and rebirth (samsara), but also freedom from ignorance, leading to self-knowledge and self-realisation. Moksha can be attained through the destructive anger of Kali, as well as through sex.

So sex can be a way of knowing yourself – of *becoming* yourself, even. And that includes angry sex, the kind of sex you have after a fight, or with certain people. But who and why?

'Some women enjoy the performance of sex,' I read somewhere recently – of being looked at, 'perved over'. If my affair taught me anything, it's that I am, in certain circumstances, among them. But I want to be looked at only in the heat of desire, not in ownership. That's what M taught me. Because he couldn't let himself be owned by me – because he'd allowed himself to get owned by someone else, through his sense of duty and worthlessness – he didn't aspire to own me. There was a kind of freedom in that. For him it was all about the enjoyment of the moment. After all, he was old. He was racing the clock, dancing towards his grave.

Yet the body is also a jail, a trap. Desire is a trap. As a woman your body starts crying out for babies and you wrap your tentacles around another human being, and they wrap themselves around you, and you get all tangled up. Inextricably so, sometimes.

It took two years to sort out my dad's affairs. A lot of money had been lost through carelessness and strange decisions and priorities, through his collecting of weird, ugly, expensive things that no one wanted to buy after he was gone. But I was lucky enough to be left sufficient to pay off our substantial debts and to pay a sizeable deposit on a house. Finally, I could dig us out of our financial hole.

It was me who found the house, as I found everything, from work opportunities to lost wallets, phones, notebooks, toothbrushes. It wasn't the house I'd dreamed of, but it was a good house, on a good street with good people – *real* people: teachers, NHS workers, taxi drivers. People of many different races and backgrounds. Kids played out on the street. It felt right.

But immediately after moving in I went into freefall. I felt miserable, trapped, on the edge of some kind of breakdown. I was awake before five each morning, belly churning, staring out of the window and feeling rabidly anxious. Everything I'd thought I'd wanted and that would 'sort everything out' was crowding in on me. My dad had bailed us out by dying his horrible lingering death and making me pull the plug on him. He'd died by not taking care of himself, and now I was using his money to continue feeling captive to responsibilities and generally overwhelmed.

That's when I started to run away, to bury the pain and the anger. That's when I went to Valencia with a group of girlfriends for a few hedonistic days of eating paella and ogling sexy butch women flamenco dancers and flirting with young waiters. And after that I went on that trip to Ibiza for my fiftieth birthday – the trip that led S to jump ship on her marriage.

And I started to go on more press trips, and meet interesting people from all kinds of different places and backgrounds. The children were older now and school rules had tightened, so I couldn't insist on travelling with at least one of them as I had before. They needed me less at home, too. And in any case, the trips were paid assignments. They were still paying the entire mortgage and all the bills. I was not on some long holiday.

In India, my crying in my cottage is not about a man as such, but much of it is about the frustration that men seem to stir up in me. I feel let down or even damaged by so many of them, and lonely, existentially lonely. Will anyone ever understand me?

K, the 'Camino Casanova', had, of course, got dumped by his new French girlfriend (for not agreeing to give her a house and a job-free life). Crying his eyes out in a voice message to me while driving back along the Languedocienne, he told me he needed me to be his friend.

I was in the Maldives with my youngest son. I said fine and, a few weeks after I got home, K and I finally met in person for the first time since the Midwest trip.

He'd written me a short story, a story about our last night together in the States, and in a hotel bar in London he read it to me and I laid my head on his shoulder and sobbed. Then we went back to our small room with its big bed we'd agreed we could share as friends.

Neither of us made any movements towards sex. I kissed K on his bald head as I used to kiss the shiny pate of my beloved grandfather, the first father I ever had (because my own was at that point still married to someone other than my teenage mother), and we went to sleep hugging.

The next day we woke up and I cried again and K held me, and then we went downstairs and I worked on my piece about my trip to the Maldives in the lobby because I had a deadline. While I was doing so, I caught sight of K pacing about in the street outside, phone clamped to his ear. I finished my piece. His call went on and on. When he finally came back in, he was flustered. It was the French girl. She knew he was with me and she'd gone berserk with jealousy.

But the only way she could know he was with me was because he'd told her. He must have wanted to provoke her.

We went on to have the perfect day – until it turned into the worst day. We headed to Borough Market and nibbled on lots of delicious food, we walked the Thames towpath, and we stopped at the Globe, where K bought us tickets to see Shakespeare by candlelight the following day. Then we went back to our hotel to nap.

I was woken up by K leaping out of bed and dashing out of the room with his phone. When he finally came back, he said he 'had a situation'. The French girl was losing it. I told him he was an idiot. She'd treated him horrifically, she'd tried to use him, and he needed to stop taking her calls and being her puppet.

We went out for dinner, but it was broken, again. When we got back to our room and went to bed, I tried to explain again why what he was doing with the French girl was making it worse for both of them in the long run, and in response he screamed in my face in the darkness and I had no option but to make him leave, because I didn't feel safe.

Now, in my clifftop perch in Kerala, I'm months and months, and miles and miles, away from K and all his nonsense. In fact, after London, we did renew contact, but he never apologised for yelling in my face in the dark like an animal. And then one day he went on the Camino again, and he met yet another lost girl, an American this time, and he ignored a message or two or three from me, and I just picked up the phone and told him I was done.

Now I watch vast container ships float in and out of the nearby port, heading out into the Indian Ocean on their mysterious courses, and these days it's Sandesh I think about, not so very far from here, in the Maldives. Sandesh who messages me every night after he's finished work, or who often tries to call me – to the extent that I'm glad to have the excuse of no WiFi here.

Sandesh, dreamboat, bane of my life…

I was drunk when I met him, at a pool party at the end of the previous year, on a press trip to Dhigurah island (Siyam World). He was working the bar. I was bored of talking to the other journalists by this point. Sandesh was making everyone medusas (floater cocktails that look like jellyfish) and I got chatting to him, asking him all about himself.

He was from Goa, where I'd spent a month during my backpacking trip around India, long before he was born. He was twenty-six now and devastatingly beautiful.

We linked on Instagram so I could send him a few pictures I'd taken of his pretty drinks, and I thought little of it. In the buggy on the way back to our villas, some of the other journos ribbed me about it all. Was I going to invite the sexy barman back to my villa and have my wicked way with him?

If only, I thought. But no, of course not – in any case, I didn't think staff would be able to get away with that.

Fast-forward a month and Sandesh was messaging me on Instagram. He'd been waiting for me to call him that night. He'd stayed awake, hoping I would summon him to my overwater villa.

I was a bit taken aback. I wasn't even sure if I'd fancied him. He was *so* young, even younger than the Italian ex-sommelier Luca. I'd been genuinely interested in hearing about his life.

He asked if I was still going to India the following month, which I didn't remember having told him. When I said I was, he said he was hoping to go back to Goa for a family wedding that same month. Would I, he asked, like to go off with him for a couple of days?

Hang out with me, will take you on my bike and we'll go to South Goa. South Goa is good to relieve mind.

Well, I thought, I did want my mind relieving, and I very much liked the idea of going off on the back of a motorbike with a sexy young Indian. This was the kind of invitation that only comes along once in a lifetime. So I said, **hell yes, let's try to make these dates collide and the stars align.** I was even prepared to pay to change my flight home yet again to make the dates work.

Everything fell to pieces after that, because Sandesh couldn't get leave for those dates. But just as I was about to leave for India, he called me and said he'd been sacked for getting in a fight with another member of staff. I knew he got drunk a lot after work; frankly, I would if I was trapped on a tiny island, however gorgeous. I really felt for the people who worked in the Maldives and had nowhere to go in their down time.

Then Sandesh told me he needed to get himself home and would try to fly via Mumbai – my first stop-off in India – so we could hang out there. But by this time I was getting weary of the calls and dramas. I'd only wanted a bit of fun – those couple of days on his motorbike. Nothing was ever going to come of it all, with that age difference, and this was all just so much effort and fluster.

Mumbai doesn't work out, nor Sandesh's subsequent idea of flying to Kerala. Part of me is relieved. But I do feel lonely in my room, or when I'm listening to the prayers. Lonely and sad, but also happy and grateful. It's all very strange and discombobulating.

And then all too soon it's time to leave my new girlfriends and head back to Mumbai. By now Sandesh has got back to Goa, via Bangalore. He almost literally flew over my head one day. It's absurd how close we got, yet how impossible it all seemed to actually get together. But it's about to get more absurd.

I leave Thiruvananthapuram station on a sleeper train bound for Mumbai, scheduled to take twenty-nine hours to travel through four states. I did this back in 1994 with L; this time I'm relishing doing it alone. But when I look at the timetable of stops, I do a double-take: I will pass within ten miles of Sandesh's town. What were the odds? What is the universe doing to me?

You can't have what you want, it seemed to be saying. Perhaps it was taunting me, or perhaps it was protecting me from what I wanted, or what I *thought* I wanted.

I message Sandesh telling him how close I will be to him. I guess I'm sort of hoping he'll say he'll come to the station to see me when I stop there, or even try to persuade me to jump off and go off on that motorbike ride with him. He doesn't.

As we get to the station nearest to him, I feel physically sick. We tried so hard to get together, and now here I am, so close, and it isn't going to happen. I want to have the daring to just get off, but my train is arriving into Mumbai at 5 am the next day and my flight out is at 2 pm. If I get off now instead, I'd have a few hours with Sandesh and have to try to get on the first flight tomorrow morning. If I don't manage it, I'll miss my flight, or at least have to change it, at even more expense.

But as soon as the train has passed that stop, the sadness lifts. It wasn't meant to be, it was a ridiculous flirtation during which we both lost our heads.

And my solo train ride is pure delight. On the first morning, I wake to the sight of an ant-like human figure wading across a river as a fat orange sun rises behind it, and to views of farmers leading buffaloes across marshland, wild peacocks strutting around, and egrets impassive as statues. I feel blessed.

For most of the journey, I share my portion of the train with two late-teen girls and a young man, Sangeena, returning from a wedding in Kerala. Sangeena translates for me so I can chat to his mum and his grandma. I learn that they live in a Mumbai hostel, yet they insist on sharing their jackfruit chips with me and on helping me hop off the train at stations to buy meals on the platform. Sangeena also writes directions for me on how to get to the airport.

Mumbai at that time of the morning is a head-fuck, even though I spent two days in the city when I arrived in India, in the company of two amazing women. The first, Anjali, is a tour leader for Intrepid, a firm that has helped make India (and other places around the world) more accessible to women travellers – their trips include women-only tours and also specialist ones that both offer unique perspectives on the lives of Indian women and help them earn a living through tourism.

Anjali, much younger than me and very much in love with her husband, was a delight to hang out with as she showed me sights including the Gandhi Museum and Dhobi Ghat, Mumbai's somewhat confronting open-air laundry and slum. As we ate together, we chatted about our lives – she about living with her in-laws, about how that would always be the case in a country where the generations look after one another. Her in-laws would help look after her children while she and her husband worked, and in turn the couple would look after their elders when they got infirm.

I'd never had parents or in-laws close enough to offer very much support with my kids, so I saw the benefits, while also feeling how constricting such a life could be. But we agreed it was all about expectations. Anjali also talked about what it was like growing up as the first girl in her family to be educated and to leave their very rural village – the effect that had had on her mother and sisters.

The second woman offered a whole other perspective. Rarely for an Indian woman, government guide Sangeeta had never married and had travelled widely by herself, as well as having her own film production company. Sangeeta took Anjali and me around Dharavi, the world's biggest slum; she knew many of the people who live and work there personally, which gave me the chance to talk to some of them and learn about the complexities of slum life – many of its inhabitants are fighting it being razed to make more space for Mumbai's super-rich. And many of the people who live there also take real, justified pride in their work, some of it in factories and workshops that recycle plastic and other garbage.

In the midst of all this, Sangeeta and I had a very deep conversation about community – about the need to spread your money around, when you have it. About what money, and ultimately life, is for – helping one another and the less fortunate.

I relive all this in my head on the outskirts of Mumbai at five in the morning, with the boy Sangeena's instructions on getting to the airport in my hands. Walking out of the station, I feel my mouth literally drop open at seeing the open-air concourse littered with bodies – those of women, children and even babies sleeping on the concrete ground. Some of the babies are starting to stir, sit up. My heart feels like it's cracking open. *Oh India...*

I have some rupees left. They are nothing to me and everything to someone. I'd only spend them on overpriced crap at the airport. I walk around, slipping them under lengths of sari spread out from sleeping women's bodies. There isn't enough to go around, but then is there ever?

Then I get into a women's carriage. These were the first of their kind in the world when they were introduced in Mumbai in 1992, to make women's journeys easier and more secure. This one is rammed with women of all ages already on their way to work, some carrying huge containers of food they must have got up even earlier to make, presumably to sell on the streets of central Mumbai. Some are already falling asleep where they stand.

It's hard not to let the pity show on your face. Many of them keep sneaking me shy looks, probably wondering where I'm from and what I'm doing here, with a lungi wrapped around my bottom half over my denim cut-offs, a T-shirt with a 'Yoga Punk' logo, Converse trainers, and only a small backpack for luggage.

But you can't show pity. Pity is not the answer. Pity is condescension.

And despite their tiredness, they, like Sangeena, reach out to me, look out for me – some of them ask if I know what stop I need, and look at my ticket, and tell me exactly when to get off. Showing curiosity but no envy of this privileged Western woman in their midst, free to flit around the world at whim. Perhaps not even imagining what that would be like, that freedom, because how can you envisage something you can never expect to have?

Sandesh's Insta posts from Goa reveal that he's in a relationship and has been for quite some time – since long before we met.

Of course he is. When I message him, Your girlfriend looks nice (which she does), he asks if I am mad at him, and I ask him what she would do if she knew that he had invited a much older woman to spend a few days with him on his motorbike, and he says, 'She would fucking kill me.'

I tell him to be careful and not to risk hurting her. That doesn't stop him carrying on messaging me, and sometimes asking me if we can make a plan to somehow meet. As if I could just nip over to the Maldives at the drop of a hat.

About eighteen months later, he starts posting dramatic Bollywood-style videos featuring him chasing his girlfriend along windswept beaches and exchanging loving gazes and hand-holding. It's all very performative and highly cringe. There's even drone footage. My eyes swivel in my sockets.

A bit tipsy one night, drinking pisco sours in Cusco with Tracey (as you do), I reply to one of Sandesh's WhatsApp status updates with the tongue-in-cheek exhortation: 'Please send dick pics'. He'd sent me plenty of those in the past, and wanking videos too – completely unbidden, I might add; as previously mentioned in relation to Tracey's BW, I loathe that kind of nonsense.

By this point I've gathered from his posts that his wedding is five days away, and I fully expect him to block me for my ridiculous, provocative behaviour. But *au contraire* – and even though I explained to him that I was JOKING – he messages me in extreme keenness to send me further photographic evidence of his manhood.

When I then ignore him, he starts trying to video-call me on WhatsApp, and then on Instagram – causing Tracey and me to re-christen him The Horny Groom on my WhatsApp contacts list. Which, like the Camino Casanova, he remains to this day.

But deep down, Sandesh has only ever been another distraction/amusement, albeit the most handsome one. (God is he handsome, the bastard.) In India, I was sad and I cried a lot and I did regret missing out on going off with him. But I think it was ultimately more about the motorbike than him, and there really was nothing to stop me learning to ride one and getting one of those between my thighs instead of Sandesh.

In reality, K, and Sandesh, and any previous man for that matter, turned out to be the least of my worries, because on the way home from this trip that was all about sorting my head out – on the flight home from India itself – I met chaos in human form.

PART II

ON THE RUN – IN SEARCH OF ANSWERS

CHAPTER 11

TORCH SONGS – OUR GLOBAL KARAOKE TOUR

Rhonda

That unofficial gay bar in Penang, a Korean tourist board party at a boutique hotel in Covent Garden (from which Tracey nigh-on got banned), a night at the infamously seedy Gerry's Bar in Soho, with a younger American man I'd picked up in a techno club in Berlin [facepalm], a student cabaret bar in Montpellier with F and her medley of friends…

However terrible the racket we make, and there have been some literal howlers, karaoke has always proven a great way for attention-seekers like Tracey and me to take the pulse of a city – and maybe, unless they take violent offence at us, make new friends.

Karaoke is also the ultimate leveller. No matter how good or bad you are, nobody cares. It's all part of the fun. In Manchester's dark and sweaty basement Vina, for instance, we performed a truly dire version of Spandau Ballet's 'Gold' and a slightly less horrific one of the Pet Shop Boys, 'West End Girls' amid a motley crowd of blow-ins: students, office workers, rockers and pin-up girls, K-pop boys, and even a couple on their very first date. Some were awesome, some were terrible, but we all had an absolutely scorching time with strangers, some of whom fast became mates.

Hence, upon landing in Saint John, New Brunswick, after nine hours in the sky, we had only one thing on our minds

– to locate the nearest karaoke joint and immerse ourselves in local bar culture. This fog-prone Bay of Fundy city might be best known for its high tides, whale-watching and hip craft breweries, but those could wait.

In Saint John, it seemed, there was only one karaoke option open to us, and a distinctly unsavoury one it turned out to be, when we finally located it on a dark backstreet: ill-lit to the point of lugubriousness, with sticky floors and a musty whiff. Not that karaoke bars *should* be stylish, fragrant affairs: quite the opposite – their very charm lies in their insalubriousness or at least their tackiness. But this was other-level fleapit.

Still we persevered, heading for the thronged bar as locals eyed us curiously as if we'd just blown down from Mars. Some of the men haltingly attempted to chat us up, while clearly not knowing quite what to make of us. We ourselves were giddy with jet lag and somewhat disorientated. But we were resolute in our mission to take this city by storm, so we put our names down on the long list to get up on stage. It was clear to us we'd trounce the locals.

Within a few songs, we were shooting each other nervous glances. While the clientele here looked like they were 90 per cent jailbirds or hoboes, each individual or group who got up to sing seemed even better than the one before. There was some serious talent behind these care-worn faces – some were almost stadium-level good. They belted out the Canadian classics – Bryan Adams, Celine Dion, Shania Twain – with confidence and panache. They seriously knew their shit.

We couldn't hope to compete. I was all for not even trying, for going with something quintessentially British that we knew really well. The Smiths, perhaps. Or Oasis ('*Because maybe…*'). But there was the risk that, if the audience didn't know it, they'd heckle us off for bringing down the vibe. In any case, Tracey had her heart set on covering something by her beloved Cher, and who was I to argue?

Only there wasn't too much choice left on the playlist, and so that's how we daftly came to sign up for a song Tracey didn't know too well and I'd never heard. We instantly regretted it. Happily, the crowd had the decency to politely look away from the car crash unfolding on the small stage and to talk among themselves while Tracey caterwauled and I just bumbled along; there were no hurled glasses.

When we got another turn, we felt like we redeemed ourselves with our rendition of 'Total Eclipse of the Heart', but it was probably only better because the crowd were singing over us this time – a genius strategy on their part. We admitted defeat.

And meanwhile, the Canadians just kept belting out the hits, the tear-jerkers, the all-American classics about axe murderers and serial killers and ill-fated love and heartbreak and deception, until by the end we were all waving our hands in the air as we sang along with a 75-year-old absolute queen crooning 'Nights in White Satin' with the full force of someone whose whole life history is encapsulated by these lyrics of unrequited love. Some of us were welling up; well, I know I was (*DAMN those perimenopause hormones*).

Because isn't that what karaoke is really all about – catharsis? Hence mine and Tracey's love of women's heartbreak/break-up/divorce songs. Some of our favourites: Cher's 'Believe', Dolly Parton's 'Jolene', Beyoncé's 'All the Single Ladies', Gloria Gaynor's 'I Will Survive', Lorde's 'Green Light'...

And then, of course, Florence & the Machine's *Mermaids*, about sea-maidens climbing Brighton Pier to dance and to make a romantic sacrifice, and about the legendary drinking propensities of English girls.

Hic...

And we are getting better, slowly. Or at least we think we are, and that's all that matters. One of our most triumphant performances came a couple of years back at the marvellous and magical Monster Ronson's Ichiban Karaoke in Berlin's hip Friedrichshain, where – after watching a new friend, Elissa, perform a kick-ass tribute to Tina Turner, who'd died the previous week, and a trans woman sing a heart-rending take on 'Hey Jude' – we were delighted to get our first chance to sing with a live band.

This time we picked the Fleetwood Mac banger 'Go Your Own Way', written by Lindsey Buckingham about his break-up with Stevie Nicks. It was another dangerous choice, given that Tracey barely knew it. But fuelled by peppermint schnapps and negronis and swagger, we gave it all we had in the way only heartbroken, divorcing, tipsy fifty-somethings can give a song all about loving the wrong person.

And the packed crowd lapped it up. As I thrust my mike-stand around and Tracey prowled the stage like a voracious cougar, a line of young dungaree-clad lesbians stretched their hands up at us like adoring groupies, eyes all puppy-like. And after we'd taken our bows and were fighting our way out through the crowd, we were high-fived and bought rounds of drinks by all and sundry.

For a brief time, I *was* Stevie Nicks – and in the words of another great songwriter, George Gershwin, 'You Can't Take That Away from Me'. Not least because, with no video evidence of this particular show, we'll never know just how bad we really were.

Leap forward a couple of years, and Tracey and I are pinching ourselves as we are flown down to the southern tip of Argentina to board an expedition ship to Antarctica – a vessel we have no reason to suspect will be the scene of one of our most outlandish performances.

It's the trip of a lifetime, involving an overnighter each way in Buenos Aires, where we eschew the tourist joints in favour of a gay tango evening, or rather a Queer de Queer *milonga* (a faster version of tango, with smaller steps) in a club called Atroden. It's beguiling and sexy. I straight out fan-girl perv over the organiser and dance teacher, Mariana Docampo, who initiated Buenos Aires' Queer Tango Festival to counter the macho image of tango, where women are 'led' by men. In Atroden, women dance with women and men with men, and it's as hot and sultry as hell. Yummy!

From there we fly to the former penal colony of Ushuaia, the world's southernmost city, to board our ship, the MS *Fridtjof Nansen*, one of two hybrid ships within the HX Hurtigruten Expeditions fleet, which was built to explore the White Continent in a sustainable way. We're both a little nervous at being so far away from our kids, and glad we're doing this together. We plan to keep ourselves to ourselves and get lots of work done while ogling penguins, humpback whales and seals.

As always with Tracey and me, things don't go according to plan. The first two days are relatively calm as we cross the infamous Drake Passage, which can be as still as a millpond or the world's roughest stretch of sea. You take your chances. We luck out and encounter only three-metre waves; they can be up to ten metres, which is when you just stay in your cabin and pray for mercy (although it's all perfectly safe).

Late in the second day, we spot our first, ghostly iceberg in the distance, through grey gloom, and that's when Tracey loses her shit – the excitement tips her over the edge. Shortly afterwards, a group of ladies from China (who turn out to be a choir holidaying together) gather around the piano and belt out a few songs, concluding with something in Chinese to the tune of 'Auld Lang Syne'.

It's not New Year for another three weeks, but the anglophone contingent, many of them (including us) now several cocktails down, all sling their arms round one another and start singing the Scottish lyrics. And suddenly Tracey and I are full-force socialising with the other journalists on board, and with some of our fellow guests too. The cocktails are strong, and these combined with the excitement of being on the brink of getting to Antarctica instil a kind of madness in us.

Tracey starts loudly denouncing her ex to anyone who will listen, in the foulest of language, while I gaze hazily but adoringly at a Filipino barman far too young for me (*quelle surprise*), and eventually send a very drunk Tracey on an errand to convey my lustful thoughts to him and enquire as to whether he reciprocates them. She returns with the news that he does indeed. I cringe – only another eight days aboard this boat to dwell on my cougar-esque outburst and avoid the poor youngster. What is *wrong* with me?

I've come to Antarctica heartsore (yes, yet again). And it's all (yet again) through my own stupidity. On my way back from India, where I'd gone to meet my former self/fix myself, I'd caught a glimpse of a man at a pub table as I walked through Heathrow Terminal Five to my connecting plane to Manchester. With his dark-rimmed glasses and salt-and-pepper hair, he sparked a surprise association.

'If I ever see M again, it will be running into him at an airport,' I said to myself.

It was the first time in forever I'd thought of my ex-lover and the man who'd helped me nuke my marriage.

Normally, when flying, I choose a window seat and am lost in my music within seconds of boarding, but this time I didn't get a choice and ended up in the dreaded middle seat. It was also the emergency-exit row, so I had to keep my headphones off while the cabin crew gave us special instructions on what to do should we get into a pickle.

It was at this point that the man who put the idea of M back into my head boarded the plane – he was the last passenger – blundered up the aisle like a rambunctious bear, sat next to me and started bombarding me with words. It was like being hit by a tsunami.

We talked and laughed non-stop before take-off and for the thirty-minute flight. We found out we had both come from the same flight back from Mumbai, on which we'd both watched the same film (*Wild*, based on the Cheryl Strayed book that Tracey and I love so much – it had been the film open on my seat-back screen when I switched it on, despite it being last in the alphabetical list, as if it was waiting for me…). And we quickly established that we were both separated.

At Manchester we walked through the airport together, and we hugged goodbye at the baggage carousel. He messaged three times from the car park while waiting for his lift.

I texted Tracey from my train home and told her the whole weird story about glimpsing him and thinking of M. So *this* was my *Eat Pray Love* moment, I told her – not Raj the masseur at Kovalam. Not someone in India. Someone actually my own age and from the UK. The novelty of it all! Was it fated? Could it be that I had sorted my life out, and the universe had recognised that?! Was the astrologer at Somatheeram right?

Although he wasn't my type physically, V and I went on our first date a week after the flight, because we had had a good laugh together and it seemed daft not to. And he was very, very keen.

By this point I hadn't touched a drink for a miraculous (for me) two and a half weeks, since arriving at the Ayurvedic retreat. But rather than ease myself back in, which would have been the sensible option, I arrived at my date and waded in on the double G&Ts. A couple of negronis on the back of those and I found myself completely smashed.

Already I knew that V and I wanted very different things – that he was fully up for a new life partner. Alarm bells were clanking away, but the booze clouded my vision and before I knew it I had agreed to go back to his hotel room for a sobering cup of tea (*I know, I know…*). It was a mistake, on my part, that would end up doing both of us a lot of damage, but maybe also teaching us both some valuable lessons.

The problem was that, after the ruse of the sobering Tetley's and an impromptu foot massage that he threw in with it, V got me, sexually, immediately. That's how he reeled me in. I don't know how he knew to, but he went straight in where M had left off and then took it further than that.

Fucking V was like having a drunken brawl in a prison cell. He was big and he was burly and he was rough, and I somehow liked that.

I didn't know where it was all coming from, why they (M, then the Maltese Bumble hook-up, and now V) liked it, and why I liked it. I didn't know whether, for me, it was shame, guilt and the desire for punishment, or whether it was something I'd have always liked had I been with someone who drew it out of me. The loss of control. Maybe, as I said, it was a relief after having had to be responsible for so many things for twenty years. Perhaps this was how I relaxed now.

The hotel we started going to was right on the flightpath to Manchester Airport, and at 5 am we'd lie sleepless and listen to the planes float in over our heads and laugh about how we'd met up in the clouds.

Sex was all I wanted from V, really. Like M, he was too different from me. He was another Tory, and he was rich – so rich that, while only a year older than me, he was already retired. And for that reason he was bored.

Six years separated, he decided right off that I was *it*, for the rest of his life. When I told him I really only wanted to see someone once a month at the most, if I was going to have a relationship at all, he battled me down to every two, then quickly started saying he 'wouldn't accept' less than once a week. He told everyone, including his kids, about us after our first date.

Already I was spooked as he bombarded me with calendar invites and suggestions for things to do, some of them involving sitting around in pubs with his mates. Sometimes I struggled, with my travels, to make enough time for my own friends.

Meanwhile, V ditched his antidepressants because he was 'so happy'. He shouldn't have been on them while drinking anyway, or rather the other way round – he needed the meds and he needed to stop drinking.

The drinking was something I was only just starting to realise was the real problem, for him. It also started to become what we did together – our dates and our nights together were boozy and wild. I started to match his energy because I had that side to me too.

V has a big personality and we laughed a lot and the sex was addictive if maniacal. But I also think he was cross with women, or at least with the wife who had booted him out. And I think that's at least partly what the rough sex was about. I think many men are cross with women, because we are not the devoted angels that they want us to be, that they build us up to be in early childhood before they realise that their mother is actually a woman in her own right. We disappoint them when we choose ourselves, as ultimately we all have to do if we're to really live.

V was all over the place mentally, and I quickly saw that. Like M, but in a very different way, he was all about control. He sulked about me going away, which was a big problem given that it's my job; he was annoyed about me going out dancing with a close male friend; he got snitty when he tried to be spontaneous, like inviting me to drive over for a beach walk on a sunny day, and I wouldn't/couldn't go along with it, because I had a busy life and wouldn't/couldn't just drop everything.

Worse, he tried to persuade me to start divorce proceedings even though he was still not divorced himself, and when he stopped to pick me up in his big, shiny, ridiculously expensive 'Batmobile', I found him on Rightmove looking at house prices on my street so he could try to convince me to sell mine.

Still I didn't end it. As a storyteller, I wanted our meeting to make some kind of sense. I didn't want to see that we were both stuck in the clouds where we'd met.

The week he drove the shiny, defective car of us into a brick wall, he was furious with me. Furious I'd called him out on his drinking, furious I'd gone on a work trip to Bordeaux, furious I wouldn't see him that week even though we had a hotel booked for two nights the following one. After cancelling everything, he announced he was going to go back on his meds. He also hinted he was bipolar.

V was right about us. It was shit and I shouldn't have even gone there. I should have had better boundaries when I knew it wasn't right for me. Because then I started to care. And mixed in with that was guilt – that I'd encouraged him to go off his meds and made things worse.

In fact, I didn't. He kept in touch, a bit; he started drinking less, he took up yoga, and he went back to consultancy work. He said I'd made him realise what he didn't want to be any more.

And what he was, of course – I saw it now – was a carbon copy of my dad: a twice-divorced, early-retired alcoholic. Chaos in human form. A ghost.

When was I going to stop trying to save men the whole time?

That same week that V and I crashed and burned, I failed to save another father, my 'French dad' Daniel – father of one of my oldest friends, Sophie.

I'd spent blissful, formative, life-changing summers with her and her family in the Vendée region of France in my teens. Daniel introduced me to jazz, talked to me about books, shot rabbits and hung them in the kitchen to break down the muscle fibre and make them more tender. Daniel liked wine but wasn't a drunk. Sophie and Daniel and his wife Rolande showed me another world.

On meeting Sophie while I was on the press trip in Bordeaux, and hearing that Daniel's Parkinson's was worsening, we made plans to go and see him. Sophie felt he wanted to say goodbye to his *fille anglaise*.

But before two weeks were up, and before we'd set a date, he'd been overcome with shame and helplessness at his condition and shot himself in the mouth in his garden.

That was a tough spring and summer because of both V and Daniel, but Tracey was there for me, for which I will always be indebted and endlessly grateful. Tracey listened to me sob and snot down the phone on many occasions, including when

I travelled out to be with Sophie and her mum, sit by Daniel's body with them, support them at the funeral, and also say goodbye, on some levels, to my teenage self and the girl who had become me.

And while all that was happening, V, wobbling violently, was breadcrumbing me then disappearing again, over and over. I didn't know what he wanted and seemingly neither did he. Flying into Manchester once a month or so, I'd look down, in spite of myself and my aching heart, at the hotel where we'd lain wrapped in each other, at the gardens where we'd walked, the café where we used to have breakfast. Remembering him telling me afterwards how he'd nearly cried when I linked my arm through his.

This all went on until one day, having said he desperately wanted to stay friends and inviting me over for dinner, he cancelled within twenty-four hours, saying 'the line between friends and more' was 'too blurred'. I would tolerate no more of him.

Something was very wrong with the men I was getting involved with. It was time for a complete reset. Perhaps I needed to become a nun?

Even India hadn't sorted me out. In fact, it had somehow made me worse. Lessons weren't being learned about boundaries and about pulling back from complicated situations and unsuitable men.

It was time to follow a new road and find my way without men sending my compass spinning like a weathervane in high winds. And only my girlfriends could help get me out of my mess.

But it would take a while. While I was still with V (if I ever really was with him – it now seems like a weird dream), I got back in contact with a man I'd met two years before at a work event. He was in his sixties and married but in a sexless 'brother–sister' relationship with his wife. Sound familiar?

This man and I went on from the event to spend a drunken night on the terrace of the Groucho Club during which he a) kissed me, a lot and wildly b) tried to get us a room c) went to great pains to point out that we were soulmates. At 4 am, pissed and deciding I was fed up with married men jumping on me and also men in general trying to seduce me with the line that we were some kind of kindred spirits, I concluded our encounter by telling him where to stick it – and it wasn't in me. But we exchanged occasional messages and I never forgot him.

When I saw him on TV two years later, one night while I was having a text conversation with V, I messaged him and he messaged right back. I still don't know why I did but it felt right. It wasn't right and I'm an idiot.

A couple of months later we managed to meet up, and this time, as I ran out of the Groucho Club to get the last train of the evening home to Manchester, he pulled me down a cobbled alley, pushed me up against a wall and told me how much he wanted me, before kissing me savagely.

What followed was another long dance of despair. We saw each other again four months later, at Halloween, again in the Groucho, at a party. I was his plus-one. I dressed in a mask and devil horns. We drank strong grapefruit cocktails and danced together and he told me I was dangerous – he who had jumped on me on our two previous evenings together.

Out in the street, he hailed a pink fluffy rickshaw. I protested that we were only five minutes' walk back to my hotel.

'Come on, Rhonda, it's fun,' he said, as if I needed to lighten up. As if I don't know how to have fun.

At my hip hotel, we finally slept together – drunken, emotional, un-rough sex that oozed guilt, at least from his side. Then he attempted to lay out some ground rules that involved him not losing any of his financial security and the companionship of a woman he 'got on really well with', while having fun all around the world with me, in secret.

Why the fuck had I not only allowed this to happen but

invited this man, this situation, back into my life? Why could I not stop returning to unfinished stories to try to make them make sense? I did think I might actually be in love with him, but it was becoming clear that he was not going to sort out his issues, that he was too comfortable in his own life.

He left the door open to me though; he left a trail of crumbs in his wake. He had got himself into my head and it fell upon me to somehow be strong enough, as I hadn't been for so long with M, to say, *No, this will not be good for me. I am worth more.*

There were several other travel writers aboard the MS *Fridtjof Nansen*, from around the world, and many of them turned out to be as unhinged, in their different ways, as Tracey and me.

A fabulous thirty-something gay couple from Germany wasted no time in instigating threesomes with passengers in their room (Grindr was apparently in full operation aboard the ship). A French journalist in her late thirties drunkenly announced that she was miserable in her marriage back home, to a Moroccan surf instructor she'd met on a trip, and never wanted to go back – especially after she developed a fixation on one of the other journalists on board, from the States.

And we all worried about Clara, an elderly Canadian being dragged around the world by her influencer niece with the aim of being the first octogenarian to visit every country in the world – we feared it would kill her, and debated staging an intervention.

Together, some of us commandeered the poor onboard pianist Davon, who hailed from Saint Lucia and was frankly going out of his mind tinky-tonking ballads night after night to travellers sipping Malbec as they pondered the icy landscape through binoculars.

It was Tracey, again, who set it all off, when she requested Davon play Cher's 'Believe' for us. Suddenly all hell broke loose as we all took to the floor and began flailing around, Tracey herself trying to mount the furniture like some kind of interiors erotomaniac.

'*Don't* fuck the map table,' hollered Seb, one half of the gay German couple. 'Show some respect.'

The Malbec drinkers gaped like fish, although some of the other passengers were infected by our madness, or had their own madness unleashed by us, and joined in on the dance floor in a joyful mash-up of nationalities.

The following night Davon, having swotted up on Kylie Minogue (Seb had requested one of her songs that first evening, but the pianist had somehow never heard of the Aussie pop goddess now in her mid fifties), started playing 'Can't Get You Out of My Head'. Before I could think better of it, I was up next to him on the mic. To be fair to myself, I had expected Tracey and Seb to join me. But they were too busy squawking with laughter as I battled to find my pitch and keep up with the lyrics of a song I barely remembered. They even filmed me for posterity, goddamn them to hell.

Reader, I completely slaughtered it and I die inside anew each time I think about it. God only knows what my young Filipino waiter crush Angelo must have thought of the whole spectacle.

More successful was the girl-band we formed, for one song only, with the explorer and climate activist Sunniva Sorby, who happened to be the *Fridtjof Nansen*'s 'godmother' – this being an honorary title given to a prominent woman who is invited to bless and name a new ship.

Sunniva was among the most inspirational women Tracey and I have met on our travels. Born in Norway and raised in Canada, she left her husband in her twenties in search of more meaning in her life. This included spending two winters living in total isolation with one other woman on the Norwegian Arctic island of Svalbard to raise awareness of climate change, and prior to that being a member of the historic all-women's Antarctic polar expedition in 1993.

This four-woman, 700-mile expedition to the **South Pole** on skis unlocked a new era of women's history in **Antarctica**, a place hitherto famously inaccessible to women. This history was delved into in a fascinating onboard talk by one of the ship's female scientists, who range from glaciologists to cetologists. Such talks are part of HX's amazing education programme, which can help you while away your time when you're not singing karaoke and knocking back super-strong cocktails or Baby Guinnesses.

Women were considered either physically unworthy of living in Antarctica or at risk of distracting the men tasked with the Mr-Big-Bollocks important work. Interestingly, however, the Argentinians weren't beneath airlifting a hugely pregnant woman to the continent to give birth there in 1978, in an attempt to strengthen its territorial claims to the continent.

Together with the epic Sunniva and two Austrian sisters (one in her late twenties, with whom I had some thought-provoking chats about living with men and settling down versus possibly being bisexual, and versus freedom in general), Tracey and I took over the mics, threw our arms around one another, and belted out a wild and joyous rendition of 'Ain't No Mountain High Enough' – the absolute classic by the wife-and-husband team, Valerie Simpson and Nick Ashford, who wrote Chaka Khan's break-out hit 'I'm Every Woman'. It was pure female bonding at its most glorious, in the most unexpected of places.

And Angelo, a man, in all this? Well, let's just say that my eight-day unconsummated romance with The World's Cutest Filipino Barman™ was a painful delight, an ongoing tease that at least took my mind off Groucho Man and what I was going to do with him – dive into an affair that I knew would drive me crazy, or break my own heart by refusing to see him.

A day or two after Tracey announced my lustful feelings to Angelo, when I was in the bar alone, feeling slightly too queasy to go out again in one of the RIB inflatable explorer boats, he came up to me. I was sitting alone gazing at icebergs over a coffee, feeling slightly the worse for wear – the unlimited booze situation was already getting to us. He said he was glad to see me alone; blushing wildly, I forced myself to make conversation, ask him about his home, his family, when he would next get to go back to Cebu City, etcetera. Then he headed off.

A minute later the grand piano started up. I turned my head, expecting to see Davon on the keys, but it was Angelo, smiling over at me as he played the most soulful rendition of John Lennon's 'Imagine' I'd ever heard. I smiled back, butterflies going berserk in my belly. Was this for real or had I slipped back into Richard Curtis territory? Then he played something classical, maybe Bach, still shooting me winsome smiles.

As I sat there, a hot mess, with no idea what was happening or how best to react to all this, he strolled back over. For a few minutes I questioned him about his music and about where he had learned to play like that. He told me how he'd taught himself the piano, and the guitar, and the saxophone. And then, ridiculously, he told me I was beautiful and I told him he was beautiful too. I was not lying.

Days went on like this. Stolen smiles. Coming over to tell me he'd loved watching me dancing. And in the end very openly seeking me out and putting his hand on my arm while the other staff looked quizzically on. Every day it got a bit more awkward and a bit more frustrating. I wanted to nail him, and hard, but I was pretty sure inviting him to my cabin would risk getting him sacked – and what was the alternative?

One night when ordering cocktails from him, I told him I'd drunk too much the night before and 'needed something weak', and he said to me, 'I'm weak,' and his lovely face looked like the face of Groucho Man when he knew we were finally going to sleep together. An attempt at deadpan, barely concealing guilt and even terror.

Another evening, Angelo told Tracey he was going to come to my cabin when he was done. That night, a bit freaked out, I went to bed early, before his shift ended, and managed to find him on Facebook and discover he was massively Catholic and also most probably had a girlfriend he seemed to conveniently forget about whenever we came within a couple of feet of each other. For the first reason alone, I decided to keep a lid on it from now on. But could I trust myself? Based on previous experience, *hell no I could not.*

Meanwhile, I also tried to let Antarctica itself give me some perspective on my life and my feelings of being caught between a proverbial rock and a hard place. One night, Tracey and I were lucky enough to be among those who got to camp on Antarctica itself – an experience both thrilling and horrific. Dumped on land by the *Fridtjof Nansen*, which immediately fucked off into the distance, we pulled our sled up a steep hill covered in snow that kept giving way beneath us to the height of our thighs, and wondered (yet again) about our sanity.

After struggling to put up our tent only to take it down again because it was facing the wrong way, we finally got it erected and collapsed inside it, on a 'ground' so uneven it felt as if we were going to fall into a crevasse during the night. Not much sleep was had.

There was no night-time here, no darkness. Whales quested across the bay in search of food, the sun danced down towards the horizon but then swam back into the sky, and glaciers calved around us, tearing the holy silence asunder. We slept a couple of hours, peed in front of each other on portable toilets, and swore. We swore a lot.

Back on ship with a breakfast Tia Maria in hand, full of swagger, we proclaimed ourselves warrior queens. Then we went and curled up in our posh beds for a few hours.

And then there was the polar plunge. Now, we all know that Tracey Davies is a massive show-off in general and a cold-water and wild-swimming junkie to boot, but I've been known to have trouble getting into the English Channel on a sunny July day without a wetsuit to hand. So as our ship somehow squeezed through Neptune's Bellows, the narrow channel affording access into the flooded volcanic caldera of Deception Island, I very much doubted I would join her on an icy dip in the Antarctic waters.

However, off a black-sand beach against the eerie backdrop of the collapsed metal structures and whale bones of a former whaling station, the two of us stripped down to our swimmers (with me also wearing a fetching bobble hat) and sprinted side by side into 0.1°C water.

It was so cold, it felt almost as if it burned. Or it felt like something I'd never felt before, something neither hot nor cold – a new category of existence. That's how I managed to do it. It was unearthly.

Unsurprisingly, the cruise ended in chaos as we sailed back across the grey and penguin-free Drake Passage. The comedown from leaving the shimmering, shattering beauty of Antarctica was sharply felt by us all, giving us all the more reason to huddle around Davon and his piano. There, guests and staff alike – Filipinos, Chinese, American, Germans, Austrians, Brits and plenty more besides – all merged in a gigantic group hug as we joined in a raucous chorus of perhaps the ultimate and most melodramatic of power ballads, Bonnie Tyler's 'Total Eclipse of the Heart'. A song described by its writer, Jim Steinman, as a 'vampire love song'.

As our plane home ascended from Ushuaia, I looked down at the MS *Fritzjof Nansen* as it was transformed into a toy boat in a playground replica of a harbour, and I cried. I cried because it would never happen again. I cried because I would never see Angelo again or get to nail him. But most of all I cried because I couldn't distract myself from my heartbreak any more.

Every now and then I fall apart...

CHAPTER 12

MIDLIFE MAGIC

Tracey

'Come on, universe. Get a wriggle on,' I say to the tarot cards scattered across my bed. 'I should be drinking margaritas by the sea with my *mamacitas* by now!'

It's been four years since I separated from my husband. Two of those have been spent going through a long and unnecessarily protracted divorce, which is nowhere near as much fun as Hollywood makes it out to be. Despite seething with incandescent rage that I pulled the plug on our there-but-for-the-grace-of-God marriage, my ex is reluctant to move on and I've been stuck living under the same roof as a man I'm no longer in love with, one who has become a hostile stranger who seemingly bears nothing but ill will for me.

I feel trapped, helpless but mostly furious. And it's now I realise I have no option but to resort to witchcraft.

Forget the wayward witches of *Macbeth* or Sarah Jessica Parker in *Hocus Pocus*, it was Sooty and Sweep who were my gateway drug into the dark arts. I was obsessed with the mute yellow bear who'd wave his magic wand while a grown man and a sappy panda chanted 'Izzy-wizzy, let's get busy.'

Sweep, the squeaky dog puppet – my favourite – would always pull a string of sausages out of an empty box. It was pure magic. I particularly enjoyed the episodes with Psychic Soo, where Soo the panda would dress up like Gypsy Rose and tell fake fortunes for hard cash. That was the beginning.

While I've always been a big fan of astrology – I'm Sagittarius with Virgo rising, in case you were wondering – it was Rhonda who introduced me to that other world of divination, tarot, after she read an article by CJ Hauser, author of *The Crane Wife,* a brilliant memoir about living a non-conventional life beyond marriage and relationships, while she was in Sydney airport.

Hauser uses tarot cards to check in and talk to themself – something Rhonda describes as like 'taking your emotional temperature and working out what you really think and want'. I'm immediately sold.

One of my best friends, M, is an oracle when it comes to this kind of woo-woo. She gave me my first cards, the Original Rider Waite Tarot Deck, saying they had presented themselves to her as mine (your deck has to choose you). She also once turned up at my house with a jam jar, a tiny candle and a spell, because 'it's a new moon and this might get rid of the fucker'.

This is the kind of friendship all women need.

'Try this. It's vetiver oil. It gets rid of bad energies,' says P, thrusting a tiny bottle into my hand. Then she rummages around in her handbag and pulls out a bag of shiny stones.

'I carry these around with me. I feel it when people have bad energy,' she says, clutching them to her chest. 'Oh and get obsidian, it's a black stone, it will protect you.'

In magic, the herb vetiver is used to ward off negative energies, purify spaces and attract abundance. Obsidian does the same. Using both creates a shield against negativity and harmful energies, which is exactly what I need right now.

Hailing from Colombia, P is the beautiful neighbour I mentioned earlier, a self-proclaimed 'white witch', a Mormon, and a simply glorious human being. I call her my spiritual nana because she guides me using rituals, spells and other divine aids

– all of which she says helped her through her own divorce more than twenty years ago.

When I first told her my husband and I were separating, P waited until I was alone and then rocked up at my door with a pair of nail scissors, a clove of garlic and a sage brush, and performed a cleansing ritual in my bedroom (my only private space) to protect me from the dark, toxic influences that flooded the house.

In Colombia, witches are called *brujas* and have different roles. Some are respected healers, some are worshipped as shamanic figures, supposedly capable of transforming into supernatural beings. And then there are others who are feared for using their spiritual talents in a more malevolent way.

'Like casting quick-working curses to get rid of toxic exes, maybe?' I enquire.

While I don't think my beloved P is capable of such dark tricks, or shapeshifting for that matter (although you never know), her cleansing rituals have become a monthly habit and allow me to have some sense of control over my spiritual destiny.

More and more women are dabbling in divination, the practice of seeking knowledge by supernatural means. And tarot cards are the entry drug, in my opinion. Women – particularly women like Rhonda and me, who are of a certain age and going through separation and divorce – are using tarot cards and witchcraft for guidance and emotional support. I suppose it gives us a sense of empowerment during these challenging times.

My tarot deck has become my spiritual mentor. I travel everywhere with it, even though it always gets flagged up at airport security because it has the same density as explosives. 'Oh, that will be my woo-woo,' I joke every time.

And in a way, tarot cards are like bombs, in that they can be a tool in blowing up your life and starting over again.

I turn to my deck when I'm seeking clarity in something. The cards can help me understand my emotions and my worries, and often reassure me that I'm on the right path. In the early days I'd pull the Three of Swords, which symbolises separation, heartbreak and betrayal, on an almost weekly basis. The cards know, you know.

I have friends in the deck. I love the Empress with her flouncy feminine energy and nurturing loveliness, while the High Priestess, who I think has a touch of the Tilda Swintons about her, is about knowing and harnessing one's own power.

I've got enemies too. I'm looking at you, the Ten of Swords, a bad boy of betrayal, loss and painful endings. And you, the Tower, who just throws everything up in the air and then sets fire to it all. And we don't discuss the Devil, my old nemesis – a demon for temptation and toxic habits.

I know! Shut up.

My favourite card is the Fool because I fully identify as such. The Fool is all about exploring your potential, new opportunities and new beginnings. It's about taking that leap of faith, blindly sometimes, even if the path ahead feels unknown. This very much appeals to the Sagittarius me.

Sometimes I'll notice the same card turn up in a reading time and time again. This is the universe saying, 'Trace, you're not listening!' I've recently been pulling the Nine of Wands, which is about resilience, persistence and facing my challenges. It's the universe's way of saying, 'Keep calm and carry on, you're on the right track,' and I feel comforted by that.

But while my tarot deck brings me much comfort, I really need my home situation to move the fuck on. So I'm calling in the big guns, the sea witches. Since our Florida road trip, Rhonda and I have been obsessed with mermaids and sirens and their mystical life ruling the sea, so, when we come across sea witchcraft, we're on it like a couple of barnacles.

That's how I find myself on Bournemouth beach with Jennifer Heather. When I first arranged to meet her, I wasn't sure what to expect – witchcraft can attract a curious bunch. But this beautiful, erudite and serene young woman swathed in sea-greens and blues is the very vision of a modern sea witch. I fall under her spell immediately.

'There's a formula to witchcraft and understanding symbolism is the key,' she tells me. 'To do a sea spell, I use my own ink, which I crafted with love, energy and seawater from this beach.

'I have a glass pen, which I use solely for my sea spells. I write my intention on a piece of paper, roll it up like a scroll and put it into a chalice of seawater and let it dissolve. It's the sea equivalent of lighting a candle,' she says. 'Once it's dissolved, I empty the chalice into the sea, returning my intention to the sirens.

'I'm an atheist, so witchcraft to me is like energy work. It's not tangible. It doesn't rely on any belief in something other than outside of yourself, not like a deity,' says Jennifer. 'I see witchcraft as like raising energy. If you feel really enthusiastic about something, you'll feel an intensely energetic peak. I think doing spells is like raising your enthusiasm, your energy, your passion.'

Jennifer was born and bred by the sea here, and sea witchery was the natural next step for her. In her *Sea Witch Book of Shadows* she explains that the siren is the dark counterpart to the mermaid, as both hold magic drawn from the mystery of the sea.

Sirens first featured in Homer's *Odyssey*, as 'formless voices summoning sailors to their island where they would meet their doom'. But in modern times, the word is used to describe – in Jennifer's words – a dangerously enigmatic woman.

'All archetypes have something to tell us about the human condition, meaning that if you're currently drawn to the siren archetype in a spiritual sense, it may be indicating that this is a side to yourself that needs to be explored and understood.'

Maybe this is what Rhonda and I are becoming? The sirens of our modern times.

I ask Jennifer if we can do a sea spell, and she leads me down to the water's edge, dodging bare-chested lads playing volleyball, to a quiet-ish spot along the shore.

We begin by standing close to the water and trying to time our breathing with the waves.

'Just lose your mind in the sea and get into that meditative state – it's all about getting into the right mindset,' says Jennifer.

I listen to the white noise of the waves and start zoning out.

'When you're relaxed, just centre yourself, ground yourself in the sand and become really clear what your intention for the spell is.'

Freedom.

'A witch's ladder is a very simple spell,' Jennifer goes on, picking up a length of thin seaweed she calls mermaid's hair. 'You can use a length of string or this seaweed and tie nine knots in it, and recite a rhyme: *By knot of one, spell's begun, by knot of two, my spell will come true* etc... all the way through to nine. With each knot, I say my intention and then, when I get to nine, I cast it into the sea.'

Then she picks up an oyster shell and starts binding it with the mermaid's hair.

'Another spell is to find a shell that calls to you, say your intention into it, and bind it with the seaweed. This is more a binding spell, which is probably not what you want.' She grins.

'But essentially, it's a ritual, it's about how it makes you feel. You could bind up the shell as a representation of your situation, and then slowly unbind it and cast it into the sea then, to encourage your ex to leave, to move on.'

She explains that we also have the option to bury our intentions. I don't say I've thought about burying him many, many times, but somehow I feel she can hear my thoughts. She's that type.

'If I wanted closure on something, I would bury my intention. I would find two similar shells like this [oyster shells] and speak my intentions into them. If I had my special sea ink, I would write on the shells. I'd then bind them together with mermaid hair and then bury them in the sand. And that would be very symbolic of putting it to rest, returning it to the earth.'

After we say our goodbyes, I linger on the beach for a while.

Silently, I look out at the horizon. My new life is so close. I want real closure on this part. It's been sometimes wonderful, sometimes hurtful. But it's time to say goodbye now.

I throw my shell into the sea and breathe out.

Only a few weeks later, I'm inching up the Kuychicassa Pass, one of the steepest parts of the Quarry Trail in Peru's Sacred Valley. Tears are streaming down my face. At 4,450 metres, this is the highest peak on the trail. Emotionally speaking, my skin feels as thin as the air at this altitude.

Adrian, our guide, puts his hand on my arm and asks if I'm okay.

'I'm fine! Don't be nice to me!' I stutter, fearful that any kind words will make me dissolve into a snotty mess on the floor so that I have to live here among the llamas.

To quote the youth, I'm 'raw-dogging' Peru. More or less overnight, I've come off Prozac, HRT, lion's-mane mushrooms and all the various supplements I pop into my husk on a daily basis. It's now been ninety-six hours since I popped my last pill and I'm struggling a little.

I wasn't planning to come off my daily SSRI Skittle until after my divorce was finalised, on doctor's orders, but, with an ayahuasca ceremony looming, I have no choice – Mother Aya does not mix well with modern medicine.

Ayahuasca is a Quechua word that means 'vine of the soul'. It's seen as the mother of all plant medicines – in fact, author Cory Firth describes it as a 'stern grandmother' because, like Grandma, she heals you with her love but also gives you tough love when you need it.

I need a stern grandmother right now. I'm still lost, spiritually and emotionally. I'm not entirely sure where I'm meant to be going in life. Leaving my marriage has left me rudderless. As a freelancer with ADHD, I bumble aimlessly through life, taking it week by week, month by month, crisis by crisis, with little thought for the future.

Pensions? Pah. Annual tax return? *Que?* Retirement? I don't think that's for people like me. I often joke that I'm only ever moments away from living under the pier giving handjobs to tramps.

Except it's not a joke. It's a near-constant fear.

I'm hoping Mother Aya will change my mindset a little and help me find a better way.

But first, Rhonda and I have to conquer the Andes. We're spending three days and two nights trekking through the Sacred Valley with Intrepid Travel, one of our favourite companies for their work in empowering women around the world. Before we reached the Andes, they took us to spend time with the K'intuy Ocutuan community, where the female leader Urpi told us about how much tourism benefits the families around the lake.

It was fascinating. As well as learning about medicinal plants – no, not aya – local farming and the food they grow, Urpi spoke to us about her community and how climate change is affecting the valley. We learned snippets of the Quechua (Inca) language and talked about female empowerment, particularly in the light of Peru's rather machismo culture. We also had coffee and cake in a restaurant and café in Urubamba in the Sacred Valley, called AMA, which hires single mothers so they can support their children and the local community.

And part of the Quarry Trail itself was developed by another awesome Peruvian woman – Intrepid's inspiring operations manager here, Maritza Chacacanta. Maritza's work goes beyond the Quarry Trail – she's been on a huge mission to clean up the Andes hiking trails and to make trekking more sustainable here. Like most Andeans, she has a deep reverence for Pachamama – Mother Earth. And she did such a good job of training hundreds of staff about preserving the trails that the government wrote to her congratulating her on her work.

With nine or ten hours of walking a day, painfully uphill for much of the time, and two nights' camping high up in the peaks, the Quarry Trail gives me plenty of headspace to think about our upcoming ayahuasca ceremony.

As the final traces of Prozac start to leave my body, I ruminate over everything: how I've brought my children up, whether they are happy, what I have and haven't achieved in my career, whether I've made my parents proud, and, of course, my failed marriage. Endless hours stewing over that.

By the time we eventually get to Machu Picchu town, I am exhausted – mentally, emotionally, physically – and yet also somewhat cleansed. The pre-ayahuasca diet of no booze, coffee, meat or sweets has done its trick. I whip out my tarot deck and pull the Ace of Wands, which assures me that I'm on the right track.

Driving up to Machu Picchu itself, winding up through the jungle, the river raging below, it feels like we are climbing through the clouds to another land far, far away – like I'm in Enid Blyton's *Magic Faraway Tree*. My favourite book as a child – one all about escapism, wanting a different world to retreat into when yours gets too much.

I think that's what I'm looking for in ayahuasca, a little luxury minibreak from life. Little do I know.

At the peak of Machu Picchu, I try to centre my mind and find my intent for the ceremony tomorrow. I think this trip is the quietest I've been in nigh-on fifty years. Coming off the drugs, pushing my body to its limit and having endless time in my head has forced me to be introspective – to be honest with myself.

I have lived with shame for as long as I can remember. My earliest memory of it is at my beloved uncle's wedding. I can't remember how old I was, maybe seven or eight. I was the only bridesmaid and I assumed I would have my hair done by the hairdresser to make me look pretty. After the bride was done, I waited patiently for my turn, but everyone laughed at me and said no. I felt ashamed. Who did I think I was expecting special treatment like that? I couldn't shake that feeling, that embarrassment, for the whole day.

I was only able to name the feeling as shame during a three-year stint of therapy when my depression had surpassed itself and Prozac wasn't even touching the sides. I was blessed by the God of Good Therapists when Rob came into my life and slowly put me back together.

Our first six months of weekly sessions were spent unpicking my all-encompassing sadness, the anger towards my husband, the guilt and shame I felt for failing. Sometimes all I could do was cry all the way through my fifty-minute session – an unexpected breaking-through of the Prozac barrier. I'd return home exhausted and fall to sleep immediately.

It was my marriage counsellor who'd suggested I had my own therapy, to 'work through' my anger. After six months of my crying, Rob and I started the long journey of unpicking me, releasing that trauma and rebuilding me.

During Covid, we had a few online sessions then took a break for about six months. By the time I returned, I had pulled the plug on my marriage, and I wanted Rob's help to guide me through the next chapter. But already he had seen that I had changed. The dimmed light in me was starting to come back brighter.

From the second I said, 'That's it', I could breathe again. I'd made the final decision, one I'd been wrestling with for several years, and I was free. Well, almost.

You need an intention when you take ayahuasca, and I decided mine was 'to let go of the things that are holding me back and to let go of shame.'

I repeated it. A lot.

I was nervous and excited about the next day's ceremony. I wasn't going to read any more about it. After digesting the entirety of the Reddit/ayahuasca thread, I was sure I could nail being a shaman myself.

I wasn't exactly sure what I was hoping to achieve. I was just hoping it would be a positive experience and that I'd come out of it without any lasting mental damage. Taking ayahuasca was supposed to be as good as having ten years of therapy, so I had high hopes.

On our bus journey back to Cusco, Rhonda and I chatted with our fellow trekker Suzanne from Boston, who had spent the previous week at the Alta Sanctuary in Los Prados in the Amazon. She heard about it in an interview with naturalist and explorer Paul Rosolie on the Lex Fridman podcast and immediately booked a trip, leaving her husband and children at home. Along with others on the retreat, Suzanne did an ayahuasca ceremony, and she talked us through her experience.

I asked her if she would do it again. 'I think I would,' she said.

We arrived back in Cusco about 9.30 pm. The high altitude had brought on yet another headache, plunging my sense of humour to an all-time low. I fell into the hotel room and almost immediately into bed. Without a thought about tomorrow, I sank into a deep sleep, only waking when my lungs gasped for oxygen (aka I snored myself awake), and was mainly out for the count for nine hours.

I had lovely comforting dreams – dreams of being liked and loved by those all around me. This was a far cry from the dreams I had had in the mountains, when everybody hated me and I went through life disappointing every person I met. Something was already changing.

I wake up the calmest and most at peace I have been for a very long time. Rhonda wakes up shortly after, also feeling strangely calm. We look at the ominous three-litre bottle of volcanic water we must consume in its entirety in the next twenty minutes. It's a little murky but, dutifully, we each pour a cup and down it. It's neither delicious nor unpleasant – slightly salty and not entirely unlike an Alka-Seltzer. Looking at each other, laughing, we down about eight cupfuls each in quick succession, as we've been instructed to.

And then we wait.

The volcanic water is to purify us. Within minutes we're both shitting through the eye of a needle, and it barely stops for the next five hours. Weirdly, it's not unpleasant at all, and, once we get over the cringe factor of what sounds like a trumpet section echoing through the room each time one of us uses the loo, it feels cleansing. Enjoyable even. Well, sorta.

When we feel ready to leave the comfort of proximity to a bathroom, we slowly, silently walk to the shaman centre, where we're led up two flights of stairs to a vaulted attic room laid out with rugs, one stained – maybe a sign of what's to come. Looking at Rhonda, I feel nervous and excited.

In the corner is the shaman's paraphernalia: long gnarly bits of wood, strings of beads, a washing-up bowl and various plastic bottles. After a few minutes, we're joined by Johanna, who runs the show and welcomes us warmly. She pulls out some padded mats, more cushions and rugs, and arranges them around the room. We're the only participants in the ceremony today, something that both reassures and worries me.

Outside are twin babies, maybe a little over a year, trying to crawl into the room. Is this a sign? I start to worry that my own twin babies might feature in my ayahuasca experience and can feel the pricks of tears start to threaten.

Johanna explains they're her twins and says they got into this room once and drank some ayahuasca. Our faces must say it all, because she reassures us that the babies were fine, just had diarrhoea and a dazed look on their faces for a few hours. She also informs us that she did ayahuasca all the way through pregnancy. And there was me giving up coffee.

Johanna then introduces us to Shaman Christina 'from the jungle', a tiny, wizened old woman in shawls and smocks who comes in and sits cross-legged on the floor, pulls out a smartphone and lights a cigarette. Rhonda and I glance at each other and grin. Ah we've got a modern shaman who's probably checking Bumble.

In front of her is a series of plastic bottles that all look like they've been dug up from the jungle. She picks up an old

Gatorade bottle that has maybe three inches of dark brown liquid in it. After shaking the bottle, she unscrews the lid and blows cigarette smoke into it.

I wasn't expecting my portal into the otherworld to come in an old Gatorade bottle, but here we are.

Johanna asks us what our intentions are for the ceremony. Sitting cross-legged in front of Shaman Christina, I repeat my new mantra: 'I want to let go of the things that are holding me back. And let go of my shame.'

Johanna translates for me while Shaman Christina nods her head and carries on smoking. She asks if I have had any addictions? No, I shake my head. I don't think 1980s power ballads counts. She asks if I have depression, anxiety or any trauma. I'm a soon-to-be-divorced woman in my fifties, Johanna, who doesn't? I think. So I admit to bouts of depression, increasing anxiety, and a little trauma here and there.

Johanna repeats what I've said to Shaman Christina, who stares ahead, nods and continues smoking. She beckons me over and, after one last puff of smoke into it, she hands me a long shot glass of the brown liquid and I drink it down. It's not hideous. It's been described as nectar, which is a step too far, but if I was being kind I'd describe it as like a syrupy espresso martini that has been used as an ashtray and left out in the sun.

Johanna asks Rhonda the same questions and the shaman hands her the same shot glass, refilled with ayahuasca and smoke. One glance at me and then she downs it.

There's no going back now.

I lie down on a rug, propped up by cushions, as Johanna puts a bucket and some toilet roll in front of me. After a while I curl up into the foetal position and stare over at Rhonda, wondering if she's feeling it yet. She looks so still and peaceful, I briefly panic that she's dead.

After a time, Johanna touches my shoulder and asks if I'm okay and if I'm feeling anything yet. I shake my head. Shaman Christina, who is chanting throughout, hands me the glass again.

The second shot of ayahuasca has an effect almost immediately. I close my eyes and it's like stepping into a neon maze, all green and pink tiles pulsating like a heartbeat. I feel disorientated. I feel dizzy, confused and a little scared. What the fuck have I done?

It's like I'm in a fast-moving film exploring the darkest corners of the grimiest nightclubs in Ibiza. Rushing through endless corridors and rooms in search of something, anything. Although I can't hear anything apart from the rushing in my head and Shaman Christina's chanting, it feels like it should have a soundtrack of hard, dirty techno.

Remembering the intentions I told the shaman – 'to let go of what is holding me back, and to let go of shame' – I have no choice but to go with it.

Suddenly, the throbbing disco tiles disappear and I have a flashback to my dad in the 1970s. He's grinning at me with smoke emanating from his teeth like a cigarette advert at the cinema. He has Tarbuck-style hair, lamb-chop sideburns, tobacco-stained teeth and six fags on the go. He never looked like this, by the way. I feel both comforted by his presence and scared that it's a sign he's going to die.

I also have a brief flashback to London Bridge and Borough Market in the late 1990s, where my ex and I both worked, but oddly this is his only appearance. Instead giant triffid-type plants are growing up and around me, wrapping themselves around my limbs and torso until I can't breathe.

I run the full gamut of emotions during the trip. I have fleeting moments of feeling high and elated, only for loneliness to seep through my body. Tears stream down my face and I hold my own hand for comfort. 'This will end,' I chant to myself. And eventually it does.

After four or five hours that seem like thirty-six, Johanna gently rouses us and I wander out onto the street in a daze.

Rhonda, on the other hand, looks like she has found her God. The only sense I can get out of her is that she found it incredibly erotic. I give her a death stare. I'm not sure I even want to know.

Never again, I say to her as we wobble our way through the bustling early-evening buzz of Cusco, the dregs of the drug making everything seem brighter, weirder and more surreal. Rhonda is floating on air with a blissed-out look in her enlarged pupils, while I look like I've spent a month on meth.

'I need soup,' I beg. We wander in and out of restaurants, checking the menus for *sopa*, the only thing I want. But when we find the required soup, a delicious creamy bowl of steaming corn, I can only manage a few spoonfuls before having to ditch Rhonda and head to bed, desperate for darkness so I can process the day. Instead the WiFi kicks in and immediately one of my daughters calls in floods of tears and motherhood kicks back in too as I talk her through her angst and settle her down.

Weirdly, this helps me come back to earth and I fall into a long, deep and surprisingly peaceful sleep, with no flashbacks to the ceremony at all. I wake up feeling calm and refreshed, like a minty hurricane has blown through my messy mind and cleansed it.

As I fly home, leaving Rhonda to spend a couple more days in Cusco by herself, I reflect that, while ayahuasca was confusing and scary, it's already feeling as if meeting my stern grandmother has had a lasting positive effect. I feel calmer. Less mental. Together, almost. I tentatively prod my soul looking for signs of shame and I feel less sensitive than before.

Has Mother Aya achieved the impossible? Only time will tell. But I'm determined to stay off the Prozac.

Meanwhile, I assume Rhonda's going to entertain herself in Cusco with a few Bumble dates and an avalanche of pisco sours. But no. Turns out she enjoyed the ayahuasca so much, she goes back to the shaman centre and asks them to take her up to their temple in the mountains for more of the stuff.

I worry for her, of course, but reason that she's a big girl now. And when she returns she regales me with hilarious tales of sharing a taxi up into the middle of nowhere with an Australian guy called Dave, an acid-head in his thirties, of having her coca leaves read (and finding them weirdly accurate), of being spat in the face with *agua de Florida* and beaten with a condor's wing by a shaman during a purification ceremony to cleanse negative energies, of being showered with flowers and then crowned with blooms to align with the spirits of the universe and allow her life to blossom, and of making an offering to Pachamama – Mother Earth. And that was before she took even so much as a sip of ayahuasca.

When she finally did, this time her trip was wilder, more psychedelic and scarier, she says. But she felt that, by taking control of it, she proved to herself that she was mentally stronger than she thought. And overall she felt that the two trips had taught her both to let go and have faith in the universe, and to assert dominance over situations when she needed to.

In fact, she laughs, she feels so proud of everything she'd done over her ten days in Peru that she got up that morning and took herself off to get her very first tattoo.

She holds her left inside wrist up to the camera of her phone and I see a little mountain range.

'I'm proud of myself, and I'm even more proud of you and what you got through,' she says, and we both have a little cry.

CHAPTER 13

BALI OR THE ART OF SELF LOVE

Rhonda

'Have you slept with me yet?' giggles Ibu Fera, a self-professed former 'naughty nun' who when she first learned to meditate would close her eyes and see a parade of her past lovers passing before her.

'There were so many of them!' she exclaims with a giggle as she tucks me into an aerial hammock for my 'Sacred Nap'.

I laugh in recognition. I've not been a saint myself. But with all my man troubles, is it time to become an actual nun?

That's what I'm here in Bali to find out. I'm only half-joking.

Having nearly lost my mind in the madness of penguins and eerie abandoned whaling stations and polar plunges and karaoke and my frankly unhinged flirtation with Angelo the Filipino barman of a far too tender age, I flew home from Antarctica and, laughing in the face of jet lag and time zones, picked up my youngest son and flew him and his friend over to Australia to spend Christmas with their best friend.

When I arrived in Sydney, I was a basket case. Crashing out of the distraction of Angelo, I had convinced myself that Groucho Man was the first eight out of eight I'd ever met, based on that list of things I'd want from a relationship that I'd written after meeting Young Daniel. And by extension maybe the only perfect eight I'd ever meet, given that I was cruising towards sixty.

But if there was a number nine on the wish list, it would be that the person was single, and Groucho Man was married and seemingly in no mind not to be, despite his issues. Meanwhile, my own husband had moved back into the family home to save himself money, causing me huge anxiety.

In Australia, I cried on my girlfriends' shoulders while trying to decode messages from Groucho Man. His communication was half-assed at best, as if he was trying not to encourage me even though it was he who was always jumping on me IRL. I felt torn: damned if I did, damned if I didn't. Whatever I chose, I felt, I would be unhappy.

Every day, while the kids ran wild, tombstoning from the harbour walls, exploring abandoned mansions and smoking weed, I worked in the daytime and then went and lay on the rocks on North Wollongong Beach and cried. My Oz-based girlfriends were very much there for me, patiently catching me again and again in this long slow fall, learning not to play London Grammar songs in front of me in case I spun out.

Together we danced, ate in hip restaurants, headed to hot springs and went on road trips, singing along to the radio and our own playlists, sleeping in cabins by ponds and lagoons where I could fall asleep to the sound of water (or lie awake to it, crying).

We'd all been through the wars since we'd met in Manchester nearly twenty years before. Canadian MN was finally divorced after years of struggle and had also survived one cancer diagnosis and another medical catastrophe. G had finally left her husband too and was juggling two lovers in their thirties, alternately bedazzled and bewildered by her new life and relationships with men from a different generation with different ways of going about things (polyamory being now very much a thing).

I surprised myself by largely stopping drinking, traumatised by the excesses of the Antarctic and also annoyed by my menopausal weight gain. Inspired by yoga bunny G, I started doing kundalini again every morning. It made me feel instantly more empowered in body and mind. I started eating more mindfully too.

I could see so clearly all the abundance in my life and be grateful for it, but at the same time I was drenched in grief for the fact that I couldn't have the man I thought was the first ever perfect one for me.

I came home, trying to find some resolution in my mind. It felt like I never would and that I was going full-on gaga. Peru helped – the headspace while climbing and the sense of achievement of actually doing it, and also the first ayahuasca trip, when I envisioned Groucho Man boarding a train down into the underworld and my saying goodbye to him without regret, because he was making his own choice. But there were still sticky bits in my head.

When I was back home, he chased me up. It had been many months, mainly due to my travelling, and we had said we would see each other again. We arranged a date when I would next be in London, and I finally managed to convey to him with some degree of self-conviction that it could be only on the basis of being friends, because the rest was too much of a head-fuck. He didn't reply to that comment in any way, just agreed to the suggested date.

I was flabbergasted, on my knees by now with indecision. All he had to do was say that was fine, that we could do that. He clearly didn't believe that that was what I wanted. What was going to happen if I did see him? Could I trust him? Could I trust myself?

So I clicked my heels and magicked myself over to the other side of the world.

My soul sister A, an American I'd met at the Ayurvedic retreat in Kerala, was renting a villa in Bali, learning sound healing to complement her yoga teaching. She also happened to be in the process of 'consciously uncoupling' from her husband of fifteen years, N. She was my age, he was seventeen years younger – thirty-nine.

A said she didn't want to worry about her ageing body; the physical side had mainly gone and she wanted to age gracefully with someone of around the same age.

She and H were doing it in a very slow and elegant way, with much love and respect. Why couldn't Groucho Man and his wife do the same, I wondered? Was it only about money and security? Or as with M, was I maybe too wild for him? Did he not trust me as a potential partner, only as a good-time girl – fling material?

Bali was my reset, but this time I was determined there would be no *Eat Pray Love* entanglements at any point, despite the Elizabeth Gilbert connection. I would *not* meet a Felipe, or any man at all. I would do copious yoga and sort my head out.

It kind of worked, although on the first night, delirious with jet lag, I sat watching local musicians jam in a plant-food café and thought how much Groucho Man (who was also in a band) would enjoy it, and I couldn't help but message him to that effect.

But then I gave myself a good metaphorical punch in the face, and, drinking lion's-mane coffee on the back of a moped as N drove me through Ubud's chaotic traffic to a sound-healing session in a replica of the Pyramids of Egypt, resolved to throw myself into the glorious ridiculousness of Bali: the wonderful madness of man buns and Masculine Presence circles and cacao ceremonies and therapy speak and 'Relearning Love' classes.

Was everybody here heartbroken, like me, I wondered? Is Ubud where all the lost souls of the world eventually converge?

In fact, Ubud derives its name from the Balinese words 'ubad' and 'usada', meaning 'medicine' – reflecting the history of the surrounding area as a source of curative plants and herbs. And today this messy, scrappy and joyfully *alive* town is full of healing places such as yoga studios, massage parlours and vegan restaurants and cafés, dotted amid the temples and shrines and houses over which monkeys clamber and lizards scramble.

Adjoining A and N's little pool villa, my guesthouse, which had just two rooms, was within the garden of a family home – a garden filled with their own private shrines. As I had at the hot springs of southern Australia, I fell asleep to the sounds of water – this time, the fountain of the koi-carp pond shrine right beside my window. In the mornings when I opened my door, the pregnant young wife of one of the brothers who ran the guesthouse would be laying out the *canang sari* – daily offerings of palm-leaf baskets filled with flowers, rice and sweets – and lighting the incense before the Ganesha statue in front of my room.

Ganesha, the guardian of temples, patron of arts and sciences, and bringer of good fortune – the Hindu god to whom people pray for wisdom, knowledge and the ability to overcome challenges…

Never had I needed this more. Just like in my clifftop cottage in India, listening to the prayers in Malayalam, I felt I'd been called here. I was being cocooned and protected. Lessons were waiting for me here. This time I absolutely had to listen, and change.

As thunder crackles over the rice paddies where chickens roam like happy zombies, I let Ibu Fera fold me into a womb-like cocoon of a silk hammock suspended from the ceiling of her Dharma Shanti ('Path to Peace') Bale at the Four Seasons Sayan resort on the outskirts of Ubud.

There, with the day's tropical downpour cascading over the Sayan Valley (*water, water everywhere!*), I melt into a meditative state as Ibu Fera reads the life story of the Buddha against a background of meditative music and I drift into and out of consciousness.

This resident wellness mentor at the resort's remarkable spa, but more importantly a one-time 'naughty nun', is among the people I have to listen to on my path to self-understanding and change. A fascinating forty-something woman overflowing with life wisdom and also compassion for life and humanity in all its contradictions, she was inspired to design 'the Sacred Nap' I am enjoying by rocking her own baby to sleep.

Afterwards, as we chat as two women from very different backgrounds but with, it turns out, so much in common, I find out all about her remarkable life story, including how she went from being a nun to the single mum she is today.

I learn how, from being born in Java to a Buddhist father and Muslim mother, she was caught in what she describes as a 'world war' between the two families – until her parents 'finally, *finally*' divorced and the two families became great friends and her father and mother became 'like brother and sister'.

From there she went to Hong Kong, where she became a wild child, sleeping around even after she met a lovely Bostonian Irishman called Jerry who was happy to support both her and her family.

It seemed like she had it made, but as soon as she asked him to marry her (because all her friends were getting married, and also because he was *lovely*), 'the confusion came dramatically.' She couldn't work out the cause of her unhappiness or what she wanted, especially when all her friends said how lucky she was. She started drinking and smoking, a lot.

Finally, after changing her phone number and making herself uncontactable to Jerry, she fled to Jakarta, with no money. There, a Canadian nun on a silent retreat introduced her to meditation as a way to find out what she really wanted, and it turned out what she really wanted was to go even further – to change her number again, so that this time none of her friends knew where she was either.

After ten months working with a community of volunteers, she decided she was ready to dedicate herself to her practice. Myanmar was safe and full of people willing to support her to become a nun – and a good not a naughty one. Using the money she got from selling the engagement ring Jerry had given her, the badass headed for Myanmar (writing Jerry a long letter to explain what she had done but giving him no address to reply to).

I think about how it must be to live solely among other women. I'd loved sleepovers at my divorced friend T's house;

such a woman's domain, free of men's presence and demands. And I love sharing a space and beds with my girlfriends in Ibiza. We often talk of living in a commune together in our dotage. Even my still-married friends get a dreamy look in their eyes as they talk about how their husbands might die earlier than them and they'll live a life of freedom with their mates, like the Barbie dolls do in their cul-de-sac in the movie.

But becoming a nun went further than just desire – to practicality or even finding a new role in life. In some parts of south-east Asia, many elderly women, especially widows, become unofficial nuns or *donchees* so they can live together as they ready themselves for death. But some of these 'wat grannies' have also been trained to spread health messages to younger women about the likes of breastfeeding and pregnancy. Some become so revered that they go on to lead male monks.

Ibu Fera thought she'd stay a nun for ever (and intends to be one again), but after a few years she felt the need to teach others, and also to return to Indonesia to look after her mother – it felt like another natural juncture. Working at another hotel in Bali, she was discovered by the equally inspirational Luisa Anderson, who oversees all the Four Seasons spas on this side of the world, and who is described by her staff as a 'source of light' (Ibu Fera says she should be a nun herself).

But back to Ibu Fera, whose young daughter asks her why she never married and how, if she didn't, she conceived her. Ibu Fera chuckles. Pema's father was a Burmese Californian she met in a monastery, and a 'nine out of ten' – the missing one in this case being that he 'said bye bye' when he found out Ibu Fera was pregnant.

She shrugs and smiles. 'Perhaps it was karma for breaking Jerry's heart.'

Ibu Fera and I spend much of our time together laughing hysterically – not something I'd have expected of meeting a nun. But like me, Ibu Fera is in her heart a rebel, a lost girl, someone who struggles to live a conventional life. And though she seems to have found her way, she's at pains to point out that, while people tend to come to nuns and monks because they perceive them as having fewer problems, often they are no more sorted than anyone else. Life is messy but the answer is inside you, she points out; you need a mirror, not judgement.

It's like travel, I say. The best thing about that is meeting other people, being exposed to different points of view and *listening, really listening*, even if you have thunder overhead that feels like it's ripping open the skies above you.

The only constant is the uncertainty, the irresolution. You make it up as you go along.

At the hotel's Sacred River Spa I also indulge in a Restu Bumi treatment, designed to spiritually cleanse me (god knows I need *that*) and take me 'deep into the soul of Mother Bali' with all her sacred energies. This is done through the use of traditional instruments (a huge gong, a 'chest sheet' that receives the sound waves from the gong and sends them deep inside me, and a genta bell), local herbs and a gemstone massage with Indonesian moss agate.

It's two hours of indescribable bliss, but what's even more lovely is the chance to chat to my masseuse Nimah, a local woman whose genuine care and kindness makes me feel as if I've been dipped into a bath of warm orange sunshine. I ask Nimah about her daughter, and about her husband – the latter, it turns out, works in a luxury resort 18,000 kilometres away, in Turks and Caicos, and comes home only once every two years. Nimah shrugs cheerfully and says she's used to that.

The politics of a migrant workforce and its moral implications for my job as a travel writer and my feelings as a human being aside (let's just say, it sometimes does keep me awake at night, but I'm not sure what the solutions are), in Bali I feel like I'm taken in the arms of a number of incredible women and held tightly and made to feel like it's going to all be okay. A tarot reader from Jakarta called Tiara pulls me a set of tarot and oracle cards that seems to explain my current life to me – and that culminates in a Mermaid card promising that 'Magick awaits', which of course delights me.

She also tells me I have to stop doing it all myself and start letting myself be guided by others, as well as allow myself to be taken care of with massages and other treatments. As Ubud is such a healing place, I have no problem letting myself be persuaded to head out for near-daily massages and facials – yes, they are cheap by UK standards, but I always tip heartily, and these lovely, empathetic, smiling women need my money.

I strike up friendships with charming young waitresses in the restaurant down the road, where I go to write and keep up with other work. I ponder ceaselessly my wonderful luck at washing up here in my weird floating life of trying to work out who I am now and what I want. Ubud, or the Ubud that I experience, is a joyful, inclusive place, one where shopkeepers chirp 'Hello, sister' as you pass them while they're leaving their *canang sari* out on the pavement, and everyone greets you with one hand held to their heart.

But it's not just the humans who speak to me. After checking in to my guesthouse, I find in my room a dead butterfly being eaten away by ants – an act I see as symbolic of transformation and rebirth. When I'm chatting on my terrace with A one morning, eating breakfast, a lizard drops onto my shoulder – something viewed as an omen in Kerala, where I first got to know her and N.

And that same morning, having walked to the end of the garden to have a peek at the ornate family temple (not knowing that that part of the grounds is out of bounds to non-Balinese), I hear a thud and see that a white-headed munia has fallen out of the sky onto the stone path in front of me.

I stand and look at it, knowing it can't be helped but unable to put it out of its misery. I glance up and, when I look back down, it's closed its tiny eyes for the last time. I open Google and read that a bird dying in front of you is a symbol of grief but can also symbolise the end of something – and change.

I bring it a flower as an offering. I can feel myself becoming different.

There's even a tarot restaurant in Ubud. Of course there bloody is! In the ludicrously named Merlin's, you can opt to let your choice of dishes be determined by the cards you pull. *Of course* mine are bang on: they tell me a) I need to stop my balancing act and being a people-pleaser, b) I need to start listening to signs from the universe, *good and bad*, and *acting on them* and c) that my job is to be a muse and an inspiration to others.

The restaurant also has a book of wisdom on a plinth to consult. I open it to a page that tells me that the Magician (a tarot card I've pulled several times when thinking about Groucho Man) 'will never be obedient'.

He'll never leave his wife, or at least not because I want him to. And in fact that's not what I do want. I don't want anyone to get hurt. I just don't want to live in dishonesty and deceit.

And also, people have to make their own minds up about what they'll put up with and what they'll sacrifice.

Ubud is even more than all this; so much more. One night I go to an ecstatic dance event and rave soberly with a couple of hundred other seekers-of-something, and it's actually *fun* and liberating. I'm being shown that I don't need booze to enjoy myself. I go for lots of sound-healing sessions, including an oceanic version with Katrina Blackstone, 'The Singing Oracle', a vocalist and voice activator who, having struggled herself, helps people with self-confidence, overthinking and feelings of overwhelm, by activating the vagus nerve.

As I walk toward the yoga mat where I want to place myself, I see there's an oracle card on it and ask Katrina if that means the mat is reserved. She says she doesn't think so, doesn't know why it's there. She comes over to pick up the card. It's the Healing card. She says that if I've come here for that, then that space has been held for me.

Accompanied (*surprise!*) by the sounds of torrential tropical rain all around the open-walled yoga studio, Katrina's 'Siren Soundbath' immerses me in the sounds of the sea accompanied by the mesmerising vocals of her jazz-trained voice. All this can be just about relaxation, she says, or it can be a way of tapping into our hearts and receiving messages from ourselves.

Have you been listening? she sings. *What wants to come through to you?*

I remember that my astrology reading for 2021 said that I am giving birth to a new soul, a whole new me. That's why it's so painful, and why it's taking so fucking long.

And of course there's yoga, which I've started doing again every day since I was at the hot springs in Australia with G. It was she who'd introduced me to kundalini several years earlier, when we first met as mums to tiny kids in Manchester.

I've already talked about *ajna*, the third eye, the chakra of intuition and inner knowing. Another chakra is sahasrara or the crown chakra, and the crown chakra meditation features my favourite mudra. The word means seal or closure: by connecting your fingers to make a seal, you link your energy centres, causing various very cool things to happen.

The crown mudra involves spreading your fingers apart like the petals of a lotus; the seal is created by bringing the outer edges of your thumbs and your little fingers together. You then bring the 'flower' you've formed with your hands to rest on the crown of your head, to function as a kind of antenna or satellite dish that channels universal wisdom down to your pineal gland – that third eye. For French philosopher and erotic writer Georges Bataille, this 'pineal eye' represented a blind spot in Western rationality.

I've done yoga for decades, on and off, but the younger me pooh-poohed all the mantra stuff, the chanting, the chakras. The older me is not so sure. The older me is open to anything, actually. Anything that will put me back in the right place on the road map of my life, or take me back to the place or places where I took a wrong turn and found myself walking blind. Walking blind into a marriage that nearly took me out.

I'm open to anything that will help me find my way back to myself – the self that I mislaid twenty-two years ago when I had my first child and lost touch with my dreams and energies and the governance of my own time. Or rather, whoever that self is now that I'm in my late fifties and my children don't need me so much any more.

I don't believe there's one self throughout life, or even one self at any given time. I believe that we are like the lotus flower that I form with my hands when I 'pray' – or whatever it is I am doing when I meditate. Many-petalled – in fact, a thousand-petalled in the case of the sahasrara, each and every petal a different colour.

Whatever it is that I am doing when I meditate...

Channelling wisdom, seeking the oblivion of my ego? Crying out for help, maybe?

Mother. Wife. Friend. Lover. Writer. Breadwinner. Cleaner and Tidier. Finder of lost things. Watcher in the night: of babies, first, and then later of wandering teens.

Adulterer. Liar.

Who am I in all of this? I am all of these, and I am none.

Adultery. Such a harsh word. Hurled at me. *Thrown* at me like a weapon. The implication being that I have committed a crime.

Adultery: an outmoded idea? Certainly not a crime. An unrealistic expectation? Are human beings made for lifelong monogamy? Scientific studies seem to suggest there's a biological basis for the 'seven-year itch'.

And in my husband's writers' circle of friends and acquaintances, the married men who were known to be sleeping around were looked upon indulgently, jokingly dismissed as jack-the-lads, 'a bit of a player'. Meanwhile the women they slept with were regarded as slags and potential home-wreckers. The same tired old story.

There were no vows at our wedding. We tore up the rule book and made no promises beyond that of our mutual commitment to bring up our son, who was at that point more than eight months cooked inside me, according to our values.

I never promised that my vagina was off limits to other men, but I had no thoughts or expectations of ever sleeping with anybody else. I was thirty-three and had been sexually active since my mid-teens. I'd had 'more than my fair share'. I had no aspirations to sleep with other men.

And in the eighteen years that followed, ditto. Barely a thought of it. The occasional stolen glance and *what if?*, but really... *Really?* Who can ever be bothered?

And besides, the thought of ever getting naked in front of another man mortified me. Breasts that had fed three babies for a total of more than three and a half years, the scar from one emergency Caesarean, a uterus bulging with fibroids, the menopause coming on thick and fast. Just *no*.

Yes, he's angry and hurt, my husband. And so would I be, if he'd done the same. Vows or no vows, it's not the ideal way for a marriage to pan out. An affair is not a healthy way to address resentments and injustices and dissatisfactions. But for a time, it can be an escape from that toxic swirl of emotions.

And I was so lonely in my responsibilities, so lonely lying awake at night worrying about the bills and the credit-card interest, and about what would become of the kids if I turned out to have cancer.

The me that fell in love with an older, married, Conservative businessman was different to all the other versions of me. Whereas sex within the marriage had become another chore, something else to feel guilty about, sex with M was wild and hedonistic because it was on my terms. And so in that sense, it was myself I was falling back in love with: my body and its pleasures.

From being a baby-making, baby-feeding, husband-pleasing machine, my body was being repossessed. I was on a new journey, one for which I didn't want to look at the map. Why spoil the surprises in store?

I've always thought of myself as a feminist, by default. The question of whether one is a feminist doesn't even seem worth asking of a woman – or at least a woman who hasn't been brainwashed. All those books I read at uni and throughout my twenties – *A Room of One's Own*, *Le Deuxième Sexe*, *The Beauty Myth* and many, many more – were only telling me what I already knew.

But then... Biology. The trap of the body. You work your way through a few relationships, you fall and you get up and try again, and then suddenly one day you're slightly broody and, if like me you have slightly older friends who are struggling with infertility and the pain of repeated IVF failures or phantom pregnancies, you panic about time running out. But instead of it taking a year to conceive, it happens the very first time you don't take precautions, and nine months later you're walking hospital corridors trying to breathe through the contractions, thinking: *Wow, am I really ready for this?*

There is so much that I would like to say to the eighteen-year-old me who went to live in Hong Kong alone, to the 24-year-old me who travelled overland to India, to the possibly-broody 32-year-old me, about men, about relationships, about the world and what it wants of you. What it takes from you.

There's much pain that I could save that girl and woman I was, so much wasted *time*. But then I think: no, it's like with your own children. You can't really ever tell them anything. They have to make their own mistakes. I had to make my own mistakes.

And in any case, out of mistakes come good things too, things one wouldn't want to go back and undo. One's children, mainly, of course. There's the rub of it all. You wouldn't efface it even if you could.

It was during Covid that finally, in my bones, I became a feminist. For the first time, I had the chance to read and to think – *really* read, *really* think – about the things I'd chosen or that had happened to me, or a mixture of the two. About how, whatever choices you make, the system is rigged against you because of your body and because as a woman *you care more*. We are designed that way.

Caring more makes you more thoughtful, dutiful, responsible. Why else, under coronavirus, was it generally countries with female leaders that fared better than those with men, in terms of the response to and overall handling of the crisis? Countries with female leaders who looked at all sides of the picture, who spoke from the heart and from intuition and instinct, who *empathised*...

But caring more is also a trap. Just look at Jacinda Ardern.

It was all about biology again, at my time of life. Your baby-making days come to an end and all the serotonin is gone, your levels of oestrogen, progesterone and testosterone are dropping fast, and you're left drowning in the stress hormones cortisol and adrenaline. You're left neck-deep in anger for all the things that the fuzzy-warm hormones made you able to accept.

You're out of all that kindness, that patience. You're done with self-sacrifice. You stop thinking things will get better: your boss's incompetence, your teenagers' vile moods, your friend's narcissistic self-absorption. The Tories. The economy. Society. Injustice.

You're done with forgiveness.

In India, I'd begun to understand, for the first time, that I had depression. Dysthymia, in fact – low-level but persistent, chronic depression. It's always been there, really. It's part of the fabric of who I am; partly existential.

But under the circumstances that I tolerated for the sake of the kids, for the sake of harmony, this 'high-functioning' depression was both a form of survival and my downfall. You 'get on with it' because you have to. You are the coper, the breadwinner, the person who can and therefore should do things.

It's a vicious circle. The more you do things, the more you have to do, because you do them the best or care to do them at all, because you have standards. But inside you're withering. You don't want sex, you don't read novels, you don't really even want to travel, despite your job. Your appetite for life is drying up.

All you really ever want to do is stay in bed and cry under the duvet, go to bed for a year under the guise of some kind of long-lasting but non-life-threatening 'condition'. But you never allow yourself that. There are always things that need attending to. Children, bills, a dirty kitchen, a toilet to be cleaned.

Biology was my worst subject at school; in fact, I failed it on purpose, in umbrage at having been forced to take it at all. I should have paid more attention. I didn't understand then how it would dictate the course of my life.

I left Bali. I could have easily stayed there for ever. It was cheap; I was in many ways happier than I had ever been. Life was relaxed and good, the weather was warm, yoga was coming out of my ears.

From that I had to go back to the stress and unhappiness of my ex being back in the house I'd paid for, and it being an unholy mess, and despite that needing to somehow fix it up and sell it…

There was also my wretched love life to fix. Was I now, finally, ready to do what was good for me, long term, even if it hurt like hell in the moment?

CHAPTER 14

ROAD-TRIPPIN'

Tracey

'I feel awake. Wide awake. I don't remember ever feeling this awake. You know what I mean? Everything looks different. Like I got something to look forward to.'
Thelma

'Look! That rock looks like a massive penis. And that one. And that one. Christ Almighty, Utah is a veritable forest of cocks,' I exclaim to Rhonda as we drive through Arches National Park in Moab.

'Do you think this is why Ridley Scott filmed *Thelma & Louise* here? As a metaphor, because men can be such dicks?'

'Freedom, I won't let you down...' belts out George Michael as we drive along the I-15 in our silver Ford Mustang.

I look over at Rhonda, her hair whipping up vertically like it did in Florida, and grin. Fuck, we are some lucky bitches.

As with our seminal road trip to meet the mermaids of Florida, Rhonda and I are teased with some delicious freedom, this time in Utah, driving south from Salt Lake City to southern Utah to live out our *Thelma & Louise* fantasies. No, we're not taking revenge on all the men we've ever been aggrieved by – although that's tempting. We're on a girls' road trip through the rugged red rock heart of rural America where much of the iconic women's buddy movie was filmed.

It's now been more than four years since I separated from my husband, and the divorce is all but rubber-stamped. My three children have largely left home, each is happily entwined in their own lives, and all that's left is to sell the house and move on. And as these final strands of our marriage are severed, like Thelma I start to feel awake. I mean like, really awake. Four espressos awake. Line of cocaine awake.

After years of doubting myself, feeling less than, I know one hundred per cent that I've made the right decision. I've chosen me. And now everything, my life, my future, looks entirely different. Like I've got something to look forward to.

With five national parks and more than forty state parks, Utah is one hell of a place for a road trip. There's some confusion leaving Salt Lake City – naming no names, Rhonda Carrier – but our detour is a chance to take a peek at Capitol Reef National Park, famous for its mammoth copper-coloured monoliths topped with white dome-shaped rocks. A few hours south of Salt Lake City in south-central Utah, it stretches for a hundred miles like a fat wrinkle in the earth.

Legend has it that 'the devil dragged his pitchfork on the road to Las Vegas'. It's proper Wild West out here and I fully expect the Marlboro Man to swagger out in leather chaps and lasso a wild burro before us.

We eventually arrive in the desert city of Moab just as the sun is setting, and check into our tipi at the Moab RV and Glamping Resort in Spanish Valley on its outskirts. I thought Moab would be packed with feisty middle-aged women in hot sports cars paying homage to our heroines, but it seems we're the only ones.

I was nineteen when *Thelma & Louise* came out in 1991. I walked out of the cinema with my friend Sarah and we just looked at each other and laughed like loons. It was, hands down, the best thing I had ever seen. Not only did it make me a dyed-in-the-wool feminist and a firm believer in the strength of female friendships; it instilled in me a lifelong obsession with road trips.

For the rare few who haven't seen it, please put this book down and go and watch it immediately. The story is centred around the friendship of the titular women from Arkansas, played by Susan Sarandon and Geena Davis, who are going on a weekend trip to a cabin in the mountains. After an altercation in a roadside bar, the two women become outlaws as they drive across America in a '66 Ford Thunderbird in a bid to reach Mexico.

Women, particularly women our age, have been obsessed with *Thelma & Louise* for more than three decades. It's not hard to see why. There are few films, even now, that show women taking agency in their lives in this way. Yes they commit crimes, but they also unleash their power, they choose themselves. They are in charge.

And aside from depicting female friendship in all its glory, the movie has the gorgeous car, the epic scenery, a baby Brad Pitt and a dreamy Michael Madsen. It's also angry and violent at times. Thelma and Louise are the epitome of the rebellious woman.

Of course, we can thank another woman for this cinematic masterpiece, American screenwriter Callie Khouri, who was working as a production assistant at an LA studio when she came up with the idea for a movie about two women going on a crime spree across America.

While it's centred around friendship and female empowerment, it also shines a light on the challenges that we women have to face every day – the stereotypical gender roles, the threat of sexual assault, and then, if something does happen, the fear that the police won't believe us. Sadly, these are something more of us than ever before can identify with.

I think it's fair to say that men do not fare well in the movie. An immature husband, a predatory rapist, a robbing gigolo, a leery trucker all make an appearance. But our queens take no shit. I particularly love the scene where they put a road cop in the trunk of his police car and he begs for his life.

'I've got a wife and kids,' he pleads, and Thelma says, 'Well, you better be sweet to them, especially your wife. My husband wasn't sweet to me and look how I turned out.' Glorious.

As we drive through Utah's rougy rugged landscape, I daydream that Rhonda and I are the modern-day Thelma and Louise. Rhonda claims Louise, and I see it. Strong, mouthy, takes no shit from men. She would have definitely shot Harlan for saying 'suck my dick'.

I have more Thelma vibes: chaotic, naive, big hair. I idly wonder if I could turn my hand to armed robbery. When we stop to fill up with petrol, I look at the gas station through Thelma's eyes and think, yes, I too could be a polite armed robber if push came to shove.

I've long been a fan of road trips. It's a trait I inherited from my parents, who thought nothing of flinging an old mattress in the back of the Vauxhall Chevette for us kids to sleep on and traversing the country.

My folks upped their road-trip game when I turned twenty, and took my brother and me on holiday to California, where I finally realised my lifelong dream of going to Disneyland. It turned out twenty was the perfect age to go: with my hot-dog legs and cute English accent, I spent my day in the Magic Kingdom telling American boys that I went to school with Princess Diana.

And while meeting Mickey and Minnie was fun, it was the following week of driving along the Pacific Coast Highway from LA to San Francisco that was the real dream. My folks had hired a big old station wagon, like the Griswolds' jalopy in the National Lampoon movies, to hit the road. The ocean views, the roadside diners, the gallon-sized Slurpees… I fell in love with all of it. Ignoring my younger brother beatboxing beside me, I'd sit with my head pressed against the back-seat window listening to the Beach Boys on my Sony Walkman and daydreaming about living in Malibu with my imaginary American boyfriend, Brad.

Twenty-four years later and I was allowed behind the wheel for my own Great American road trip after bagging a commission to write about a women's road trip through Nevada and Utah, hooked around the twenty-fifth anniversary of *Thelma & Louise*.

I was travelling with my friend M, a fellow travel writer who was writing for an airline magazine. We'd known each other for around five years but this was our first trip together. We flew into Las Vegas with a plan to drive through Nevada to check out the national parks in Utah, hit Death Valley and then roll back into Vegas for a night of gambling. I was in charge of the driving – a Ford Mustang, for authenticity you understand – and M was in charge of the itinerary and the playlist, both of which she nailed.

As Jack Kerouac said in his 1957 novel *On the Road*, driving through America evokes a sense of freedom rarely felt anywhere else. And the first time I got behind the wheel of that Mustang, I felt that anything was possible.

We filled the stereo with Nineties bangers, waved goodbye to the Las Vegas Strip and hit the road, chatting easily about everything and nothing. The Mustang smashed 1,200 miles that week as we explored four national parks, survived the night in a B&B with a potential serial killer, visited an eerie ghost town and drank margaritas with real cowboys in Tonopah, an old silver mining town.

A year or so later, M and I blagged more road-trip commissions, this time to drive along part of Route 66, again in a Mustang. Built in 1926 to connect the east and west coast, what became known as the Mother Road stretched for 2,448 miles and crossed eight states and three time zones. Sadly for us petrolheads, much of the original road had been decommissioned by 1984, but there are still some sections to be found.

The nearest to Las Vegas is Kingman, Arizona, which has the longest remaining stretch of 66 running through it. A proper dusty desert town, it makes you feel like you're stepping back into Fifties America – all low-slung motels and retro roadside diners with flashing Route 66 neon signs. I particularly enjoyed eating a really filthy cheeseburger at Mr D'z Route 66 Diner and feeling like I was in a Tarantino movie.

Although we only did a small part of it, we were following in the tyre tracks of another epic female, Alice Ramsey, who in 1909 became the first woman to drive across the United States, at the age of just twenty-two. It took her fifty-nine days to drive the 3,800 miles from New York City to California, which she did with her two sisters-in-law and a young friend in a 30-horsepower 1909 Maxwell DA touring car. And without a playlist too.

The first-ever recorded road trip was by a woman too. Bertha Benz, the wife of Karl Benz, who invented the first gas-powered car in 1885, got bored of her husband's procrastinating and in 1888 took his three-wheeled Benz Patent-Motorwagen and drove to her mother's. The 56-mile journey between Mannheim and Pforzheim is now documented as history's first long-distance car trip. Along the way, Bertha and her young teenage sons faced various challenges including having to push the car up hills, cool the engine with water and find ligroin, an early form of petrol usually only available in pharmacies.

She also did various roadside repairs, from fixing a blocked fuel line with a hatpin to replacing brake linings with leather, effectively inventing the brake pad. The journey not only saved her husband's business but was a historic milestone in automotive history. The resulting Bertha Benz Memorial Route between Mannheim and Pforzheim is now on my European hit list.

But my love of road trips had started well before my Americana phase. When we were travelling, my husband and I criss-crossed Australia on some brilliant trips. He caught up with me from Hong Kong six months after I left and we continued our love affair.

From Cairns, we relocated a Britz campervan down the east coast to Sydney, stopping off in Airlie Beach, Byron Bay and

Surfers Paradise. A second big trip was following the hallowed route of *The Adventures of Priscilla, Queen of the Desert*, another epic road-trip movie, from Sydney to Alice Springs, and then back again via the Great Ocean Road between Adelaide and Melbourne.

And it didn't stop when our kids came along. Most summers we'd pile the gang in the car and drive down to the Dordogne for a week holed up in a farmhouse with a bunch of friends. And who could forget the Herculean family road trip from Brighton to Bologna in central Italy in a £700 Saab procured from the internet only weeks before. The red engine warning light flashed before we'd even reached the Channel Tunnel but, incredibly, the old girl made it there and back, and lasted three more years before succumbing to the red light of doom.

I'd also take the kids on solo jaunts up and down the country, visiting friends and family or taking them on work jollies to castles and fancy hotels. One particularly memorable road trip was to Yorkshire to see my old neighbour N, who'd since moved there. The twins were around three at the time and we didn't even make it out of London before their signature who-could-stick-their-fingers-down-their-throat-the-furthest competition resulted in a tsunami of banana-scented vomit washing through the Volvo.

I wasn't afraid of a solo road trip either – far from it. Once I was commissioned by the *Daily Express* to write a story about a revolving B&B on Prince Edward Island off the Atlantic Coast of Canada. When I landed in Halifax, the car-hire company gave me a massive Dodge sedan and I drove 400 kilometres across Nova Scotia alone, with nothing but my own thoughts and a Celine Dion/Bryan Adams playlist for company.

At a camp along the Shubenacadie River, I stopped off to go tidal bore rafting down the Bay of Fundy with a bunch of medical students. Squeezed between New Brunswick and Nova Scotia, the bay is described as the birthplace of the Atlantic Ocean, as it's where the ancient continent of Pangea cracked apart a million lifetimes ago. It sees 160 billion tons of seawater rushing through twice a day, causing tides up to five storeys high. Because of this it attracts the adrenaline crowd, who come to raft down these towering tidal bores.

It's not for the faint-hearted, as I soon found out, especially if you're on a raft with a bunch of gung-ho lads on a jolly from Dalhousie University, all determined to scare the shit out of/ potentially murder a poor middle-aged woman by threatening to overturn the raft.

I survived the ride – and the night in an obviously haunted wooden cabin in the forest – before happily hopping into my huge Dodge and the warm embrace of Celine Dion to hit the road again. That week I covered more than a thousand kilometres in the Dodge, and hence spent an inordinate amount of time in my head.

Things were ticking along at home. I still felt unseen, undesired, unheard, but I assumed that was just marriage for you. I look back now and feel sad for younger me. As Louise said to Thelma about her husband before the weekend took a turn, 'You get what you settle for.'

'Remember that the light we hold is very, very bright'
Honey

Road trips are not just about the sexy car and epic scenery, they're about the people you meet along the way. Our mermaid sisterhood in Weeki Wachee Springs, the women from West Virginia on Anna Maria Island, Darryl the crayfish in Crystal River... It's the brilliant women, the marvellous men, the colourful characters you meet that really elevate a trip.

On our first night in Utah, we booked into the boutique hotel in the Maven District, a super-cool corner of Salt Lake City with a community of 100 locally owned businesses, 75 per cent women-owned. They include boutique bookshop

Lovebound Library, which only sells romance and erotic novels, and cool cafés Early Owl and Tandoori Taqueria, which does Indian-inspired tacos and fancy chais. Maven also has a Pilates studio, a co-working space and apartments, and it's hugely dog friendly. It buzzes with entrepreneurial women and is our kind of place.

Although Salt Lake City and Utah as a whole are notorious for their Mormons, one of the most interesting people we meet is a thirtysomething Native American woman, who first introduces herself in her native language, then translates.

'In English, I said, "Hello, my name is Rhonda DuVall or Honey. I like Honey."' She grins. 'I'm representing my Tangle relatives [one of the clans in the Navajo Nation] and I'm also half African-American. I consider myself a Navajo African American woman. I'm a community member and inspirational advocate, I also do R&B and soul singing, and my performances entwine music and Native American dance. I also do a lot of storytelling.'

Of course, Rhonda Carrier and I are smitten.

Although Honey now calls Salt Lake City home, she was raised on a reservation in California and grew up splitting her life between the two. Today she works at the Urban Indian Center of Salt Lake and is the founder of the nonprofit organisation Natives Aiming to Succeed Education Resource Center (NASERC), where she works with younger members of the community.

I ask her about the role of women in the Navajo community.

'Diné women are the key holders to the community. They're the ones who make the decisions, based on feeling and emotion. They're also the ones who hold the power. The feelings and emotions that women experience are very, very powerful.

'In other communities, in some powwow drum groups, young women aren't allowed close to the drum because they're believed to hold so much power, but in the Diné culture women are included.'

She tells me she believes women are most powerful during menstruation. I'm assuming that's not just because I walk around carrying a hammer.

'We hold so much light and so much power, to the point where it can make somebody sick. So when it comes to ceremonies, the men will always ask the woman if they are on their moon [menstrual period], and say we cannot have you in here. We cannot have you around. We need you to go inside and take care of something else, because you just hold so much power and so much energy and so much grace that we can't handle it.'

I love that idea that we are so powerful, especially when we're on our periods, that men literally can't handle us. I mean, you can try and wrestle that king-size Twix off me, but I wouldn't rate your chances, mate.

'When I say women are so powerful,' continues Honey, 'I mean that in the sense that sometimes we're a bit too much. The space that we hold is a bit too much, and not everybody can understand or accept that, which is totally fine.'

This hits hard. I'm often described as being 'too much' and I'm not quite sure how to feel about it. I'm very tall, I can be loud, and, as a Sagittarius dickhead, I'm naturally very 'enthusiastic' – I get excited about everything.

I'm also a big show-off, hence my foray into stand-up comedy, an arena notoriously overcrowded with those who are 'too much'.

I've read that being a show-off often stems from having a deep-seated insecurity – a desire for external validation to compensate for a perceived lack of self-worth.

I once overheard someone say, 'Oh my god, that woman. What is wrong with her?', because I was being loud, silly, overexcited. I *was* being a bit of twat, to be honest.

I *was* being too much. Which is weird when I've lived a life of not feeling enough.

But after years of trying and failing to dial it down to an acceptable level, I'm trying to embrace it. Like Honey says, it's my power. And if it's too much for some people, I'm sorry, but that sounds like a you problem.

Honey also talks about how every culture has its way of preparing the next generation for adulthood.

'The people who have supported us during those transitions become our anchors – our ancestors continue to walk with us wherever we go. We have the Kinaaldá, a coming-of-age ceremony that prepares girls for adulthood. For four days, we help young women experience what their future might be like and we pray for their success, kindness and resilience.

'One tradition is that each day a young woman gets up and runs east, as far and as long as she can, and all the women present run behind her. She can't stop, and neither can we, until she turns back. That teaches us that our support is always right behind us – we are never alone.'

If that doesn't demonstrate the power of the sisterhood, I don't know what does.

It's our last morning in Moab and we're reluctant to leave. 'Why can't we just stay here for ever?' says Rhonda. Which, to be fair, she says on almost every trip we do together.

We spent the night at Red Cliffs Lodge on the banks of the Colorado River, where I passed most of my time gazing up at the massive cliffs surrounding us, feeling petite, for once. While I feel we've paid suitable homage to our heroines, I'm a little disappointed that we failed to commit even a tiny crime. But the day is young and, of course, there's always the chance for a spot of polygamy in these parts.

Moab started out as a Mormon mission in 1855 but was abandoned soon afterwards because the Ute tribes didn't approve of their practices. While it has its fair share of members of the Church of Jesus Christ of Latter-day Saints, it's actually one of Utah's more diverse areas. That said, I find out there's a fundamentalist Mormon community thirty miles south of Moab that practises polygamy.

Pack your veil, Rhonda, we're going daddy hunting.

Founded in 1977 by LDS fundamentalist Robert Dean Foster, Rockland Ranch is a small private community with giant houses built into the rock face, where Mormons can practise polygamy away from the eyes of the law. Although plural marriage is illegal in the USA, and also very much frowned upon in the Mormon Church, there are still around 35,000 Mormon fundamentalist polygamists in the West, with many communities found near here, around the Utah–Arizona border.

In 2020, the Utah State Legislature passed a law to decriminalise polygamy, reducing it from a third-degree felony, which meant prison, to one on a par with receiving a speeding ticket. But hold on to your hen dos – this is not to say that polygamy is legal in Utah. It does not legally recognise plural marriages, but a married person can take additional spouses as long as they enter the union voluntarily.

Hmmm, I fear the term 'voluntarily' is doing a lot of heavy lifting here.

In the early days of the Mormon church, polygamy was accepted as a way to stop men being tempted sexually. A kind of *eat* the cake, so you're not tempted *by* the cake approach to marriage. And with 99 per cent of polygamous marriages actually being 'polygyny', where a man is married to multiple women – often much younger women – we ladies do not get the same deal.

But to be honest, which sane woman would want more than one husband?

'Or any at all,' pipes up Rhonda. She has a point.

Public interest in the Mormon lifestyle has been excited by TV shows such as *Keep Sweet: Pray and Obey*, *Sister Wives*, and that voyeurs' favourite *The Secret Lives of Mormon Wives*. The latter follows the lives of eight #MomTok [Mormon TikTok] influencers in Provo and Salt Lake City. Clips on YouTube reveal it to be a fairly saccharine montage of heavily curated 'aspirational' friendships, family dance routines and parenting tips. Meh.

However, in 2022 the MomTokkers went viral when one of the stars announced on TikTok that she was getting divorced after the group's soft swinging antics went a little too far and someone overstepped the boundaries. Soft swinging is a kind of ethical non-monogamy, where couples hook up with each other but don't have full sex.

Naturally, the ratings rocketed. Now it seems that anything goes, and the last clip I watched showed one of the mums celebrating her recent labiaplasty by throwing a party with vagina-themed mocktails and party games where the women designed their ideal vulvas.

Our road trip fittingly reaches its finale in Dead Horse Point State Park about a 45-minute drive from Moab, the road unfurling like a ribbon of dusty liquorice rippling in the heat.

Skidding up to the gate in a cloud of dust, I lean out of the car to pay the entry fee, and watch as the young ranger on the desk checks out our sexy Mustang. Despite probably being older than his mother, I ask him in my flirtiest Thelma-esque way if he gets many middle-aged women driving hot sports cars through the park.

'Ahh. Thelma and Louise!' He grins. 'Yeah, we do get some…'

'I bet you do', I say with a wink and put the pedal to the metal. We speed off howling like loons.

After driving a further ten or so minutes, we both lose our shit when the road opens out to the canyon. Shimmering in the heat, the mesa looks like the Grand Canyon. Except it's not. It's right here where the runaways' Thunderbird is finally surrounded by the police, the FBI and 'the goddamn army'.

'How many times do women have to be fucked over?' asks Hal Slocumb, the cop played by Harvey Keitel, and then the friends drive off the cliff into the 'Grand Canyon'.

Rhonda and I sit on a pale-stone ledge overlooking Fossil Point, the clifftop where that final scene takes place, and discuss whether the film would end differently today. Her novelist friend from the South of France, F, wrote about *Thelma & Louise* for her university dissertation three decades ago and reckons it would still be the same now. She says there's nowhere for wild women to go in society – apart from off the edge of a cliff.

And I kind of agree with her. I'd have loved to see the friends get away with it and get to Mexico, with the final scene being of them drinking margaritas by the sea.

But in reality, it could never have happened. The controversy it would have caused – women being seen to get away with crimes against men? Not on our watch, lady. Not like with *Buster*, the 1988 film about the Great Train Robbery, in which Buster Edwards flees to Mexico and *does* get away with it. Well, he does until his wife insists he returns home to face the music.

For me, Thelma urging Louise to 'just keep going' was the best possible ending in this scenario, because this way our heroines are in charge of their final destiny. And that final shot, with the green '66 Thunderbird flying (but not falling), still hangs in the air now.

Keep going...

And that's exactly what we do. We keep going to New Orleans, the original Sin City, to continue our journey.

What could possibly go wrong?

As with all questions of this nature, I look for guidance in my tarot deck. 'What will New Orleans bring?' I ask as we wait to board our flight from Salt Lake City.

Vanity Fair once called New Orleans the 'Wicked City', and it still holds a certain reputation for its debauched party scene and deep-seated belief in voodoo. I'm excited and a little fearful. Not least because I am weak-willed – I simply cannot resist a good time – and susceptible to the suggestion of anything woo-woo.

I pull the Judgement card, which suggests rebirth, a spiritual awakening, as if 'all the pieces of the puzzle of your life are finally coming together'. And as an almost-divorced woman, it resonates. With the end in sight, I can feel the final vestiges of the real me coming back to life, with all her big-haired dickhead energy.

The humid heat hits like falling into warm soup. And it smells just as delicious, like gumbo and good times. Soft jazz emanates from the doorways of antiques shops while the Southern drawl of those trying to draw us in pours over us like Carnation cream. The sheer sultriness of this city is intoxicating. It feels like the polar opposite to preppy, clean-cut Utah.

We're staying in the Vieux Carré, the French Quarter, where it seems as if every other shop sells bone altars and voodoo dolls, where some of the haunted Creole houses have wrought-iron balconies designed like penises that prostitutes used to signal themselves to potential clients, and where nearly everybody saunters around with all the time in the world, sipping lurid cocktails out of cheap plastic urns.

Already, it's our kind of place.

One of the reasons New Orleans has been on our wish list is because of its connections with voodoo and the spiritual underworld. Oh, okay, it's because we wanted to make voodoo dolls of our exes and learn bad curses. So bite us.

Voodoo is a religion and an integral part of life in Louisiana, particularly in New Orleans, and yet it gets a bad rap at times. I blame Hollywood, which tends to depict it only through black magic and harmful curses.

Voodoo originated in West Africa and came to Louisiana via Haiti, with the enslaved West African people who were shipped here. They merged their religious rituals and practices with Catholic ideas, the saints and icons and so on, and borrowings from the beliefs of Native Americans. Voodoo connects the everyday and spiritual worlds, letting us interact with our ancestors and the spirits through rituals, music and dance.

As we walk around the sultry streets of the French Quarter, sipping urns of rum-laced voodoo juice, Tanya, whose family has 'lived in this swamp' for more than 300 years, shares with us the entrepreneurial tales of the prostitutes who made this city. We learn about Brick Top Mary, America's first female serial killer, and also Delphine LaLaurie, a socialite turned torture-happy tyrant, and, of course, Marie Laveau, the 19th-century voodoo priestess who is still hero-worshipped here.

We stop outside a shop called Hands of Fate NOLA, where Tanya introduces us to her cousin, Sam, who owns it. A medium, shamanic and sound healer – we're incredulous to learn he's worked with our shaman Christina in Cusco – he takes us into his seance room, decorated with the skulls of his husband's French ancestors and even that of a Knight Templar. The second voodoo juice we have must have been a strong one because Rhonda books herself a seance for later in the week.

After Tanya leaves us, we're magnetically drawn to Bourbon Street – loud, bawdy and suitably sleazy in parts. We watch as drag queens throw strings of beads at pretty boys from a wrought-iron balcony while an octogenarian dressed head-to-toe in neon tie-dye dances to the music emanating from a bunch of kids armed with tubas and trombones playing the blues.

New Orleans is next-level nuts.

'I want to live here for ever,' announces Rhonda, eyes flickering with mischief.

We've arranged to meet one of Marie Laveau's disciples, Bloody Mary, a psychic, spiritualist and 'psychopomp' – someone who guides the spirits in their transition to the afterlife. She runs the Haunted Museum and Voodoo Shop on North Rampart Street.

In hindsight, drinking an untold number of cocktails at the micro-distillery and museum Sazerac House beforehand was probably not a good idea, not least because the faceless effigies and spooky dolls in the Haunted Museum might take advantage of our tipsy souls. But sitting round her seance table, we manage to hold it together to find out more about her work.

'As a Priestess of the River – the Mississippi is the mother and the bayous are her children – I work with mermaid energy a lot. I like giving fruit, honey and coins, and writing wishes on eggs and sailing them down the river,' says Mary in her silky Southern drawl.

'It's like sea witches – although I don't use the term witch. I'm a priestess and a voodoo queen. Although I quite like "swamp witch", because we use the land, the water and mud for our magic.'

She talks us through her life communicating with the spirits. 'My family has been here since 1718, I've got a deep root system goin' on. When I was tiny, they were talking to me, the ancestors, the land spirits. They were waking me up and I wanted to know why.

'I stopped getting the correct answers from the Catholic Church, so I went on my own adventure to find out. I questioned a lot of people and the answers seemed to always be in voodoo.'

Mary then sends us on our own mission. 'I want you to go upstairs alone and introduce yourselves to the spirits, then come and tell me what you feel. I like people to go in naked, you know, without me front-loading them with all the information.' She grins.

Rhonda and I creep up the stairs into a room lined with empty chairs, piles of dolls and a mannequin draped in a black widow's veil. We peek into the kitchen, which has shrines strewn with dollar bills, empty bottles of liquor and cigarettes.

When we get back downstairs, Mary explains that the house is haunted by the victims of a murder–suicide pact and that people can often feel their presence upstairs. Sadly, I think that last mai tai numbed me to any visits from the spirits.

Rather embarrassingly, I ask Mary if she's seen the 1990 movie *Ghost* and whether she thinks it's a true representation of the spirit world. Yes and no, she says before quickly moving on to talk about the effect Hollywood has had on the city. *American Horror Story: Coven* was set in New Orleans and told the story of the

LaLaurie Mansion at 1140 Royal Street, with Kathy Bates playing Madame LaLaurie. It's considered the most haunted house in the South, and Mary was called in to do an exorcism on the set.

'But Madame LaLaurie was no Kathy Bates – she was a hot cougar! She was forty-five years old and married to a younger man, and she held the purse strings. She wouldn't like how Hollywood depicted her. She was a Demi Moore or a Courtney Cox.'

Manifestation is also a big part of voodoo culture. It's believed that focused intention combined with specific actions can channel energy and influence the material world.

I've dabbled with it myself over the last few years. Desperate to move on from my toxic living situation, every night I dream about and decorate the (virtual) seafront flat I wish to buy. It gives me something to focus on during my sleepless nights – I've changed the colour of the sofa four times. This is manifesting in a simple way, picturing what I want for future me.

And maybe that goes for men too. When I separated from my husband I wrote down on a tiny piece of paper what I wanted if I was to have another relationship. My man-ifestation, if you will. It had just three things on it:

Must be kind.
Must take an interest in me and champion all my nonsense!
Must like sex. And lots of it.

After decades of not feeling enough – or too much – particularly in relationships, I'm starting to think that I do deserve a bit of that delicious love pie. I do deserve happiness. And yes, I deserve a good sex life. As my fizzing libido regularly reminds me, I'm not dead yet.

From New Orleans we have a last road-trip hurrah (for now) out into wider Louisiana, where we meet fantastic female chefs such as Madonna Broussard of Laura's II (her grandmother began the first one in 1968 and it now involves five generations of passionate women) and Holly Goetting, the executive chef at Charley G's.

We meet entrepreneurial women such as Colette Bernard, who has been paying off her student debts by founding an affordable art collective, Cocodrie Collective, in her native Lafayette. And artist Roz LeCompte, who got herself through her divorce and other trying life circumstances by creating her own oracle deck (a divination tool similar to tarot cards) and is also starting an art collective of Acadian women artists past and present (Acadians being French immigrants to Louisiana via Nova Scotia; the word eventually became 'Cajun').

And we learn about enslaved women and those who ran the cotton plantations they worked on, and last but not least meet a trio of female alligators on an airboat ride through the Henderson Swamp, where these dazzling creatures choose to live in peace away from the bolshy males.

I'm reluctant to leave this glorious place, but I need to go home and work. Lucky Rhonda decides to stay in New Orleans a few more days. When I land I pick up a voice note from her. The first thing she did was go back to Bloody Mary's and buy herself a bona fide voodoo doll, made from Spanish moss (which is not actually Spanish or moss, but an air plant related to pineapples).

You can't kill anyone with it, she tells me – there's a misconception around voodoo dolls. They are actually supposed to be a version of yourself, for you to manifest with. You put them in the fridge if you are feeling hot-headed. You put coins in them if you need some extra cashola, you dress them up all sexy if you want some action. And so on and so forth.

She had to name hers and baptise it with Florida water and blow onto its crown chakra, in a way eerily similar to what our shaman Christina did to us on our ayahuasca ceremony in Peru. She then had to spank it to bring it to life, and will have to regularly 'feed' it with essential oils or herbal teas or even beer.

Then she'd had her psychic reading with Sam in his seance room. She asked about our much-missed S, and also about her dad, and her French 'dad' Daniel, and she received messages of peace from them all. S told her, via Sam, that she will always be walking by our sides.

But more than anything supernatural, Rhonda experienced the session as a kind of therapy and the chance to talk about how to manage and protect her energy and her heart.

And it was actually another Daniel she had uppermost in her mind, a living one. Young Daniel from Florida, with whom she had that now-distant and dreamlike 'Richard Curtis' day in London, had posted a brilliant poem about serendipity on Facebook. She'd commented on it and he'd replied that he'd posted it hoping she would see it – in fact that it had been inspired by their day in London and the typewriter poet. He said he was fascinated by her travels and hoped they would get to see each other again one day, someplace, and talk…

'Fat chance,' she'd thought. She'd long reconciled herself to never seeing him again. But then she realised how close she'd be to him while she was in the USA – just an hour or so's flight away.

'I don't suppose you fancy coming out to join me for three days in New Orleans?' she'd ventured, not expecting him to say yes. He replied that he was looking up flights and could hardly wait.

As for me, the first thing I do when I get home from the freedom of the open road in Utah and Louisiana is check my emails and find out that, as if by magic, my divorce papers have finally come through.

CHAPTER 15

MERMAIDS ON DRY LAND: SLITHERING TOWARDS SANTIAGO

Rhonda and Tracey

Sitting on a bridge just outside Santiago de Compostela, we're nearly at 'Kilometre Zero' – the city's cathedral, where you finish walking the Camino de Santiago.

In days gone by, it was pilgrims who followed this ancient network of routes converging from all over Europe, to seek redemption for their sins at the cathedral, which is the alleged burial site of the Biblical apostle St James. Today it's more those who are at some kind of turning point in life, like us, who walk the Camino – people in search of answers or guidance about a new direction in life. Hence the 'Camino Casanova's' obsession with it, bless him.

Our original plan was to go to Mauritania and join in with a divorce party to celebrate our new start along with other women doing the same. In this huge but sparsely populated north-west African country, 90 per cent of which is Saharan desert, divorce is not seen as a failure but as a positive new start, and men seek out divorced women as wives for their life experience and wisdom, while, for Mauritania's younger women, divorcees are repositories of fantastic advice.

We thought we would go party with some of them, but it proved too difficult to get there and to infiltrate such an event –

and also we got the ick the more we found out about Mauritania's human rights record.

Instead, we decided to celebrate ourselves and our friendship and new lives by doing a very long walk together – 135 kilometres over five days, across northern Spain. Up to ten hours' walking a day... Perhaps the ultimate test of friendship.

Rhonda: My god, hasn't this last week been THE most amazing adventure? And we haven't killed each other! How have you found it, genuinely? What have the best bits been for you?

Tracey: Well, watching your tight butt marching in the distance was a real highlight, Carrier. What with you listening to your filthy German techno, I couldn't keep up the pace. I found it hard, way harder than I thought I would. But also, I think it's one of the best things I've ever done.

Books like *Eat Pray Love* and *Wild* have become bibles for middle-aged women. Legions of us are signing up for big physical challenges like a marathon or a charity trek, because the toughness makes you feel alive. It's ace that we now have thighs like Serrano hams and also that we could fill our faces with huge piles of steak and chips and bucketfuls of *vino rosso* every night.

My highlights? Obviously, that first cold beer in Chandada. That first day was tough. I was doubting my life choices at kilometre twenty, and lost my sense of humour when that dog was chasing me, trying to nip my ankles. And then we added six miserable kilometres on to the day by getting lost. But two beers down and it felt like the best day ever. It felt good to really push my body.

Do you remember that nuts place in Bandeira? Vinoteca Cadeira. It was like walking into someone's nana's dining room. I think it was after day three. The family were sat round the table eating when we waltzed in and asked for *jamón*, egg and chips. And what we got was two fried eggs and a plate of crisps, and a bottle of wine. And then the grandpa, who had had a few wines himself, put Bruce Springsteen on the stereo and proceeded to dance around the bar with his young grandson, wearing a feather boa. Bonkers.

What about you?

Rhonda: Yeah, neither of us will ever forget that. I also remember that the pissed grandpa was giving you the eye as he hacked pieces of Serrano off one of the giant thighs that had been denied to us for no apparent reason. When you had to nip out to the cash machine and I had to wait there alone, I was genuinely fearful for my sanity or my life, or both.

Otherwise, the fact that we started in the vineyards around Monforte with a wine tasting with a hot viniculturist – that certainly helped ease me into the idea and feel a bit less sick about what I'd let you talk me into! You and I know as much as anyone how much wine helps menopausal, divorcing mums of teens cope with life, or the thought of walking insane distances through the middle of nowhere.

I do love walking my darling dog, but I didn't think I was capable of thirty-five kilometres a day, for sure. So for me the highlight has been both challenging myself and proving to myself I could do this – but then actually *enjoying* it too.

Bruce Chatwin once said walking was a 'sovereign remedy for every mental travail'. And it turns out to be true: I found, after the first two hours each day, it felt that all my worries started to dissolve, my head emptied of unhelpful thought patterns, and my body just took over. There are stats about all this – walking has been scientifically proven to counter menopausal symptoms and depression and also enhance physical self-esteem and life satisfaction. I did love how my body felt – strong and capable. When I woke up each morning I actively wanted to get moving again, to push myself and feel my calf and thigh and booty muscles burn.

I also felt restored by nature, immersed in it, maybe even protected by it, if that doesn't sound too wanky. It was very calming to plod along those country lanes and forest paths, through the mist, looking at, smelling all the plants – gorse, pines, eucalyptus, ferns, mosses, the wild mint growing in cracks in stone walls, the marrows ripening by the roadside. There was a kind of simple, timeless bliss to it all, this world of sleepy cats, tiny chapels, henhouses built on stilts to keep the foxes out… I got out of my head for a time but not in the way we've done in say, Ibiza or Berlin.

So what do you think you have learned about yourself while we were walking?

Tracey: Well, I've learned that I'm not as fit as Rhonda Carrier, ha ha. Seriously, I've learned that I can do big, difficult things, and largely without whinging.

Even though we mainly walked separately, it did still feel that we were in it together. It took a bit of getting used to, but eventually I enjoyed being in my head for several hours a day. I used to avoid difficult thoughts, parking them for another time, but I found that walking for such a lengthy amount of time helps shake things up. I found it gives me space to think about things I often avoid thinking about at home.

I also learned that I don't need to wear my jazz hands and entertain all the time. I'm an extrovert and a natural show-off, and I sometimes take the role of entertainer too seriously. Walking such distances and switching off, I realised that I can just be. I don't have to crack jokes or be a dick, it's okay to be quiet and thoughtful. I also enjoyed the mindfulness of walking in nature. I found I didn't need to take the piss out of every phallic rock or the size of a stray dog's balls, I could just smile, acknowledge the funny and carry on.

And you?

Rhonda: Well, I've realised from the Camino and from the Andes that I *can* like walking for a long time, but only if I have a goal or endpoint. Part of the fun of the Camino is spotting the yellow arrows and scallop-shell signs showing the way. It makes it like a quest of sorts – even if that's just getting to our next hotel for a hot shower or bath, or to a bar for cold beer. Also, making ourselves understood in local restaurants and bars with our crap Spanish and hand gestures felt like an achievement in itself.

I knew already, but I was also aware of the delicate balance between my need for company – comradeship even – and alone time. I wouldn't have wanted to do it myself – to be in my own head for ten hours a day, ruminating, And I needed someone to laugh with at the end of the day. That would have made me feel sad and lonely, walking all day and then eating and sleeping alone. But it was important for both of us that we walked separately a lot of the time, to think, but for me also to listen to music and the odd podcast.

Getting a bit lost a couple of times when we were not paying enough attention to the signs, as well as walking at different paces and needing rests at different points – those could easily have been sticky moments, couldn't they? But in fact I think ultimately they proved the strength of our bond. And chivvying each other along during the tougher moments has really driven it home to me how much female friendship and especially yours has kept me moving forward through these difficult few years. Since we lost S, I am more grateful than ever for the amazing women in my life.

I was just thinking. We've travelled A LOT together now. What do you think you have learned? What has it given you?

Tracey: We have, my love. And how bloody lucky we are! How the hell you've put up with my relentless snoring, I don't know.

Well firstly, I feel so lucky to do this as a job. I've been able to give my kids some incredible experiences, ones they would never have had if I worked in any other industry. And travelling has always given me the space that I need, that I thrive on. I struggle to function properly when I'm stuck in the same routine, day in, day out. I need the adventure, the excitement, the dopamine hits of being thrown into a new place, a new situation. I think it's why I'm drawn to performing stand-up comedy. I'm an adrenaline hunter.

When I felt unhappy, sometimes desperately so, and at times riddled with depression, it was travelling for my work that really helped me. It gave me the space to process the situation at home, to tentatively prod the sadness that I carried, and the space and time away from the situation to see what needed to be done. Of course, it often fell back into the same situation and status when I returned home, but being away allowed me some time out, a way to pull back focus and look at the bigger picture.

As for what I've learned? Christ, I'm learning all the time. Voodoo, ayahuasca, Mormonism... I'm fascinated by it all. I think that travel has helped me handle myself in most situations. It definitely arms you with some weird and wonderful life skills, like how to react when a guy sincerely introduces you to his best friend, Darryl, a live crayfish.

What about you? What have you learned?

Rhonda: I've learned that you're got a real thing for Darryl, haven't you?

But honestly, I think for me a huge part of my healing since the affair and the break-up of my marriage has taken place through travelling and connecting with other women, and learning how they live. Which is obviously often very differently to us, yet so frequently there's that instantaneous bond and discovery of shared experiences that makes you realise we're all so very similar inside – we want the same things, and they are really very simple things. It's both more and less than love, though, in my opinion (whatever love really is) – it's acceptance for who we are and a feeling of being understood and safe.

I've obviously made some big discoveries about myself. I've discovered that I have poor boundaries, that I love human connection but give too much of my energy away and also absorb too much of others' energy. The thing is, I like dynamism and people who know what they want – partly because I don't. But I've learned that, if I know in my soul that a situation is not going to be good for me, I need to put up a wall against other people's desire instead of being steamrollered by it. I think I'm pretty intuitive, yet I've also been a devil for ignoring red flags.

Travelling can obviously help me get a distance from situations too. It might look like running away or distraction, but it actually gives me perspective. Mainly, it reduces my 'problems' and obsessions to their proper size. There are billions of other people out there suffering too, and being joyous too, and fighting their own battles, and experiencing their own triumphs. I'm just one among them, and hence one with them. I'm basically a Buddhist nun after all, ha ha.

For instance, going to Peru and also to Bali was so crucial to me in terms of finding the strength and self-esteem to not have an affair with another married man, to be able to cancel a drink with him despite yearning to see him. It did help that I had a date lined up with a much younger man, a Serbian poet in his early 30s. That was wild and beautiful while it lasted – which it couldn't, for many reasons to do with his trauma as a child refugee. I'm sad about that but it in turn has made way for other things. Things always do. In this case, it made way for me meeting Young Daniel again in New Orleans.

Speaking of which, how do you feel about the future?

Tracey: I think I'm pretty excited about it, to be honest. I get a real thrill about the unknown and all its delicious potential. I think that's why I'm a traveller.

I also feel that I've finally got some agency in my life and that I'm on my own path to happiness. Yes, I chose to end my marriage, but by doing so I was also choosing myself. I'm now the happiest version of me. It's probably quite unbearable for some, I'm sure.

When I wasn't particularly looking, I matched with a lovely man on Bumble, using a picture of hairy hobbit feet to weed out the chaff. Most men found the fact that I did that inexplicable or even terrifying; he found it hilarious, so he passed the test. He's not resentful or jealous of my travels or my friends, and actually enjoys and champions all my silly nonsense – the stand-up comedy, the sea swimming, the dicking about the world with you. It's nice. It's easy. And now I'm in my barren years, there's no expectation from society for it to be any more than it is.

How do you feel about it?

Rhonda: How to say it without banging on all night and making us late? Well, at times it's felt like it's taking for ever to heal and to be happy after all my disappointments in other people (for which read: *men*). But what does happy mean? For me it means, more than anything else, freedom – the freedom I now realise I gave away too easily. For me, relationships in any conventional sense will mean doing things I don't want to do for at least part of the time, and I've got used to being incredibly selfish, and I love it.

I've thought that, together with women friends like F and C in the South of France, I'm inching towards a brilliant new normal of older females who are living largely unattached by choice – and living unashamedly for possibility, adventure and fun connection wherever they find it. If that looks messy to others, then so be it.

With the help of meditation, reiki, tarot, ayahuasca, psychic readings, reading several million books, and enduring a fuckload of heartbreak and false starts, I've finally learned to trust myself that I am on the right path *for me*. But I also know that the 'journey' is never finished, in this life at least, because what you want changes over time and in fact recedes the closer you get to it. And also, Lady Universe is in charge. She'll throw things in your path when you least expect it.

Tracey: Indeed. So what about Young Daniel?

Rhonda: [Laughs] What indeed?

Right, we better get going. Shall we hold hands as we walk to Kilometre Zero? We should be so proud of ourselves. We made it through. And the big question is – what other adventures await us? What next?

THE END

ABOUT THE AUTHORS

Rhonda has written for the *Guardian*, the *Telegraph*, *Metro*, *iPaper*, *Red* magazine, *Condé Nast Traveller*, *National Geographic Traveller*, the *South China Morning Post*, and many others. She's appeared on radio shows and travel panels and as a speaker at travel events, and she writes and translates award-winning fiction. She has also written and edited a handful of major travel books.

Tracey is a veteran travel writer whose byline regularly appears in *Metro*, the *Daily* and *Sunday Telegraph*, *The Times/Sunday Times*, the *Guardian*, *iPaper*, *Country Living*, *Red Online*, *Good Housekeeping*, *Platinum*, *Breathe*, *Teen Breathe*, and *Travel Weekly*. She was co-host of the Carry On travel podcast and is a regular panellist on radio and travel shows. She is also a stand-up comedian.

Keep checking out our Substack (https://waywardwimmin.substack.com/) for our Secret Chapter – one so devilishly naughty, we removed it for legal reasons.

ACKNOWLEDGEMENTS

From Rhonda:
To Ethan, Ripley and Zachary Williams, beautiful, unique young men whom I am honoured to have brought into this world. Thank you for embracing me as I am, in all my imperfections as a mother and a human being, for having my back, and for making me laugh like a drain. I love you eternally.

To my parents Mary and Tim Freeman for their support since forever. To my late maternal grandparents Fred and Florence Read, and my late father David Carrier – I carry you all in my heart.

To Emilie Powles for being your magnificent self and for eternally meeting me halfway when it comes to which of us can lead the other the furthest astray. And to the rest of my Ibiza tribe in its various incarnations over the years.

To Veronika, Lo and the rest of my Kerala crew of open-armed women.

To Whilder, Adrian and Christian for helping me to get up into the Andes without dying and even wearing a smile for much of it.

To Fiona, for providing sanctuary when I truly hit the floor, and for life-changing conversations.

To Marie-Noel for an early look, the encouragement and being a wise counsel in all things.

To Sarah of The Yoga Family for the reiki and the chats.

To all the memoirists and writers of auto-fiction and autobiographical novels who have lit the path with their hard-truth-telling and vulnerability in the service of living an authentic life as a woman: Joan Didion, Melissa Febos, Miranda July, CJ Hauser, Maggie Smith, Rachel Cusk, Leslie Jamison, Constance Debré, Emma Becker, Michelle Zauner, Elizabeth Gilbert, Lily Dunn, Mary Karr, Virginie Despentes, Maggie Nelson, Vivian Gornick, Jenny Diski, Noreen Masud, Stacey DuGuid, Ruby Wax, Carrie Fisher… I bow down before you all.

To Daniel, for New Orleans and for the poetry of life.

And of course most of all to Tracey, for so many frankly deranged adventures and for the wild ride of writing this book together.

From Tracey:
To Angus, Nancy and Lola, my gorgeous gang, my me and three. Thank you for making me a mum, it's the most fantastic and rewarding trip of my life. I love you more.

To my folks, Patricia and Paul Clark, for your love and endless support. Without the help from you – and Bob and Joan – my career, and this book, would never have happened.

To Patty, officially the best neighbour in the world. Megan, for her endless love, support, swears and spells. Maxine, for the friendship and brilliant US road trips. And Jean, who reminded me that I can – and should – trust my own mind, and it wasn't just my bloody hormones!

To Sarah, Lee, Rachel, Fran, Nic, Dom and Sharon, and my glorious gangs: the Wing Lok Sai Gai tribe, Southampton crew, London Amazons, my Brighton gang and my comedy family. Thank you all for always supporting, loving and entertaining this big-haired silly billy. I'm a very lucky girl.

To Toby, for championing me and all my nonsense right from the beginning. #MGL

Finally, to Rhonda Carrier, my travel wife and partner in all crimes. I'm sorry for being such a dickhead to work with! Love you.

Wayward Women

From both of us:

To Maxim Jakubowski and all the talented team at Bedford Square, who saw the magic in the madness.

To all the creatively minded PRs and other travel professionals who helped make our most outlandish ideas come true, starting with Barry Johnston and Hannah Mulvey at Gosh PR, who sent us to Florida, where all this started, and Alice Ackermann and Zina Bencheikh at Intrepid Travel, for life-changing experiences and encounters in India and Peru.

Also to Debbie Flynn, Amy Skelding and the entire team at the wonderful Finn Partners, Sarah Bolam, Rosie Barcroft at KBC working with Visit Utah, Karl Cushing and Kirsty Dillury at TTM World, Niamh Jenkinson at HX, and Francis Tuke at We Are Lotus.

To travel professionals on the ground who made us feel so welcome in their various destinations – looking especially hard at our girl Lciton Leblanc of Lafayette Travel, Devan Corbello of Visit St Francisville and Charlie Whinham of the Louisiana Office of Tourism.

To those who encouraged us in this project in its various formats from its earliest inklings, including the many people who read and expressed gratitude for our Substack pieces, Rajan Datar of BBC Travel and Jago Lee of TellTale Industries.

To our Finland and Tuscany tribes, and to our fellow travel writers and comrades for their encouragement in this and everything else, especially Adam Turner, Mary Novakovich, Lauren Jarvis and Lottie Gross.

And lastly to the travel editors who commissioned many of the pieces from which this book grew, including Connor McGovern, Katie McGonagle, Emma Featherstone, Roshina Jowaheer, Laura Millar, Lisa Minot, Jane Dunford and Adrianne Webster.

Bedford Square Publishers is an independent publisher of fiction and non-fiction, founded in 2022 in the historic streets of Bedford Square London and the sea mist shrouded green of Bedford Square Brighton.

Our goal is to discover irresistible stories and voices that illuminate our world.

We are passionate about connecting our authors to readers across the globe and our independence allows us to do this in original and nimble ways.

The team at Bedford Square Publishers has years of experience and we aim to use that knowledge and creative insight, alongside evolving technology, to reach the right readers for our books. From the ones who read a lot, to the ones who don't consider themselves readers, we aim to find those who will love our books and talk about them as much as we do.

We are hunting for vital new voices from all backgrounds – with books that take the reader to new places and transform perceptions of the world we live in.

Follow us on social media for the latest Bedford Square Publishers news.

@bedsqpublishers
facebook.com/bedfordsq.publishers
@bedfordsq.publishers

bedfordsquarepublishers.co.uk